REAL WORLD
NIKON
CAPTURE NX 2

BEN LONG

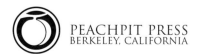

PEACHPIT PRESS
BERKELEY, CALIFORNIA

REAL WORLD NIKON CAPTURE NX 2
Ben Long

Peachpit Press
1249 Eighth Street
Berkeley, CA 94710
510/524-2178
510/524-2221 (fax)

Find us on the Web at www.peachpit.com
To report errors, please send a note to errata@peachpit.com
Peachpit Press is a division of Pearson Education

Project Editor: Susan Rimerman
Developmental Editor: Elaine Merrill
Technical Editor: Bill Durrence
Proofreader: Suzie Nasol
Production Editor: Hilal Sala
Composition: WolfsonDesign
Indexer: James Minkin
Cover Design: Charlene Charles Will

ISBN-13: 978-0-321-55359-1
ISBN-10: 0-321-55359-4

9 8 7 6 5 4 3 2 1

Printed and bound in the United States of America

TABLE OF CONTENTS

Introduction

Nikon has long been a leader in camera innovation, in both the film and digital worlds. For decades, they've pioneered new capabilities and introduced important breakthroughs in camera technology. Like most camera vendors, though, when digital photography hit, Nikon did not show tremendous prowess in software development. The original Nikon Capture, which shipped with Nikon's digital cameras for years, was a capable raw converter with some simple workflow tools built in, but it was never real competition for the likes of Adobe Photoshop, or any number of other third-party applications.

Then, a few years ago, Nikon teamed up with venerable developer Nik Software. Well known for Photoshop plug-ins such as ColorEfex Pro and SharpenerPro, Nik had developed a radical new image-editing technology called U point, which allowed the user to create complex localized edits without having to hassle with selection or masking tools. Together Nikon and Nik worked to develop the next generation of Nikon Capture software. The result was Nikon Capture NX.

Digital photographers have long had a tacit understanding of certain undeniable facts: The one lens you choose to leave at home is the one you'll need on a shoot; if you spend an evening shooting on ISO 1600 you'll forget to turn it back to 100 when you head into daylight shooting the next morning; digital zoom never works; and the software that ships with your camera is not really good for anything. With the release of Capture NX, Nikon proved that last maxim false.

Capture NX 1.0 was a great program, and its U point technology provided powerful functionality that had no parallel in any other image editor. Also, Capture NX shipped at roughly the same time as Apple's Aperture and Adobe Photoshop Lightroom, both of which were strong products that were aiming to reshape people's ideas of what postproduction should be. It's a testament to Capture NX's strength that, even in the face of this new competition, the program was met with rave reviews and a quickly growing user base.

Despite its breakthrough technology, Capture NX 1.0 still had some weak spots, as all version 1 products do. With version 2, Nikon and Nik have shown that they're committed to this product, and that they've been working hard to push it up to the next level.

Whether you use a Nikon camera or some other brand, Capture NX will greatly ease your image editing chores. The new version adds some important new features, improved workflow, better performance, and many interface improvements. We'll cover all of these details throughout this book.

IT'S THE SOFTWARE, STUPID— AND THE HARDWARE

Capture NX is *not* just for Nikon users. Because the program can work with JPEG and TIFF files, you can use it to edit images from any type of camera, or images that you've already processed with another image editor. If you have a Nikon camera that can shoot in raw format, you can use Capture NX to perform your raw conversion.

The development of Capture NX is intriguing because it's the first time that a camera maker has attempted to control both the hardware and software ends of the digital photography process. For years, Apple has shown that there can be a tremendous engineering advantage if one company controls both the hardware and software components of a product. The Macintosh and its associated operating system, for example, are extremely easy to configure because when used together they compose a closed-loop system. Because Apple controls the hardware and the software, both components can be engineered to work together smoothly. You'll find similar integration between the iPod and iTunes.

With Capture NX, Nikon has the potential to create a similar hardware/software relationship. If you're shooting with a Nikon camera, there's a good chance that Capture NX will be able to automatically perform some corrections to your image based on special information encoded in the files produced by your camera. For the shooter who needs to deliver a large volume of images very quickly, this can be a tremendous advantage.

U POINT—UNIQUE EDITING

While Nikon shooters will have access to some extra Capture NX features that aren't provided to users of other brands of cameras, all digital photographers will find Capture NX to be an excellent postproduction tool.

In addition to all of the usual editing controls that you would expect to find in a high-end image editor, Capture NX also provides unique image-editing tools, which are based on Nik Multimedia's U Point technology.

Capture NX's U Point tools allow you to make extremely high quality selective edits without ever having to build a mask or make a selection. With just a few clicks, you can create a localized edit that would require a lengthy masking or selection process if you were using a different image editor. These tools are great for users of all skill levels. They bring powerful editing capabilities to beginning shooters who aren't comfortable with the masking and selection features provided in other programs. Experienced pros will find that NX's U Point tools let them make complex edits in far less time than it would take in a program like Adobe Photoshop.

In addition to its editing tools, Capture NX provides a high-quality raw converter (for users of Nikon cameras—if you're using a non-Nikon camera, you'll have to perform your raw conversions using a separate raw conversion application), an integrated image browser, and a fully color-managed workflow for high-quality printing and output.

I'll go over all of these areas in detail throughout this book.

WHAT'S NEW IN NX 2

Capture NX 2 boasts a huge list of new features, all of which will be covered in this book. Some of the standout additions include:

- A redesigned browser that offers a better interface and easier navigation

- The ability to create and save different workspaces, to ease palette management and improve screen real estate

- Many interface changes, including a new context-sensitive Options bar beneath the toolbar and a simplified Edit List

- An Auto Retouch brush that can automatically remove scratches, blemishes and other problems

- Improved lens correction tools

- Enhanced brush tools, a new gradient tool, and many more U point and mask improvements

Capture NX sports welcome changes in every corner, from big-feature additions to interface improvements and performance tweaks. If you're a version 1 user, you'll find plenty of reasons to consider the upgrade.

HOW THIS BOOK IS ORGANIZED

This book takes you through all of Capture NX's features, providing you with explanations and examples that will help you get the most out of all of the program's features.

Chapter 1, "Installation, Interface, and Importing," will walk you through installation of the program and give you an introduction to its interface. To get you started, you'll also learn how to import images from your camera or media card reader. If this sounds like old hat, bear in mind that there are several strategies for importing, including the free Nikon Transfer, which comes with the software and that the Capture NX 2 installer can automatically download for you.

Chapter 2 is titled "Workflow, the Browser, and Color Management." Shooting and editing comprise the bulk of the digital photography process, but workflow is often one of the most confusing topics. Finding the best way to get your images out of your camera and into your computer in an organized fashion that allows for easy editing, output, and backup is no small task. Here we'll look at workflow strategies in Capture NX 2 and take a detailed tour of the Capture NX Browser. When you're facing a folder full of image files with arcane, camera-generated names, figuring out which document is the one you want to edit can be tricky. The browser's rating, labeling, and metadata tools can make the selection phase of your workflow much simpler. If you're serious about printing then you'll also want to work through the color management section of this chapter, which will guide you through configuring the program's built-in color management tools.

Chapter 3, "Basic Image Editing," will walk you through the program's basic editing features, including its raw conversion tools.

Chapter 4, "Working with Raw Files," will detail everything you need to know to get the most from Capture NX's raw features. While your Capture NX workflow is the same whether you're shooting raw or JPEG, if you are working with raw files, you'll have a few more controls and capabilities at your disposal.

Chapter 5, "Advanced Image Editing," will follow up on the basic tools presented in Chapter 3, walking you through the program's advanced image-editing tools, including its unique U Point tools.

Chapter 6, "Version Control and Batch Processing," will show you how to create multiple versions of an image, each with its own edits, as well as how to batch process your edits for speedy handling of large numbers of files.

Chapter 7, "Output," will cover everything you need to know to export digital files or to print directly from Capture NX.

CHAPTER ONE

Installation, Interface, and Importing

When you learn a new editing technique in a chemical darkroom, you usually have to learn some new theories and concepts, as well as practice and master a lot of tasks that require manual dexterity. With digital editing, your computer provides you with instant craftsmanship, so you don't have to spend a lot of time (and expensive materials) practicing particular types of exposure manipulations, retouchings, or difficult compositing tricks. Nevertheless, it still takes time to learn all of the ins and outs of a complex editing system.

Fortunately, Capture NX's interface is streamlined and straightforward, and you should find that once you've learned a few basic concepts you can quickly get up to speed on all of the program's features.

In this chapter, we'll take a quick look at installing the program and then tour the interface before moving on to a discussion of importing your images. Capture NX includes a free copy of Nikon Transfer, which you can use for managing your image transfers. Since image transfer is the first step in your workflow, it's worth considering a few different options, and Nikon Transfer is a good one if you use a Nikon camera.

INSTALLATION

If you don't already own Capture NX 2, you can download a fully functional, time-bombed trial from www.capturenx.com. This should be all you need to work through this book, and you can always buy a license later.

Installation is fairly simple. On both Mac and Windows, run the installer and follow the on-screen instructions. You'll need to pick a destination location and to agree to the license agreement.

At some point, you will be presented with the screen shown in **Figure 1.1**:

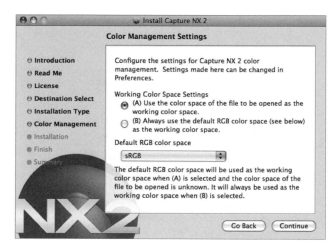

Figure 1.1 At some point during installation, you'll be presented with this dialog. Accept the defaults.

This screen specifies some color management preferences. There are a lot of different approaches to color space and color management. We'll look at color management in detail in the next chapter; for now, accept the defaults that the installer offers. Choosing these settings will allow you to control color space from your camera.

> **TIP:** As great as Capture NX is for image editing, it's still good to try to minimize your postproduction. In general, you'll be better off if you can get as much right in the camera as possible to begin with. While most any problem can be corrected later, if you're facing a shoot of 300 images even small problems can quickly become a hassle, if they exist in every image.

Finally, the Capture NX installer will ask if you want to launch Capture NX and add a shortcut (or put it on the Dock, if you're using a Mac). You'll also get the option to Download and install Nikon Transfer. Nikon Transfer is a free stand-alone application that takes care of transferring images from your camera to your computer. While you can perform these transfers using the file manager on your computer, Nikon Transfer gives you some extra features that can streamline your workflow.

INTERFACE OVERVIEW

If you've already spent a little time working with Capture NX, then you should be familiar with its interface. Just to be sure that you understand the terms and interface concepts that you'll be working with, let's take a quick look at the program's basic interface structure.

Capture NX's interface is made up of a series of interlocking palettes (**Figure 1.2**) that can be easily opened and closed using the +/- button located in the top left corner of each palette (**Figure 1.3**). Beneath this, you'll find a small button that undocks the palette, allowing you to drag it anywhere you like. If you have an especially large monitor, or work with multiple monitors, the ability to move the tool palette can help you make better use of your screen real estate. Any time you see one of these icons on a toolbar or palette, it means that that object can be undocked from its location, and moved to anywhere on the screen. Click it again and the object will snap back to its usual location.

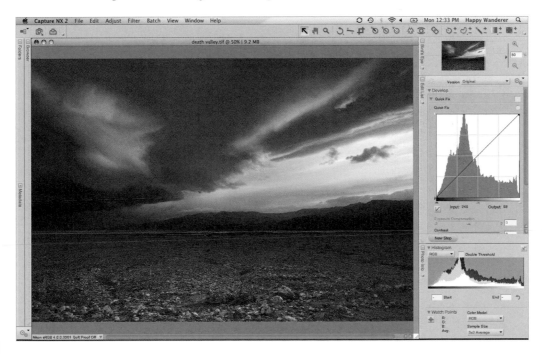

Figure 1.2 Capture NX's interface is made up of a series of interlocking palettes and toolbars that can be easily opened and closed or hidden entirely. Any palette can be undocked and moved to a new location, allowing you to configure the interface any way you want.

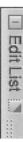

Figure 1.3 You can open and close any Capture NX palette by clicking the +/- icon in the upper corner of the palette, just above the palette name. The lower button is used to undock the palette so that you can move it to another location.

You can also completely hide and show a palette by choosing its name from the Window menu.

Tool Palettes

Just below the menu bar is the toolbar, which you can toggle on and off by choosing Window > Toolbar. The toolbar contains two groups of tools. On the left side are three buttons, which Nikon calls the Activity toolbar (**Figure 1.4**).

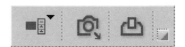

Figure 1.4 Beneath the menu bar is the Capture NX toolbar, which is comprised of two groups of controls. On the left are the activity buttons, one for changing workspace, one for importing, and one for printing.

We'll discuss each of these in more detail later.

On the right side of the toolbar is a detachable palette containing all of NX's editing tools. These tools are divided into six categories (**Figure 1.5**).

Navigation tools   Eyedroppers   Auto Retouch

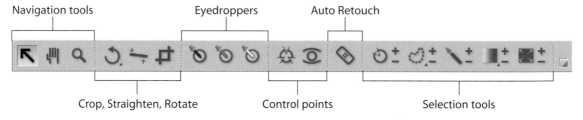

Crop, Straighten, Rotate   Control points   Selection tools

Figure 1.5 The Capture NX editing toolbar holds the program's editing tools, which are divided into six categories. Note the control at the end for collapsing the toolbar and for undocking it.

When you select some tools, such as the Crop tool, an options bar appears just below the toolbar (**Figure 1.6**). It provides context-sensitive parameters that change depending on which tool is currently selected.

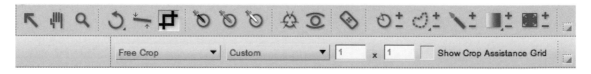

Figure 1.6 When you select some tools, such as the Crop tool, an options bar appears, offering controls and parameters for that tool.

Note that in Capture NX's documentation when they refer to "the Toolbar" they mean just the palette of controls on the right side. I'm going to stick to this convention, even though toggling Toolbar from the Windows menu hides the entire toolbar.

Browser

On the left side of the screen are three palettes: Folders, Metadata, and the Browser. Tucked at the very bottom is a pop-up action menu with some gears on it. This menu provides commands for copying adjustments from one image to another, and we'll look at it in more detail later.

To open the Browser, click the + icon. The Browser window will fill your entire screen and present you with a thumbnail display of the contents of the current directory (**Figure 1.7**). Depending on what's in the current directory, you'll probably see a mix of folders, images, and other documents.

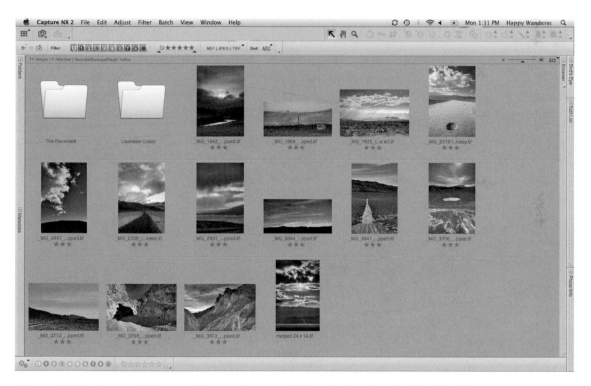

Figure 1.7 The Capture NX Browser lets you browse a folder, viewing thumbnails of all of the TIFF, NEF, and JPEG images it contains.

The point of the Browser is to allow you to browse your images in a visual way. Rather than having to look at meaningless file names, you can see actual thumbnails of each image, which make it easier to find the picture you want to work with.

Double-click on a folder in the Browser to view its contents. You can work your way back *up* the folder hierarchy by using the navigation buttons on the left side of the browser toolbar (**Figure 1.8**).

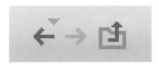

Figure 1.8 In the upper left corner of the Browser are navigation controls. Using the left and right arrow buttons you can work back through folders you've browsed. Using the Folder Up button, you can go up one level in the directory structure.

Next to the navigation buttons are controls filtering the current folder by label, rating, and file type. There's also a menu for specifying how you want the images sorted (**Figure 1.9**). We'll look at these controls in more detail later.

Figure 1.9 The Browser toolbar also contains controls for filtering the folder.

On the right side of the browser toolbar you'll find a slider for increasing or decreasing thumbnail size, as well as a pop-up menu that lets you switch between a thumbnail and list view (**Figure 1.10**).

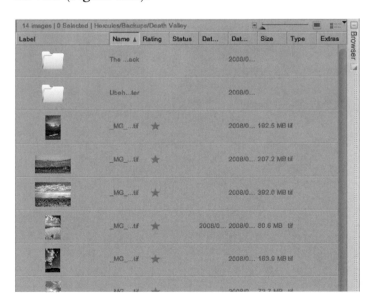

Figure 1.10 The thumbnail controls in the top right corner of the Browser let you change the size of the thumbnails displayed in the Browser window. Next to that is the control for switching from thumbnail to list view.

TIP: List view can be a handy way to spot duplicates in a folder. If you think you may have multiple copies of the same image in the same folder, switch to list view. Displaying a list of images that's sorted alphabetically by name makes it easier to spot when you've got more than one copy of the same image.

TIP: *Be sure the Direct Select tool is selected. You can only select things in the Browser if the Direct Select tool is active. This is the Arrow tool on the left side of the toolbar. If the Hand tool is active, you will be unable to select items in the Browser pane.*

Folders

The Browser makes it simple to dig deeper into your directory structure or to work your way back up a path you've already traveled down. For a broader view of the directory structure of your drive, though, you'll open the Folders palette.

Click the + button on the Folders tab to open the Folders palette (**Figure 1.11**).

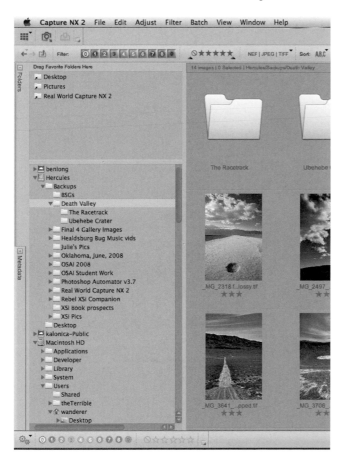

Figure 1.11 The Folders palette provides a simple way to navigate the directory structure of your drive. Click on a folder to view its contents in the Browser.

The Folders palette displays the entire directory structure of your drive. Click on the icon next to any folder to open it up and see all of the folders that are inside of it. Click on a folder in the Folders palette, and its entire contents will be displayed in the Browser.

If there are folders that you regularly access, and you want to save yourself the hassle of navigating to them (either in the Browser or in the Folders palette) then simply drag the folder from the Folders palette into the Favorite Folders section at the top of the Folders palette (where it says "Drag favorite photos here"). This provides a simple shortcut for viewing your favorite folders in the Browser.

To remove a folder from the Favorites area, right-click on it (if you're using a Macintosh with a one-button mouse, Control-click) then choose Delete from the pop-up menu.

Metadata

Every image that you shoot with a digital camera contains *metadata*. Metadata is simply a bunch of information about that image. In addition to the date and time that you shot the image, most cameras also store complete exposure details—shutter speed, aperture, ISO—as well as white balance and many other specifics about camera settings. In addition, your image metadata might contain keywords, ratings, copyright information, and more. The Metadata palette lets you view and edit the metadata for any image that you've currently selected in the Browser (**Figure 1.12**). We'll look at its controls in more detail later.

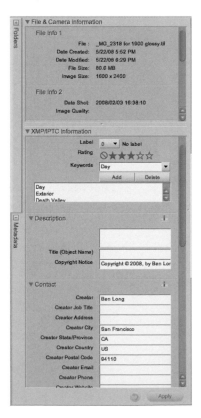

Figure 1.12 The Metadata palette lets you view and edit the metadata for any image.

Editing palettes

Finally, on the right side of the screen are Capture NX's editing-related palettes: Bird's Eye, Edit List, and Photo Info. We'll be exploring these in great detail throughout the rest of this book.

Keyboard shortcuts

With version 2, Capture NX has a much more streamlined, easy-to-wield interface than its predecessor. The program's organizational changes make it simpler to select the tools you need when you need them. For the speediest, most efficient use, though, you'll want to learn how to drive the program with the keyboard.

As with any Mac or Windows program, many menu items have keyboard shortcuts that are listed alongside the menu item.

Note, though, that many of the tools in the toolbar also have keyboard equivalents. Hold the mouse over a tool to see a tooltip, which shows the name of the tool and its keyboard equivalent (**Figure 1.13**). These keystrokes are all unmodified. In other words, pressing A will activate the Direct Select tool.

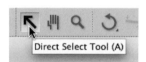

Figure 1.13 If you hover your mouse over a tool, it will show its name and keyboard shortcut.

As you probably already know, the Mac OS and Windows use different modifier keys. Where Windows uses Alt, the Mac uses Option, and where Windows uses Control, the Mac uses Command.

Capture NX's strategy for these modifier keys is fairly simple. Holding down Alt/Option while clicking on a tool does the opposite of what the tool normally does. Holding down Control/Command while pressing a key issues a command, and the Shift key modifies either a selection, tool, or the key that you're using in conjunction with Control/Command (in other words, there's a difference between Control/Command-A and Control-Command-a).

IMPORTING

No matter what image editor you use, your workflow always begins with importing. (Some people call it *ingesting* but that's a little too biological for me.) Importing is simply the process of getting the images off of your camera's media card and onto your computer's hard drive. There's no right or wrong way to import, but there are a lot of different methods.

To import images from your camera, you'll need a card reader that supports the type of media card that your camera uses. Fortunately, if you don't have a card reader, you can use the camera itself as a card reader by plugging it directly into your computer using a USB cable. Obviously, if you've been shooting a lot you might have additional cards besides the one in your camera. Each of these will have to be imported, in turn. Note, though, that connecting your camera to your computer uses up your camera's battery power, which can be an issue if you're on an extended shoot with no access to electricity. In addition, your camera may not provide especially speedy download throughput. For all of these reasons, it's usually best to import your images using a card reader (**Figure 1.14**).

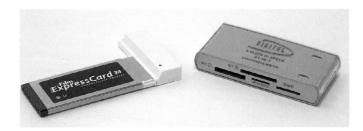

Figure 1.14 A card reader is a good way to import media without draining your camera battery. The reader on the left plugs into the Cardbus 34 slot on a laptop, while the reader on the right connects to any USB-2 port.

Most card readers come with either USB-1, USB-2, or FireWire interfaces. USB-2 or FireWire is your fastest option. Other readers can plug into the expansion slot of a laptop, and typically offer very fast performance. These days, you can get inexpensive card readers that can read several different media formats.

Depending on which operating system you use, different things will happen when you plug in a camera or card reader.

Mac OS

If you use the Mac OS, your card reader will appear on your desktop just like any other type of drive or volume. However, depending on how your Mac is configured, it may automatically launch a specific application when it detects a card reader or camera. This behavior can be controlled from several different places.

The easiest way to configure how your Mac responds to a card reader is to use the Image Capture application stored in your Applications folder.

To change your card reader preferences:

1. Launch Image Capture.

2. Select Image Capture > Preferences or press Command-, (comma).

3. In the resulting dialog box (**Figure 1.15**), you can use the When a camera is connected option to select a specific application or No application.

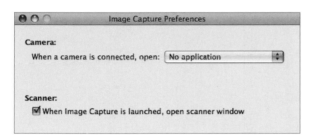

Figure 1.15 You can use Image Capture's preferences to specify what your Mac should do when you plug in a camera or card reader.

By default, your Mac is probably configured to launch Image Capture or iPhoto. If you select No application, any media reader you connect will appear on your desktop when you insert it. You can then begin manually copying images using the Finder, just as you would copy any other type of file.

This technique works fine and is often the speediest way to begin your workflow, because you can simply pull over all of the images from each of your cards and then sort through them later.

Image Capture itself is a handy import tool that allows you to selectively import images from your media cards, rather than copying the entire card. However, Image Capture offers no options for renaming images or applying metadata, and it will copy every image in a session into a single destination folder.

Using NX with iPhoto and Aperture

Apple's iPhoto and Aperture applications also have the ability to import images, and either one can be set to launch automatically when a card or camera is attached to your Mac. However, both programs maintain an internal library structure that they use as the basis of their own image-editing architectures. Working Capture NX into an iPhoto workflow is a little complicated, because you'll need to use iPhoto's export facility to export your images for use in Capture NX. If you're using Aperture, you can set Capture NX as an external editor and use Aperture's Open in External Editor command to automatically "round-trip" your images into Capture NX. See the Aperture Help facility for more information.

Windows

Windows treats a card reader just like any other type of external drive. Plug the reader into your PC and you'll be able to copy your images into any folder on your computer. When you plug in your card reader, Windows should automatically launch the Scanner and Camera Wizard, a simple app that helps you transfer your images (**Figure 1.16**).

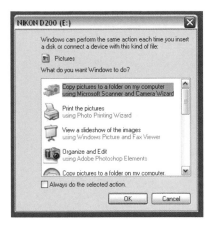

Figure 1.16 The Windows Scanner and Camera Wizard lets you easily transfer images from a card reader or directly from your camera.

Simply follow the instructions onscreen to select the images that you want to copy. The wizard asks you to define a destination directory and then copies the images for you (**Figure 1.17**). Because you can select only the images you want to copy, the Camera Wizard can serve as the first selection step in your workflow.

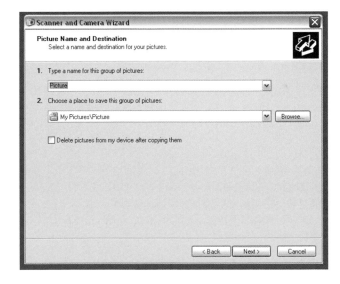

Figure 1.17 After you select the images you want to copy, select a destination directory, and the Camera Wizard copies your images to that directory.

Using Lightroom for Mac and Windows

Adobe Photoshop Lightroom maintains an internal library structure. Images can be imported into Lightroom's internal library or imported as references, leaving the original files in their current location on your drive. However, once you've imported an image into Lightroom, you need to launch it into Capture NX from within Lightroom. If you try to work with the original file in Capture NX directly, the thumbnails that appear in Lightroom might end up incorrect and out of date.

Lightroom provides a special command for sending an image to another application. Select the image in Lightroom and then click the Develop button to move into Lightroom's Develop module. From the Photo menu, choose Edit in Other Application and then select the application that you want to use to edit the selected image.

You can also use Lightroom 2's Preferences dialog box to specify Capture NX 2 as your external editor. Select Preferences, then click on the General tab, then configure the Additional External Editor controls to point to Capture NX 2 (**Figure 1.18**).

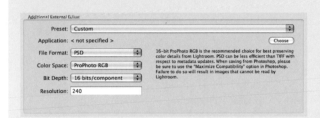

Figure 1.18 If you use Photoshop Lightroom 2.0, you might want to consider configuring Lightroom's Additional External Editor preference to point to Capture NX 2, which will provide you with an easy way to move images from Lightroom into NX for editing.

If you use Apple's Aperture, you'll find a similar control in Aperture's preferences. Look for the External Editor preference.

Organizing your image files

After copying the files to your drive, you may want to organize them into folders to ease your sorting and organizational chores. If you were *very* organized while shooting and kept separate cards for specific parts of your shoot (and you know which cards are which), you can simply import the images on these cards into specific folders. More often than not, you'll have to reorganize your images into subfolders after you've copied them to your drive.

For example, if you've just come back from shooting landscapes at the Grand Canyon and have copied all of your images from the shoot into a folder called "Grand Canyon, 2008," you might want to create subfolders for different parts of your expedition and for different subject matter. So, you might create folders called "North Rim," "South Rim," "Descent," "Canyon Floor," "Ascent," "Blisters," and "Dehydration." Or, maybe it makes more sense for you to organize your images by day, so you could create folders for "Monday—April 12," "Tuesday—April 13," and so on.

File Numbering

You've probably already noticed that your camera names each file it shoots with a sequential number. These files usually have some sort of prefix such as DSC and maybe some leading zeroes, but for the most part they're pretty meaningless. Some cameras default to always resetting the file number to zero after formatting, and others default to maintaining a sequential running order even after you format a card, or insert a new card. Most cameras allow you to change to either scheme.

If your camera always resets to image number 1 when you format your media card, this can be a hassle if you intend to copy several cards' worth of images into one folder, since the latest images on your card will likely have the same names as images you've already copied into that folder. Personally, I like to set my camera so that it *doesn't* reset the image counter to 1 when I reformat. Consult your manual for details on how to do this.

Some cameras have a manual reset feature, which automatically resets the file counter to 1 *and* creates a new folder on the card. This can be a convenient way of organizing images while you're shooting. Reset the counter every morning, and you'll know that each days' shoot will be in its own folder. If your import software of choice doesn't provide an option to automatically create subfolders based on image date, manual reset can be a great alternative.

Browser organization

The Capture NX Browser simplifies file organization because it lets you see thumbnails of the images in a folder, and it lets you make subfolders and move files.

To reorganize a folder, begin by opening the folder you want to organize in the Capture NX Browser. Try the following:

1. Open the Browser and Folder palettes by clicking on their respective + buttons.

2. Using the Folders palette, navigate to the folder you want to organize, and click it to select it. Its contents will appear in the Browser.

   TIP: You can also open a folder in the Browser by choosing File > Open Folder in Browser, which lets you use the standard Open dialog box to navigate to the folder you want to open.

The Browser palette opens, allowing you to see the contents of the folder, including images with thumbnails and any existing subfolders. Note that the Browser does not display any documents that are unreadable by Nikon Capture NX. That includes incompatible image file formats, as well as text files, applications, or any other documents. This gives you a very uncluttered view of your folder. However, if you're shocked to find that some images that you thought you had copied over are not visible, don't panic. Most likely the images are simply in a format (such as a non-Nikon raw format or PSD files) that Capture NX doesn't recognize, so it hides the images. Just to be safe, though, it's worth using your OS's file browser to double-check that the files are actually there.

Creating new folders in the Browser

You can create a subfolder inside any folder that you're currently viewing in the Browser by right-clicking (Command-clicking on the Mac) in the Browser window. From the pop-up menu, select New Folder (**Figure 1.19**).

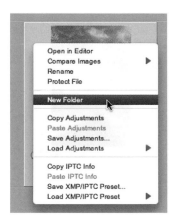

Figure 1.19 To create a new folder, right-click in the Browser window and choose New Folder.

Renaming files in the Browser

You can use the Capture NX Browser to rename individual or multiple files. When you rename a batch of files, you can specify a custom prefix, a sequential number, and a custom prefix, as well as custom separators for each of these elements. This makes it much easier to create ranges of meaningful filenames.

For example, after returning from your Grand Canyon shoot, you might rename all of the images *Grand Canyon_001_2008.jpg* through *Grand Canyon_380_2008.jpg*.

To rename images using the Capture NX Browser:

1. Select the images you want to rename.

2. Choose Edit > Rename, or right-click on one of the images and choose Rename Images from the pop-up menu.

   Capture NX will present its File Naming dialog box (**Figure 1.20**).

   At the top of the box is an example of what kind of file name the current configuration will yield. You can enter new prefix and suffix text (these are bits of text that go on either side of the file number) and configure exactly how you want the number displayed and what kind of characters you want between each element.

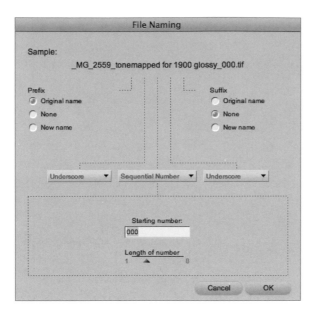

Figure 1.20 The File Naming dialog box lets you specify a naming protocol for batch renaming.

3. Once you've defined the file name to your liking, hit OK, and Capture NX will begin renaming your files.

Moving files within the Browser

If you need to refine the organization within a folder, you can move files from within the Browser itself. The Browser not only lets you view the images in a folder, it also lets you create new folders and move files around, making it a one-stop organizational tool.

To move a file into a subfolder within the folder you're currently viewing, simply drag the file on top of the folder you want to copy it into. The folder will highlight. When you release the button the file will be moved.

You can move an item that's currently displayed in the Browser to any folder visible in the Folders palette by simply dragging the item from the Browser window on top of a folder in the Folders palette. Release the mouse button and the item will be moved. This allows you to move files into folders at a different level of your directory structure.

Copying files within the Browser

Copying files works just like moving, except that you will need to hold down the Control key on Windows, or Option key on a Mac, when you drag the file to its destination. (**Figure 1.21**).

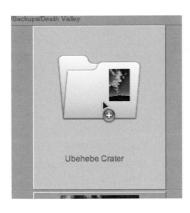

Figure 1.21 Here I've held down the Option key to copy the selected file into this folder.

Using these tools, you can easily create all the subfolders that you need and rearrange your images accordingly.

Importing with Nikon Transfer

When you install Capture NX, the installer should give you the option to download a free copy of Nikon Transfer, Nikon's dedicated software for moving images off of a media card.

If you're using a non-Nikon camera in raw mode, then Nikon Transfer won't work for you. However, your camera probably shipped with software that performs similar functions. If not, you can gain similar capabilities from Adobe Bridge. However, if you're shooting JPEG or TIFF images with a non-Nikon camera, then Nikon Transfer will work fine.

Nikon Transfer not only takes care of copying images from your camera's media card, it can also automatically build a series of folders and separate your images into different folders by date. In addition, Nikon Transfer can add metadata to your images, rename them as they're imported, and automatically create a second, backup copy.

The Nikon Transfer interface

Transfer's interface consists of a single, tabbed dialog box. Begin by clicking on the Source tab and choosing the source that you want to copy from (**Figure 1.22**). This can be a Nikon camera or any card reader. Nikon Transfer cannot communicate with a non-Nikon camera, but you can always remove the card from your camera and put it in a card reader.

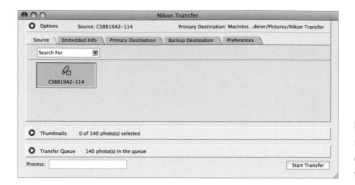

Figure 1.22 In Nikon Transfer, use the Source tab to choose the connected camera or media card that you want to import from.

If you have more than one card reader attached, or a card reader and a camera attached, click in the Source tab on the device you want to copy.

If the Thumbnails pane is not open, open it now to reveal thumbnails of all of the images on the card (**Figure 1.23**). If there are images that you *don't* want to transfer, uncheck their check boxes. You can use the Select buttons to automatically select all, or select none. You can also use the Group pop-up menu to automatically divide the images in the Thumbnails pane by Date, Extension, or Folder.

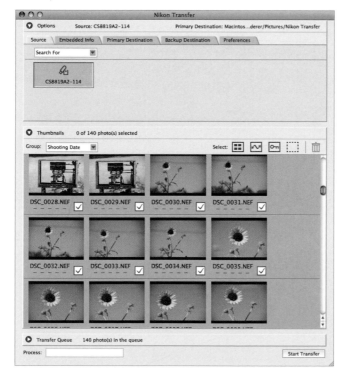

Figure 1.23 Open the Thumbnails pane to view thumbnails of all of the images on your card. Using the check box, you can opt to import only the images you want.

Adding IPTC metadata

We'll spend a lot of time discussing IPTC metadata in the next chapter. Nikon Transfer lets you add some metadata at transfer time, which can ease your workflow by reducing what can be a tedious process. Nikon Transfer's metadata editor is not meant to be comprehensive. Rather, it's intended to allow you to fill in some of the global metadata fields on the images you're importing. Using this feature, you can embed your copyright info, name, and a simple description in your imported images. If you want, you can also add a label or rating, though you'll probably want to save that step for later in your workflow.

> **NOTE:** You may ask, what's metadata for? If you're not sure why you would want to add metadata, then just skip this section for now. We'll talk extensively about metadata and its uses in the next chapter.

Click the Embedded Info tab to view the metadata controls. From the pop-up menu, you can select a pre-defined metadata template, but you'll probably want to design your own template. Click the Edit button to view the IPTC Preset dialog box (**Figure 1.24**).

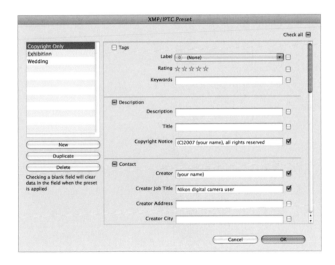

Figure 1.24 Transfer's Metadata Preset editor lets you define a template of metadata that you can easily apply to images when you import.

To define an IPTC preset:

1. Click the New button, and then give the preset a name.

2. Fill in any fields that you want to include in the preset. You don't have to fill in all of the fields. Note that if you check a box next to a field but leave the field empty, you are indicating that the template should delete any existing contents in that field when the template is applied to an image.

3. Click the OK button to save the metadata preset.

Now, when you want to apply your preset, simply select it from the Preset pop-up menu.

Defining destinations

From the Primary Destination tab you can specify where you want Nikon Transfer to copy your images to.

To select a save location, click the arrow in the Primary destination field, and choose Browse (**Figure 1.25**). Then use the file browser to select a new destination.

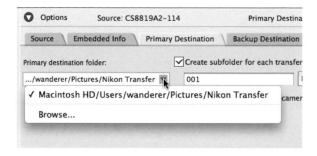

Figure 1.25 Choose a destination for your transferred images.

Until you specifically choose a different location, this will be your default destination for every transfer that you make. Nikon Transfer will remember this location even after you've quit the program.

If you want Nikon Transfer to always make a new subfolder within your chosen destination, then click the Create subfolder for each transfer button. Beneath the button is a field that allows you to specify a naming convention for each new folder. Click the Edit button to define a new naming scheme.

If you want your images automatically renamed when they're imported, click the Rename photos during transfer button. Again, you can specify a naming scheme.

The Backup Destination tab lets you specify a second destination folder. When you transfer, a second set of images will automatically be copied to this location, ensuring you have a backup. Ideally, you'll choose a different drive for your backup destination, as having a backup on the same drive as your primary set of images is not really a safe backup scheme.

Preferences

Finally, the Preferences tab lets you control a number of different preferences, including the option to automatically launch Capture NX after the transfer is done (**Figure 1.26**). Most of these options are self-explanatory.

Note that it's always better to reformat your card in your camera than it is to delete images from the card using your computer—no matter what software you're using on your computer. So, rather than checking Delete original files after transfer, it's better to leave this option unchecked and always reformat your card in your camera after you've moved your images off of it. Using your computer to erase images from your card can sometimes result in a card that's less reliable and that has trouble reading. If this happens, reformat the card in your camera, and you should be okay. If it happens consistently, consider abandoning that card and getting a new one.

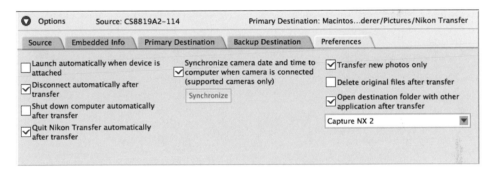

Figure 1.26 Nikon Transfer's preferences include a number of important options.

Launching Nikon Transfer

From the Nikon Transfer Preferences tab, you can check the Launch automatically when device is attached option to automatically launch Nikon Transfer any time your camera or card reader is plugged into your computer.

You can also launch Nikon Transfer from within Capture NX by choosing File > Launch Nikon Transfer, or by clicking on the Nikon Transfer button on the toolbar.

GETTING MORE HELP

Before we go any further, I'd like to point out that Capture NX installs with a full copy of its user manual. From the Capture NX Help menu, choose "Contents." The Capture NX manual will open up in your Web browser. If you're not certain about a term used in this book, or if you simply want a little more information about a topic, the Help file is a great resource.

CHAPTER TWO

Workflow, the Browser, and Color Management

Capture NX allows you to make very complex, sophisticated edits to your images, and when most people think of "image editing" it's those amazing effects that first spring to mind. But in the film days, "editing" your images meant something else. Before computers and Photoshop and Capture NX, "editing" referred to the process of sifting through all of the images you'd shot to edit out the ones that weren't worth processing.

With digital shooting, this old-school editing process becomes more important because, as you've probably discovered, it's so cheap to shoot digitally that you tend to shoot a *lot* more pictures when using a digital camera. What's more, if you understand that it's often necessary to bracket your shots, and to work a subject from many angles, it's not unreasonable to come home after a day of shooting with hundreds of images. The method you choose to manage these images—how you organize them, how you figure out which ones are keepers, which of those keepers need adjusting and correction, how you perform those edits, how you output your finals, and back them up and archive them for safe keeping—is called a *workflow*.

You may think, "Yeah, yeah, that's cool, I'll figure that out later, when I get more serious; right now I just want to correct my images." But bear in mind that image editing takes time (and here I'm using the new definition of editing, the one that refers to adjusting and correcting your images). You don't want to waste time editing an image and then discover later that there's another shot of the same subject that you like even more. Also, remember that those hundreds of images that you've imported have arcane file names and are not organized into any particular file structure. As your image library grows, it will become harder and harder to find images and to keep track of different versions you may have created (perhaps you've got color *and* black and white versions of some images, or different versions edited in different ways). If you're not careful, you can easily end up accidentally deleting images, or saving over older versions with newer files.

Fortunately, with a little planning you can make your postproduction workflow easy, and Capture NX can help.

BASIC WORKFLOWS

You can fairly easily break down the most complex postproduction workflow into seven simple steps (**Figure 2.1**).

1. Import your images. In this step, you might choose to import only images that you like. This represents your first step in culling. If you don't perform any culling at import, then you'll do it in step 4. If you do cull during import, you can refine your selections in step 4.

2. Organize your image files, and optionally, rename them.

3. Add metadata to your imported images (ownership, copyright, keywords, etc.).

4. Cull the selected images from your imported batch and rate them accordingly. (Some people call these the "pick" images or "hero" images.)

5. Edit your selects as need be.

6. Output your images.

7. Archive your images.

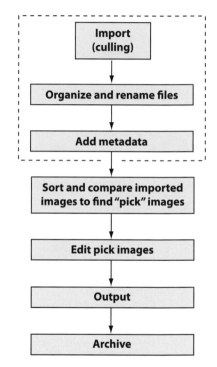

Figure 2.1 Most workflows can be broken down into these seven steps.

This workflow is straightforward, and you might already have a pretty good idea of how to do each of these seven steps. Depending on what method you use for importing, you might perform steps 1, 2, and 3 at the same time. For example, Nikon Transfer allows you to automatically copy images with different dates into different folders, automatically apply metadata to your images upon import, and it can even automatically create a separate backup copy of each image.

It's important to notice that in this workflow you don't perform *any* image editing until you've culled your images down to your selects. Because image editing can be time consuming, you don't want to bother with corrections unless you're confident that an image is a keeper.

However, the real world is often more complicated, and if you're like me, you might find yourself too impatient to perform *all* of your sorting before you start any editing, so you might do some steps out of order. Or, if you're on assignment, the final decision of which images are keepers may not be up to you. In these instances, your workflow might look more like this (**Figure 2.2**):

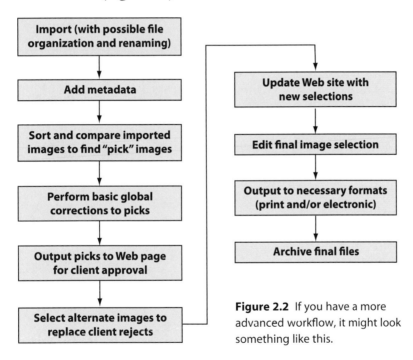

Figure 2.2 If you have a more advanced workflow, it might look something like this.

1. Import your images (possibly organizing them into folders and renaming them in the process).

2. Add your copyright and ownership metadata.

3. Cull your imported images to find your selects.

4. Perform basic global corrections to the selects that need some adjustment.

5. Create a Web site or slide show of your roughly edited selects to show to your client for approval. If the client doesn't like some images, you'll need to remove them. If the client asks for alternatives, you'll need to go back to your original image batch and try to find alternate images. This selection/presentation cycle may occur several times.

6. Edit your final batch of selects. These edits might be more involved than edits in step 4.

7. Output your images. You might have to output to several different media—perhaps a Web site for final client review followed by delivery of final electronic files or even prints.

8. Archive your images.

Many tools and functions are available to help you through each of these steps, whether you're working through a basic workflow or a more involved process. Let's take a quick look at some specifics of the basic workflow steps.

Importing/Organizing

Importing was discussed in detail in Chapter 1, "Installation, Interface, and Importing," where we also looked at organizing your images and adding an initial round of metadata. These steps are the first part of any workflow, and as you saw, there are many tools available to facilitate your importing and organizing chores.

> **Backing Up Your Image Master**
>
> After you've copied your entire shoot's worth of images to your drive, it's a good idea to back up all of your original image files. Not only will this give you a backup set in the event of a hard-drive crash, but it will ensure that you have an original set of images in case you end up making changes or edits that you can't back out of. Some photographers find it useful to preserve the original camera-generated names, since these names are guaranteed to be in the order that the images were shot. By backing up your files, you'll always have one set of images with your original camera-generated names, allowing you to freely rename the images on your drive as you please.

Adding Metadata

Depending on the tools you used for importing, you might have already made an initial metadata pass. If you haven't, or if you want to add more metadata, you can use the Metadata palette in the Capture NX Browser.

What is metadata for? In the analog world, people tend to organize images by putting them in boxes or folders, or inserting negatives or slides into sleeves. If they're good about their organization, they'll label each box, folder, or sleeve, and keep their images grouped by subject, making it easier to find particular images.

In the digital world, organization is much simpler. Because each individual image includes metadata, you can easily search your images based on their metadata tags. For example, you could search for images shot on a particular date. If you've been diligent about adding good metadata to your images, you could search for images shot on a particular date, in a particular location, and that are of a particular subject matter—landscape, for example.

These types of searches are only possible if you've done a good job of adding metadata. If your images have well-considered metadata tags, then you're not constrained to one particular organizational strategy, like you were in the analog days. The ability to search means you can view your image library by any criteria that you want, and change this criteria at any time.

An image's metadata is also where ratings and labels are stored, and these are an essential part of the selection process that you go through to determine which images you will pass through the rest of your workflow.

Choosing Selects—Rating Your Images

With your files imported, backed up, organized, renamed, and tagged with metadata, you're ready to start culling them to find the select images that you want to edit and output. In simplest terms, this process is fairly easy. You look at each image and decide which ones are the keepers. You mark them in some way—usually with a rating—and then filter out those marked images later. You can use the Capture NX Browser to make your selects, or an entirely different browsing program such as Adobe Bridge.

What should you look for when searching for your select images? Good composition and subject matter will probably be the first characteristics that attract your attention. When you see an image that you like, you'll then want to assess the following:

- **The sharpness of the image.** Is it in focus? If it's soft, is the softness slight enough that the image can be sharpened with Capture NX's sharpening feature?

- **The exposure of the image.** Is the image well exposed? Are the highlights blown out? Are the shadows too dark? Does the image have the detail, color, and tonal qualities that you want?

- **Noise problems or other lens or camera artifacts.** Does the image suffer from any of these?

- **The data in the image.** Does the image provide the data that you need for the types of edits that you want to perform? This is especially important when evaluating raw images. We'll discuss this topic in more detail in Chapter 5, "Advanced Image Editing."

Editing and Output

After you've made your selects, you're ready to start editing, a topic that will be covered in detail in Chapters 3 through 7. With your images edited, you'll then be ready for output in the form of delivery of electronic files, creation of a Web page, or printing. Capture NX provides a full-color managed workflow with onscreen soft proofing. Output is covered in Chapter 7, "Output."

Archiving

Although you made an initial backup of your original camera files, once you've finished your editing and output, you'll want to back up or archive your edited images. This topic is covered in Chapter 7.

ADVANCED WORKFLOWS

The basic workflow outlined earlier is the process you'll follow with just about any image editing program. In some cases, you might even use several programs to achieve the basic workflow that was described. There will be times, though, when your workflow needs might be more complicated because of the type of camera you have or the types of edits you want to make, or because of existing workflow strategies that you've already employed. Here are some brief examples of how you can fit Capture NX into more complex workflows.

Using Capture NX with non-Nikon raw files

Raw files must be processed using special raw conversion software before they can be edited or output. Capture NX includes a built-in raw converter, but it only works with Nikon-created raw files. If you shoot with a non-Nikon, raw-capable camera (such as a Canon, Pentax, Sony, Olympus, Panasonic, or others), you'll need to include an additional step in your workflow.

You'll still begin by copying your images from your camera media cards to your hard drive. But you'll probably want to organize your images using a different app—one that is capable of showing thumbnails of your raw files. Assuming they support your particular camera, programs like Adobe Bridge, and Photo Mechanic are well suited to this task.

You'll also want to use your browser application to rate your images and make your initial selects. Since these programs also provide the ability to edit metadata, you can tackle that problem using these apps as well. After making your selects, perform your raw conversion using your raw converter of choice and save the image as a TIFF file. You can then open the converted, processed files in Capture NX for further editing.

> **TIP:** *When processing non-Nikon raw files using another raw converter, be sure to save the finished results as TIFF files, ideally 16-bit TIFF files. JPEG files aren't capable of storing the full range of color from your raw image, and they perform a lossy compression on your image, which can leave visible artifacts in your final picture.*

After editing you can continue with your workflow either in Capture NX or move your edited files out of NX and back into your existing workflow.

Adding Capture NX to a Photoshop workflow

If you're a Photoshop user, you may think it's a little strange to talk about adding an additional image editor to your workflow. However, as you'll see in the editing lessons in Chapter 4, "Working with Raw Files," many types of edits are much easier to perform in Capture NX than in Photoshop. Once you learn more about NX's editing capabilities, you'll have a better idea of which types of edits you want to perform in NX and which you want to perform in Photoshop.

If you're shooting non-raw images (JPEGs or TIFFs), or non-Nikon raw files, your Photoshop/NX workflow will probably go something like this:

1. Find your pick images, organize them, and apply your metadata in Adobe Bridge.

2. Perform all of the edits you want to make in Photoshop (including raw conversion using Photoshop Camera Raw) and save the results as TIFF files.

3. Open the TIFF files in Capture NX and perform your NX edits.

4. Save the edited NX file in the native NX format (NEF), and then export a copy of the edited version as a 16-bit TIFF file. You'll learn about the particulars of saving NEFs and TIFFs (and what the difference is) in Chapter 3.

5. Produce your output as desired.

If you're shooting Nikon raw files, your workflow will look more like this:

1. Find your images, organize them, and add metadata using the Capture NX Browser.

2. Perform the edits that you want to perform in Capture NX.

3. Save the edited NX files in the native NX format (NEF), and then export copies of the edited versions as 16-bit TIFF files.

4. Open the TIFF files in Photoshop for additional editing.

You'll learn much more about NEF files, saving, and exporting images in Chapter 4. As you learn more about the types of edits that are possible in NX, you'll have a better idea of how to divide your image editing workload between the two programs.

Workflow Summary

To sum up: when concocting a workflow, your goal is to devise a scheme that lets you import, organize, and select your pick images as quickly as possible. Next you edit those picks, output them, and archive the whole mess—originals and edited copies. You want a workflow that allows you to move quickly, keeps you from accidentally deleting or over-writing files, and helps you to smoothly move from browsing, rating, and selecting, to editing and output. Hopefully, the schemes here will work for you.

THE CAPTURE NX BROWSER

As discussed in Chapter 1, the Capture NX Browser lets you browse the folders on your hard drive, but rather than simply displaying a list of file names, the NX Browser shows you thumbnails of all of your NEF, JPEG, and TIFF files. Because you can thumb through your images visually, it's much easier to see which files you want to work with, and how you might want to organize them.

The Capture NX Browser also provides a full suite of tools for adding and editing metadata, rotating images, rating them, applying labels, and moving or copying them from place to place.

You can use the NX Browser to perform that essential selection phase of your workflow, where you look through all of the images that you've shot, and determine which ones are the picks that you will pass on to the rest of your workflow.

In Chapter 1 you learned how to open the Browser, and how to navigate through your hard drive by double-clicking on folders and by using the navigation buttons on the Toolbar. In this section, we'll take a look at the rest of the Browser's features.

Metadata

To access Capture NX's metadata controls, you must open the NX Browser and then open the Metadata palette. The Metadata palette is divided into two sections.

At the top is the File & Camera Information (**Figure 2.3**). This panel contains all of the exposure metadata that your camera recorded when you took the shot. None of these fields are editable, because there's really no reason that you would want to edit these. After all, your image was shot with the settings it was shot with, there's no reason to edit these fields later.

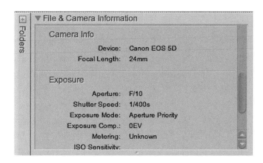

Figure 2.3 In the top half of the Metadata palette you'll find an editor that lets you view the metadata that your camera embedded in your image file.

TIP: *The metadata that your camera stores in your image conforms to a standard called EXIF. When you hear someone referring to "EXIF metadata" they are talking about that read-only camera data stored in the image file.*

The bottom half of the metadata palette shows XMP/IPTC information (**Figure 2.4**). Extensible Markup Platform and International Press Telecommunications Council are simply two agreed upon metadata standards. These days, pretty much every image editor, cataloger, and browser program knows how to read this type of metadata. Depending on which version of the Mac or Windows operating system you're using, you might even be able to access these metadata tags from your file browser.

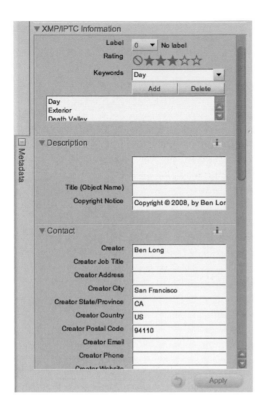

Figure 2.4 The bottom half of the Metadata palette contains the XMP/IPTC metadata editor, where you can add and edit all sorts of data about your image.

To add metadata to an image:

1. Using the Browser, select the image that you want to add metadata to.

2. Fill in the fields in the Metadata palette as desired. You don't have to fill in all of them, just do the ones that fit your organizational strategy.

3. Click the Apply button at the bottom of the Metadata palette to save the Metadata.

Any time you make any sort of change to any of the fields in the Metadata palette, you must click Apply to save the changes.

Adding Metadata to multiple images

If you want to add metadata to multiple images, simply select those images in the Browser, and then fill in the metadata fields as normal. To select a range of contiguous images, click on the first image, and then shift-click on the last image you want to select. All of the images in between will be selected.

To select a collection of non contiguous images, click the first image, then Control-click (Command-click on the Mac) on all of the other images you want to select. Then fill in the appropriate fields and hit Apply.

Change Metadata at Any Time

While I've listed metadata editing at a very particular point in the workflow, the fact is you will be constantly revising your metadata as you work. In fact, you might not apply any metadata until you've edited, simply because you're eager to see some finished images. Or, you might find that you re-evaluate an image's rating after you've edited it and some others. Don't worry about when you add and edit metadata, so long as your images end up with the metadata that's appropriate.

Obviously, the process of making selects has to occur toward the start of your workflow so that you'll know which images to pass through to the rest of your process. As such, this is almost always the best time to rate your images. But don't worry if you find yourself re-rating or adding or removing your select images later.

Metadata categories

The XMP/IPTC pane is divided into different categories. These consist of Tags, which contain keywords, ratings, and labels; Description, where you can enter a description, title, and copyright info; Contact, where you can fill in fields related to you; Content and Origin categories, which are used mostly by journalists for identifying an image's location and accompanying captions and taglines; and finally, Categories, which lets you specify different categories for organizing images.

There's a good chance that you'll only use some of these fields. So, for example, if you find that you never use the Content and Origin categories, you can collapse these by clicking on the reveal arrow next to their names. With these fields hidden, you won't have to do as much scrolling in the Metadata palette (**Figure 2.5**).

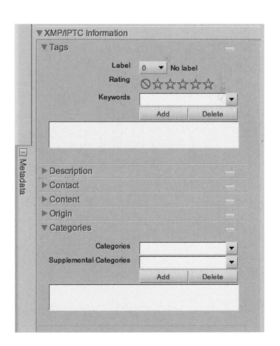

Figure 2.5 You can collapse metadata categories to get them out of your way, resulting in less scrolling in the Metadata palette.

Adding copyright

At the very least, you'll want to add copyright metadata to any image that you plan to release electronically into the world. While having a copyright tag in an image's metadata won't stop someone else from using the image, it will provide you with a way of proving ownership, making it easier to get them to *stop* using an image if you find out about it.

The correct syntax for a copyright notice is "Copyright © 2008, by Ben Long." On Windows, hold down Alt while typing 0169 on the numeric keypad (make sure the Num Lock light on the keyboard is on). On the Macintosh, you access the © symbol by typing Option-G.

In addition to Copyright symbol and date, you'll want to put your name in the Creator field.

Adding keywords

Keywords are one of the most useful types of metadata. Keywords are nothing more than words—any words you choose—that are placed in the Keywords field of the image's metadata. Keywords give you another way to search your images and provide a simple way of adding important description information.

Different people have different approaches to keyword taxonomy. Some people get very specific and use many different keywords, while others use just a few high-level keywords. What is right for you depends on the types of images you shoot and on how you like to search and organize.

I tend to keep keywords fairly general, and use broad terms such as Interior, Exterior, Day, Night, Male, Female, Animals, Landscape, Family, Event. You can search for any one of these keywords, or do combinations. For example, I can search for *exterior, day, male* to find shots taken outside during the day that have males in them. If I have a repeat client, I might tag those images with that client's name to make it easier to find everything related to that client.

To add a keyword using the Metadata palette:

1. In the Browser, select the image(s) to which you want to add a keyword.

2. Type the keyword into the Keywords field of the Metadata palette, and then press the Add button. The Add button adds the keyword to the selected image(s) and the added keyword appears in the larger Keywords field (**Figure 2.6**).

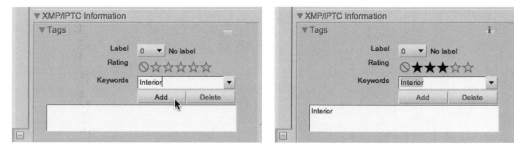

Figure 2.6 To add a keyword, enter it in the keyword field and hit the Add button. All the keywords for the currently selected image will be displayed in the larger keyword field.

3. Click the Apply button.

Each keyword that you enter is also added to the Keywords pop-up menu so that next time you want to use that keyword, you can simply select it from the menu (**Figure 2.7**). This makes it easier to maintain consistent keywords from image to image.

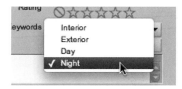

Figure 2.7 Every keyword you define gets added to the Keywords pop-up menu, making it simple to add the same keyword to a different image later.

If you want to delete a keyword from an image:

1. Select the image in the Browser.

2. Click on the keyword in the larger keywords field.

3. Click the Delete button beneath the keywords field. The keyword will be removed from the image, but will remain in the Keywords pop-up menu.

4. Click the Apply button.

Copying metadata from one image to another

Entering all of the metadata for an image can take time, even though the NX Metadata palette is easy to use. However, in many cases the metadata for one image will be appropriate for all of the other images that you took during the same shoot. Even if another image needs slightly different metadata, copying the metadata from one image can provide an easy starting point.

Capture NX makes it simple to copy the XMP/IPTC metadata from one image to another (obviously, you can't copy the File and Camera metadata from one image to another, since this information is specific to each image and can't be edited).

1. In the Browser, select the image that contains the metadata you want to copy.

2. From the Action menu in the lower left corner of the interface, or from the Batch drop-down menu, choose Copy IPTC Info (**Figure 2.8**).

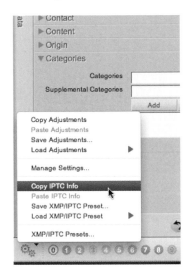

Figure 2.8 The Action menu in the lower left corner of the NX interface or the Batch pull-down menu includes commands for copying and pasting IPTC info from one image to another.

3. Select the image(s) you want to copy the IPTC metadata to, and select Paste IPTC Info from the Action or Batch menu.

4. Hit the Apply button to save the pasted data.

Using metadata templates

Some metadata will never change. For example, if you always put your name in the Creator field, that's probably not going to change. Similarly, your copyright notice is good for a whole year, and your address metadata is good for as long as you stay in that specific location.

You can create a metadata template that lets you apply a preset batch of metadata to your images, making it simple to quickly get basic metadata onto an entire batch of pictures.

To create a metadata template:

1. Choose an image and fill in the metadata fields that you want to include in your template. Obviously, you won't want to add anything that is specific to that image. Instead, fill in the more global, general properties.

2. From the Action or Batch menu, choose Save XMP/IPTC Preset.

Capture NX will present a dialog box asking for a name for the preset, and give you the option to uncheck any fields that you don't want stored in the preset (**Figure 2.9**). If a field is empty, then you should uncheck it. If there's a checkmark next to an empty field, then that field will be emptied when the template is applied to an image. This could cause you to lose existing metadata.

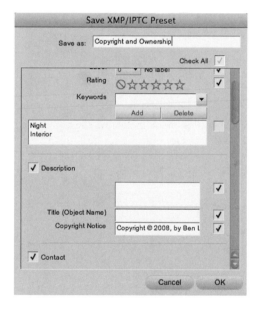

Figure 2.9 After you've filled out the metadata for an image, you can save a copy of that data as a template. Notice that I've unchecked the keywords metadata, as I don't want those included in this particular template.

3. Click OK to save the Metadata template.

> **NOTE:** *Nikon Capture and Nikon Transfer use different metadata presets, so presets defined in one program will not appear in the other.*

To apply a metadata template to an image:

1. Select the image(s) that you want to add metadata to.

2. Open the Action or Batch Menu and select Load XMP/IPTC Present. The submenu will let you choose which preset you want to apply to that image (**Figure 2.10**). Choose the preset, and the metadata fields for that image will fill in.

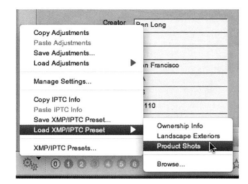

Figure 2.10 The Action or the Batch menu provide a pop-up menu that displays all of your metadata templates.

3. Hit the Apply button to save them.

> **TIP:** *If you right-click on an image (Windows) or Control-click (Mac), you'll get a pop-up menu that includes the same options that you'll find in the Action or the Batch menu. From here you can make and apply metadata templates or copy metadata from one image to another.*

Adding Metadata to Raw + JPEG

If you're a Nikon shooter and you've got some images you shot in Raw + JPEG mode—that is, you configured your camera to produce both a raw and a JPEG image—then you'll have two copies of each image that you shot. They'll both have the same names, but one will have a NEF extension and the other a JPG extension. If you add or modify the metadata of either one of these files, the other will automatically receive the same metadata change. So, you don't have to worry about making the same change to both files.

Rotating Thumbnails

Your camera should automatically add a rotate tag to any image that you shoot in Portrait orientation. Capture NX can read this tag and automatically rotate your images in the Browser. However, sometimes the camera won't properly set the rotate tag, and an image will have the wrong orientation.

To rotate an image in the Capture NX Browser:

1. Select the image(s) to rotate.

2. Click the Rotate tool on the toolbar to rotate the thumbnail 90 degrees. By default, the tool is set to rotate clockwise. If you want to rotate counter-clockwise, click and hold the Rotate tool to open its menu. Select Rotate 90 degrees CCW to select the other Rotate tool.

You can also press Control/Command-R to rotate 90 degrees clockwise, or Control/Command-Shift-R to rotate counter-clockwise.

> **TIP:** When you tell the NX Browser to rotate an image, it doesn't actually alter any pixels in the file. Instead, it sets a flag in the file that records the amount of rotation that you want. When the file is opened, Capture NX rotates the image.

Changing Thumbnail Size

In Chapter 1 you saw the thumbnail size slider, which lets you make the thumbnails in the Browser larger or smaller. You can also use the Zoom tool to enlarge or shrink the thumbnails.

To use the Zoom tool:

1. Click the Zoom tool on the toolbar, or press Z.

2. Click anywhere in the Browser to enlarge the thumbnail size.

3. If you want to shrink thumbnail size, hold down Alt/Option while clicking.

Alternately, you can zoom in and out from the keyboard by using Control/Command + (plus) to zoom in, and Control/Command – (minus) to zoom out.

Thumbnail Badges

Capture NX displays small graphic *badges* on each thumbnail to indicate a number of different image properties (**Figure 2.11**).

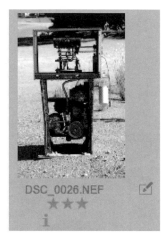

Figure 2.11 Thumbnail badges provide an easy way to see what types of edits and changes you've made to an image.

These icons give you a quick way to see what types of changes you've made to an image. In Figure 2.11, you can see the metadata badge, which indicates that metadata in the image has been edited; the paintbrush badge, which indicates that adjustments have been applied to the image; and a small lightning bolt in the lower right corner of the thumbnail, which shows that the image is cached, meaning it will load a little faster.

Comparing Images

When making your selects, you'll often find yourself trying to choose among very similar images, especially if you tend to bracket your shots or use your camera's drive mode to shoot bursts of images. To help with both of these issues, the Capture NX Browser lets you view selected images side by side.

1. Select at least two images in the Capture NX Browser.

2. Choose View > Compare > Compare in Browser.

Capture NX superimposes larger versions of the images over the Browser window (**Figure 2.12**). The size of these images will vary depending on the number of images you've selected. You can't label or manipulate any of the previews, because they are only for comparing larger views of your selected images. When you've finished evaluating the images, choose View > Compare > Compare in Browser to return to the normal Browser view or click anywhere in the Browser window.

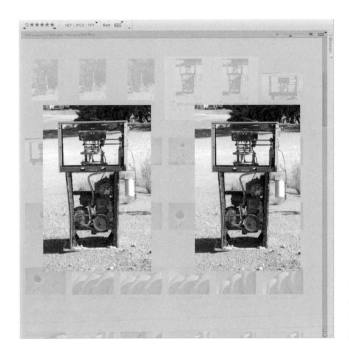

Figure 2.12 When you choose to compare images in the Browser, Capture NX superimposes them over the Browser display.

TIP: You can also access Compare mode by selecting two images and right-clicking on one of them. Select Compare Images from the pop-up menu that appears.

If you have only two images selected, you can select View > Compare > Compare in Editor to automatically view them side by side in Capture NX. With the images open, you'll have access to all of Capture NX's tools, including the ability to zoom in and out. Zooming in Compare mode zooms both images simultaneously. If the images are large, it may take a while to load them, so this is not a fix for getting a very quick view. But if you simply can't make your decision without seeing a very close-up view or a histogram, this command provides a quick way to open both images simultaneously.

TIP: Although Nikon has not supplied keyboard shortcuts for the Compare in Browser and Compare in Editor features, you can create them using any kind of macro program that works with your operating system. For example, on Windows you can use programs such as xStarter or MacroExpress. On the Mac you can use Startley Technology's QuicKeys to create a keyboard shortcut for a menu item (the Mac's built-in keyboard shortcut creator won't work with Capture NX's submenus).

TIP: The only way to accurately evaluate sharpness is to view the images at 100 percent, something you can do only in the Capture NX editor. So, to really assess sharpness you need to open the image in the editor, or use the Compare In Editor mode, and then zoom to 100 percent.

Browser Thumbnail Cache

Capture NX creates a thumbnail graphic for every image that you view in the Browser. These thumbnails are the images that you see in the Browser, and they're stored in a special cache folder on your hard drive. If you go to Capture NX's Preferences and click on Cache Settings, you can see exactly how much disk space is being used for the thumbnail cache (**Figure 2.13**).

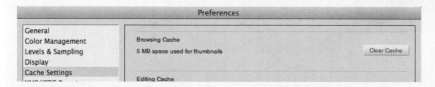

Figure 2.13 From time to time, you'll want to check your Browser cache settings, to see how much disk space the Browser cache is consuming.

If you're hurting for disk space, click the Clear Cache button to dump the cache and free up that space. This won't affect any of your image data, but next time you look at a folder you've already viewed in the Browser, you may have to wait a moment while it builds new thumbnails.

Rating Your Images

As you work through your images and identify the pick images that you want to send through the rest of your workflow, you'll need a way to mark them. The easiest way is with ratings.

Capture NX lets you apply a rating of 1 to 5 to any image. By default, your images have no rating at all.

To assign a rating:

1. Select the image(s) you want to rate.

2. Press Command/Control-1 through 5 to assign a rating. The rating will appear below the thumbnail (**Figure 2.14**).

You can also rate images using the mouse by clicking on the stars beneath the image thumbnail or by clicking on the Rating selector at the *bottom* of the screen. (Be sure to use the one at the bottom of the screen. The Ratings indicator on the Options bar at the top of the screen is for filtering, which we'll discuss in a bit.)

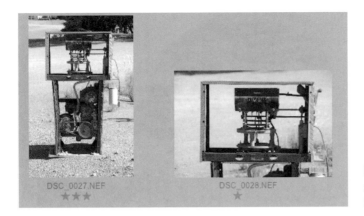

Figure 2.14 After assigning a rating, you'll see it registered below the image's thumbnail.

Note that you can also apply ratings in the Metadata palette. In the Tags section of the palette are stars that you can click on, just like the stars beneath the image thumbnails (**Figure 2.15**).

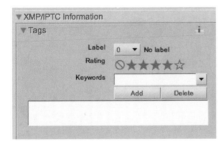

Figure 2.15 You can also apply ratings using the Metadata palette.

If you want to change a rating, just use any of the normal rating methods to assign a new rating value.

Rating strategy

Depending on how you like to organize your images, you might not need a very "granular" degree of rating control. Many people simply want a binary rating system—either an image is a select or it's not—which you can achieve by simply using one rating for all of your selects.

For example, give all of your pick images three stars; then you can easily distinguish between picks and rejects. If you later decide that you *do* want to distinguish between different levels of quality, then you still have some rating headroom.

Labeling Your Images

In addition to a rating, you can assign a label to an image. Capture NX offers nine different labels, from 1 to 9, each with a different color.

To add a label to an image:

1. Select the image or images that you want to label.

2. Type number 1 through 9 to assign a label, or 0 to remove the label. A circle will appear beneath the image thumbnail, filled with the color and number of the label you chose (**Figure 2.16**).

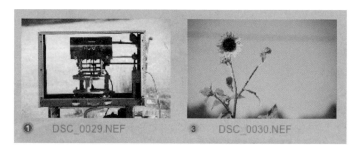

Figure 2.16 When you label an image, its label appears as a colored, numbered circle beneath the image thumbnail.

You can use the mouse to assign a label by clicking on the appropriate label on the label bar at the bottom of the screen or by clicking on the Label pop-up menu beneath an image (**Figure 2.17**).

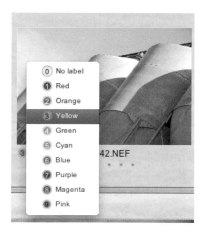

Figure 2.17 You can also label an image by picking a label from the label pop-up beneath the thumbnail.

As with ratings, you can also assign labels from the Metadata palette.

Labels are handy if you have images that you want to group into categories. Maybe you've shot a wedding and you've gone through your images and assigned ratings to indicate your selects, but now within those selects you'd like to differentiate between indoor and outdoor shots. You can do this with a keyword, or you can assign one label for indoor and another for outdoor.

> **NOTE:** *Unfortunately, the IPTC standard does not include either ratings or label fields, which means that the ratings and labels you assign in Capture NX will not be readable by other image editors and browsers. So, while these tools are great for sorting images in Capture NX, if you want to be able to mark pick images (or group images into categories) in a way that can be read by other programs, then you should use keywords or other IPTC metadata fields.*

Redefining Capture NX's Labels

You can change the name and color of any or all of Capture NX's labels using the Preferences dialog. Open the Capture NX Preferences dialog box and click on Labels. Click on a color swatch to pick a new color for that label, and enter any name you want in the corresponding text field.

From the pop-up menu at the top of the box, you can choose predefined label sets that match label colors found in other programs such as Adobe Bridge, Microsoft Expression Media, or the first version of Capture NX (**Figure 2.18**).

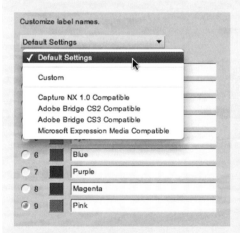

Figure 2.18 You customize label names and colors, and even choose label sets that are compatible with other browsing applications.

Finally, note the radio buttons next to each label. By default, the one next to label 9 is active. This indicates that all nine labels will be shown in the NX Browser. If that's more labels than you need, you can click a different label's button to reduce the number of labels shown in the Browser.

Filtering Your Images

Once you've assigned ratings and labels, you can filter the Browser view to show only images that have specific ratings and labels.

On the Options bar at the top of the screen is a Label selector that shows the standard selection of labels.

To filter the Browser to show only images with a particular label, click on a specific label type on the Label selector on the Options bar at the top of the screen (**Figure 2.19**). The Browser pane will immediately change to show you *only* images with that label.

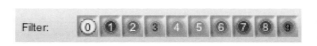

Figure 2.19 Using the Label selector on the Browser's Options bar, you can select to view only images with specific labels.

Each label button is a toggle. Click it once to add images with that label to the current display, click it again to remove images with that label. Because each label is a switch, you can turn on as many as you want, to view a range of labels (**Figure 2.20**).

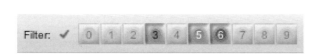

Figure 2.20 By toggling labels on and off, you can specify an assortment of labels. Here we're looking at images with labels 3, 5, or 6.

To view all images, unclick all selected labels, or uncheck the check box to the left of the Label filter bar.

You can also filter images by rating, by using the Rating selector just to the right of the Label selector on the Options bar. Slide the arrows to define a range of ratings that you want to view (**Figure 2.21**).

Figure 2.21 You can configure the Rating selector to show only images with a particular rating or within a particular range of ratings.

> **TIP:** *You can use the Ratings and Label filters in conjunction so that you can, for example, view all three- and four-star images in categories eight and nine.*

You can also filter out different file types, configuring the Browser to display only JPEG images, or raw files, or combinations. Click on the File Type filter to open a pop-up menu that lets you select which types of files you'd like the Browser to display (**Figure 2.22**).

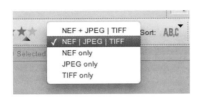

Figure 2.22 The File Type selector lets you filter for specific file types.

Note that choosing NEF | JPEG | TIFF will display all images of these types, while NEF + JPEG | TIFF will display TIFF files as well as pairs of raw and JPEG images (in other words, images shot with a Nikon camera in Raw+JPEG mode). Finally, there are individual options for each specific file type.

To return to viewing all images, select NEF | JPEG | TIFF.

Sorting Images

By default, the Capture NX Browser displays images organized alphabetically, by file name, in ascending order. You can change this by opening the Sort pop-up menu on the Options bar (**Figure 2.23**).

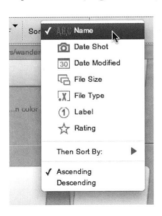

Figure 2.23 You can change the sort order of the images currently displayed in the Browser, as well as specify ascending or descending order.

With this menu, you can choose to sort by any number of parameters, as well as select whether you want an ascending or descending sort. Note that a secondary sort order is also specified, allowing you to choose a second sort parameter.

So, if you've renamed your files in such a way that an alphabetical view no longer displays related images next to each other, you might want to change to a date view, which lists the images in the order in which they were shot.

Note that if you're viewing by Rating or Label, and you change the rating or label of an image, the Browser will automatically update to show the images in the correct order for their new ratings and labels.

"Does Metadata Really Matter? Entering It Is So Tedious..."

I'm the first to admit that on the list of to-dos that I really don't want to spend time on, entering metadata is right up there with washing dishes. In addition to being tedious, it can be hard to see the advantage of metadata in relation to the workflow that we defined earlier.

When it comes to your short-term, project-based workflow, there's really only one reason to hassle with IPTC metadata and that's for ownership protection. With your copyright and credit information firmly ensconced in your image's metadata, you'll have reasonable proof of image ownership. For pictures that will be uploaded to the Web, this is especially important.

The big advantage of disciplined metadata entry occurs later when you need to search your entire image library for particular types of images. In other words, the advantages of metadata are not necessarily for the job you have now but for the jobs you may have later. For example, if you have an especially large library, finding all of your "exterior supermodel" shots can be difficult. But if you've applied good keywords and categories—in this case, category "supermodel" and an "exterior" keyword—you can easily find your images later using software that can search image metadata.

Many image cataloging programs let you search images by metadata. Your images need good metadata for these apps to produce good results, so you should be diligent about applying thorough metadata to your images.

All that said, all of this is optional. You don't *have* to assign any ratings, labels, or even metadata if you don't want to. These tools are provided as flexible mechanisms that allow you to build the workflow that's right for you and to create an organizational scheme that makes sense. Personally, I never use labels, and use a binary rating system (three stars or none), and sometimes apply a smattering of keywords. Experiment to find the options that work well for you.

Replacing the Capture NX Browser

The Capture NX browser is very capable, but it does lack some features found in other browsing programs. You can't view an image at 100 percent, for example. The Browser does not offer stacking features, and it doesn't support non-Nikon raw formats. All of the organization, rating, and selecting steps shown here are also possible in other browsers. If your camera shipped with bundled browser software, you might as well take a look at it and see whether you like it better than the Capture NX Browser.

If you choose to use a non-NX browser, it's easy enough to integrate it into your workflow. Simply perform the selection, rating, and metadata steps of your workflow in your chosen browser, and then use that browser to launch your images into Capture NX for editing.

Here are some other browsers that you might want to consider (note that, for the sake of space, I'm only listing browsers that work on both Windows and Mac).

Adobe Bridge. Adobe's browser, which ships with Photoshop CS2, CS3, CS4, and the Mac version of Photoshop Elements 6, is an excellent browser, that provides all of the capabilities of the Capture NX Browser, along with extra goodies. In addition to supporting most non-Nikon raw formats, Bridge provides additional raw workflow capabilities, and much more. To learn more about Adobe Bridge, and the Photoshop Raw Converter, check out my book *Getting Started With Camera Raw* (also published by Peachpit Press). Bridge can easily be used with Capture NX.

Camera Bits Photo Mechanic. Photo Mechanic is also an excellent browser, whose main selling point is phenomenal speed. No other browser displays thumbnails as quickly as Photo Mechanic, making it ideal for quickly moving from folder to folder as you search for and organize images. Photo Mechanic offers capabilities similar to those of the Capture NX Browser, but with more powerful metadata and rating tools. Like Adobe Bridge, it works very well in conjunction with Capture NX.

Canon Digital Photo Professional (DPP). If you're a Canon shooter, then a copy of DPP should have been included in the box with your camera. For processing Canon raw files, DPP offers a few features not found in other converters. However, be warned that the DPP browser is not great. Underpowered, its main deficiency is its glacial performance.

Adobe Photoshop Lightroom and **Apple Aperture**. Lightroom and Aperture are similar products in that they are designed to handle your entire photo workflow, from import to output. They both include a browser, editor, sophisticated Web output capabilities, and much more. However, they both also require that you import images into a proprietary library scheme. If you want to later edit those images using Capture NX, your workflow will become much more complicated, and you'll lose the benefits of Capture NX's nondestructive editing capabilities. It's possible to work Capture NX into an Aperture or Lightroom workflow, but it will be more complicated.

COLOR MANAGEMENT

If you've ever printed a photo from your computer, you've probably already discovered that your printed output never exactly matches what you see on-screen. Colors will vary, contrast will change, and your overall exposure might look a little different. This doesn't mean that you're doing something wrong—it's just the nature of translating color between two radically different technologies.

Fortunately, there is something you can do to improve the situation. Capture NX offers some simple color management tools that make color reproduction more predictable. Here we'll take a look at some of the basics of color management theory, and see how color management is handled in Capture NX.

However, before we begin, it's important to know that a print will *never* exactly match your screen. Color management technology can help it get closer, but it will always be an approximation, and you'll always have to make test prints. Color management can reduce the number of test prints, but color management technology also requires some specialized profiling hardware, and a little bit of extra time. If you'd rather dive in to the editing features of Capture NX, then feel free to move on to the next chapter, and come back to this section later if you feel so inclined.

Color management can be a very dense topic if you choose to get into a lot of the underlying theory. Fortunately, for everyday use you can get by with a few simple controls and a handful of guidelines. Keeping your system color accurate will take very little time.

Color Management Basics

A lot of factors make color consistency a difficult goal. For one, there's the simple fact that color is subjective; everyone sees color slightly differently. But there are also some hard and fast objective difficulties.

As you may have learned in grade-school finger-painting class, when you mix a few primary colors together, you can create other colors. Similarly, if you've ever set up an inkjet printer, you know that you put just a few ink cartridges in—usually cyan, magenta, yellow, and black—and yet your printer is able to spit out full-color images.

Your digital camera and your computer monitor work the same way. They combine the three primary colors of light—red, green, and blue—to create all of the other colors that they need (**Figure 2.24**). However, there's an important difference in the way your camera combines colors and the way that a printer combines colors.

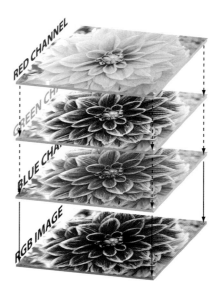

Figure 2.24 Your digital camera creates colors by combining the three additive primary colors of light: red, green, and blue.

Color systems

Your printer creates color by mixing different colored inks. The primary colors of ink—cyan, magenta, and yellow (CMY)—combine in a *subtractive* manner, meaning they get darker as you mix them together until they ultimately become a dark muddy brown. In theory, they should eventually turn black, but making perfectly pure inks is impossible, so very, very, dark brown is usually the best we can achieve. This is why black (the K in CMYK) is usually added to the printing process alongside the primary ink colors.

Like your eye, your camera's image sensor is sensitive to the primary colors of light—red, green, and blue—which combine in an *additive* manner. As you mix red, green, and blue, the result is a lighter color. Mix equal amounts of the three components and you get varying shades of gray or white, given sufficient intensity of the three.

As you might imagine, trying to translate one set of primary colors that mix together in an additive process into a different set of primary colors that mix together in a subtractive manner is a very complex process. Complicating it further is the fact that these two distinct methods of producing color have different *gamuts*. You can reproduce far more colors with an RGB mix of light than you can with a CMYK mix of ink. So, the broad range of RGB colors that your camera can capture must somehow be squeezed down to fit into the more limited range of colors that can be represented with CMYK color.

As if this situation wasn't confusing enough, different types of paper yield dissimilar results, and various monitors display images very differently.

Profiles

A color management system (which consists of software and sometimes hardware) works in the background to adjust your colors as they pass from device to device to compensate for the changes in the color qualities of each device. The practical upshot is that, with a color management system running, you should see less shift as your images pass from device to device throughout your workflow—whether that's moving the image from one monitor to another, or printing it on a printer.

Color management software works by examining special *profiles* that you specify for your monitor and your printer. A profile contains a description of certain color characteristics of each device. Your color management software uses this description to skew the colors as they pass through your workflow, so that your colors and tones appear more similar on each device.

Monitor profiles contain additional information that allows your color management system to adjust special settings in your computer's video card so that your display looks closer to an accepted standard. This process of *calibration* helps different monitors deliver similar images.

Fortunately, there is a widely accepted standard for this profiling information. The International Color Consortium (ICC) has defined a specification for color profiles. Both the Windows and the Mac operating systems provide OS-level support for these ICC profiles. Developing a working color management system begins with the process of building or acquiring good profiles for your system.

Not a magic bullet

Before we move on to profiling, I'm going to reiterate one important fact: *The images that your printer outputs will never look exactly like what you see on your monitor.*

Your monitor is a self-illuminated transmissive color device with a huge gamut of colors at its disposal. A printed page is a reflected color device with a narrow gamut of colors and a very different contrast range. As such, your colors and tones are *always* going to look different from the monitor to the printed page. So, if you're expecting that you'll be able to configure your color management system and from then on know *exactly* what will come out of your printer, you're going to be disappointed.

However, a well-implemented color management system *can* greatly reduce the number of experiments and test prints that you need to make. I usually find that on difficult images working with a profiled system decreases the number of test prints I need from six or seven to just one or two. This is better than I was ever able to do in a chemical darkroom!

Profiling Your Monitor

Configuring your color management system begins with the creation of a monitor profile. The underlying color management software uses the monitor profile to adjust the colors in your image as they pass to your screen, as explained earlier.

You can create a monitor profile by using either a software or hardware calibrator. The Mac OS has a built-in software calibrator and Photoshop ships with one for Windows. Both solutions are better than nothing, but you can now buy a hardware calibrator for under $100, and a hardware calibrator does a *much* better job than a software calibrator. So much so, that the amount of money you'll save in paper and ink will probably pay for the calibrator fairly quickly.

For getting started with color management, using a software-generated profile will at least let you see how the system works.

Software profiling on the Mac

Mac OS X includes a built-in software monitor profiler that builds a monitor profile based on your answers to some simple questions.

To use the Apple Display Calibrator Assistant:

1. Open System Preferences and click Displays. A dialog box appears with a generic monitor name such as "Color LCD." If you have multiple monitors attached to your Mac, a separate dialog box appears for each monitor. For now, pick a monitor that you want to display and move the appropriate dialog box to that screen.

2. Click the Color tab to bring up the color controls for your monitor (**Figure 2.25**).

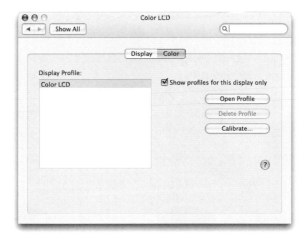

Figure 2.25 Mac OS X has a built-in software monitor calibration system that you can activate from the Displays section of the System Preferences.

3. Click the Calibrate button to launch the Display Calibrator Assistant.

4. In the Display Calibrator Assistant, click the Expert Mode check box (**Figure 2.26**).

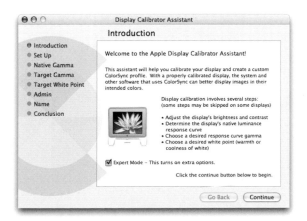

Figure 2.26 The Display Calibrator Assistant walks you through building a monitor profile for your display.

5. Press the Continue button and work your way through each of the screens that the Calibrator Assistant displays. Follow the instructions and answer each question. On some screens, the Calibrator Assistant will ask you to choose among several different patterns. You'll find this process much easier if you squint to defocus your eyes.

6. When you're finished, the Calibrator Assistant will ask you to name your new profile. You can name it whatever you want, but it's usually best to include a date in the profile name. As I'll discuss later, keeping up-to-date profiles is very important.

Software profiling on Windows

If you have Adobe Photoshop (version 7 or later) installed, or Photoshop Elements, you can use the Adobe Gamma control panel that installs with the software to create a monitor profile.

1. On Windows XP, go to Start > Control Panel. On Windows Vista, go to the Start icon, and then choose Control Panel.

2. Double-click Adobe Gamma.

3. Select Step By Step (Wizard) and click Next (**Figure 2.27**).

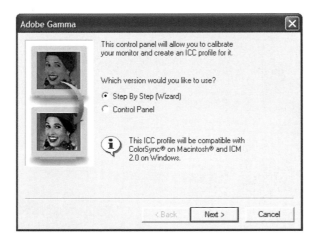

Figure 2.27 The Adobe Gamma control panel lets you create ICC profiles for your Windows computer.

4. Follow the instructions on-screen to create and save a profile.

Under Windows XP, profiles are stored in the Color directory (Windows\System32\Spool\Drivers\Color directory).

Hardware profiling

For more accurate profiles—and therefore, a more effective color management system—you'll want to use a hardware profiler. A hardware profiler is actually a combination of a *colorimeter* or *spectrophotometer*, a small device that you place in front of your monitor, and a piece of included software that uses the colorimeter to analyze your monitor to create a profile (**Figure 2.28**).

Because a hardware profile can perform a more accurate analysis of your monitor's characteristics, hardware-generated profiles are usually much more effective than profiles that you create by eye just using a software profiler.

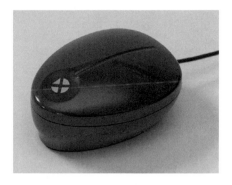

Figure 2.28 A hardware monitor calibrator generates a far more accurate profile than you can make by eye just using a software calibration scheme.

Many different hardware profilers are available at a range of prices. The Pantone Huey sells for $80, whereas the ColorVision Spyder product line ranges from $79 to $280 depending on the options you select. At the upper end, check out products by X Rite, which deliver high-end quality at higher prices. All of these devices will give you better results than what you'll get with a software calibrator, but you definitely get better profiles if you buy a more expensive calibrator.

Using a hardware profiler is very simple. After installing the included software, you simply follow the onscreen instructions. At some point, you'll be prompted to mount the device on, or in front of, your display (**Figure 2.29**).

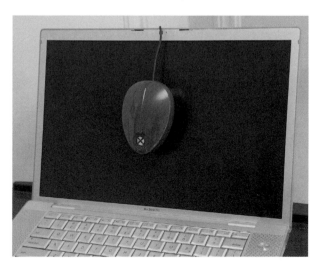

Figure 2.29 A monitor calibrator hangs in front of your monitor. Special software drives the calibrator and builds a profile for you.

Unlike with software calibration, you won't be asked to evaluate any test patterns or image swatches—that's the colorimeter's job. Profiling times will vary from device to device, but you can usually expect to have a profile within ten minutes.

Although it may be frustrating to have to spend even *more* money, you may find that the improved accuracy of a hardware-profiled display will pay for itself fairly quickly, since you'll most likely be using less printer media on test prints.

How Often Should I Profile My Monitor?

The good news is that a monitor profile can greatly improve the quality of your displayed image, but the bad news is that it won't last. Whether you use a CRT or LCD monitor, the image on your display will shift in hue and brightness over time. The older the monitor, the faster the shift. If you're working with a fairly new display, you probably need to profile your monitor only once every month or so. After about 18 months, though, you'll want to step up your rate of profiling. If your monitor is a couple of years old, you should build a new profile once a week.

The software that ships with most hardware profilers will automatically remind you every week that it's time to build a new profile. You don't need to keep the old profiles, so don't worry, you won't soon be drowning in profiles.

Also, don't think that you can just wait until you notice a difference. Your eye can adapt very well to your monitor's subtle shifts, and you may not notice how much your image has washed out, lost saturation, and shifted colors. Trust your color management system and profile regularly.

Profiles and viewing conditions

The ambient light in the room where you view your monitor has a huge impact on your perception of the colors on-screen. Ideally, you want to work in a room where you have full control over the lighting—that is, a room with no windows and no mixed light sources.

When you build a monitor profile, your profiling software will ask you the temperature of the ambient light in the room. You'll usually want to pick an option that matches the dominant light source in your room. If you work in a windowed office, this will probably be sunlight.

In a windowed office, the ambient lighting will change throughout the day. So, you might have heavy sunlight for part of the day and mixed lighting or no sunlight at other times of the day. If you're serious about color management, you should build separate profiles for each of these ambient lighting situations and change from profile to profile as the day progresses.

Some CRTs allow you to create different configurations of monitor settings. This allows you to store different brightness and contrast settings for different ambient lighting situations. You can build separate profiles for each of these monitor settings and then change the monitor setting and your profile as the day progresses.

Where Is This Color Management Software?

Throughout this section I've been talking about the color management software that utilizes your profiles to correct the color on your screen and printer. This software is part of your operating system and runs in the background. You will never interact with it directly, other than to install profiles in the appropriate places. However, you *will* alter settings in Capture NX, which in turn will handle all necessary communication with the color management software.

Printer Profiling

Just as your color management software needs good monitor profiles to be effective, it also needs quality printer profiles to accurately adjust your images for output. However, although you only need one monitor profile (unless you're creating multiple profiles for different ambient lighting situations), you typically need many different printer profiles installed, at least one for each type of paper and ink combination that you intend to print on.

Printer profiles are built using special hardware that measures printer output on a specific type of media, using specific printer settings. You then use that profile anytime you're printing with the paper and settings the profile was designed for. If you don't have a profile for a specific type of paper, you'll have a more difficult time running a color calibrated workflow.

Fortunately, these days most decent photo printers ship with a collection of profiles for all of the paper types that the printer vendor sells for that printer. These profiles are usually installed when you install the printer driver. In some cases, only a basic set of profiles is installed, with more available from the printer vendor's Web site.

Nowadays, many paper companies provide free profiles for using their papers on specific printers.

Unfortunately, profile quality can vary from vendor to vendor and printer to printer. Some printer makers provide excellent profiles for all of their printers, some provide very good profiles for their high-end printers and marginal profiles for their lower-end models, and others don't provide profiles at all.

Further complicating the printer profiling situation is the fact that not every printer that rolls off the same assembly line is identical. As such, a "stock" profile may be more effective on one unit than another, depending on how well each unit conforms to the ideal baseline.

If you aren't getting good results from the profiles included with your printer, or if you want to print on paper for which you don't have a profile (maybe you want to use hand-made paper, paper from an art supply store, or paper from a different printer vendor), you might want to consider getting a custom profile.

Several online services will make a custom profile for you for anywhere from $15–$40. To use these services, you download a few simple test pages, print them out, and mail them to the service. The service then returns an ICC profile that you can install.

For the ultimate control, you can invest in your own paper profiling hardware, but be warned: This gear isn't cheap. Starting at around $1000, products like the XRite Pulse ColorElite provide everything you need to create custom paper profiles. The process is very simple, and you can usually create a profile in about five minutes, depending on the speed of your printer.

Installing printer profiles on the Mac

Under Mac OS X, printer profiles are stored in the Profiles folder (Library > ColorSync > Profiles). They can be loose in the folder or kept in a subfolder, allowing you to keep profiles for specific printers grouped together. Simply copy your printer profiles into this folder and restart Capture NX.

Installing printer profiles on Windows

Under Windows XP and Vista, printer profiles are stored in the Color folder (Windows\System32\Spool\Drivers\Color folder). Simply copy your printer profiles into this folder and restart Capture NX.

Why Don't I Need to Profile My Camera?

Since I'm making such a big deal out of having accurate profiles for your monitor and printer, you might wonder why you don't also use a profile for your camera. As you've already seen with printer and monitor profiles, color profiles are very specific to particular situations. For example, a monitor profile is specific to a particular ambient light level, whereas a printer profile is specific to a particular kind of paper. Because your lighting situation constantly changes when you shoot, there's no way to create a usable camera profile.

However, if you're a studio photographer who works only in very controlled lighting situations, it is possible to profile your camera. Camera profiling is a complex process, involving shooting expensive test charts, and is way beyond the scope of this book. Lack of camera profiles, though, won't prevent you from running a color-managed system.

Color Spaces

The image sensor in your camera registers colors in terms of percentages. For example, a particular pixel might be "100% red." But there are many different shades of red; what constitutes 100 percent of it? A *color space* is a mathematical description that helps define the boundaries of color. So, if you map the same image into two different color spaces, the color in the image might shift, since "100% red" in one color space might be a different hue than "100% red" in another space.

The color space that you choose is simply stored as a tag in the image metadata. When displaying your image, your image editor looks at this tag to find out which color space you want to use for the image and then maps the color values in the image accordingly.

Many color space specifications are available, but the two most popular are sRGB and Adobe RGB. Of the two, sRGB is smaller; the range of colors that it specifies is not as large as the range in Adobe RGB. Probably the most noticeable difference is in the reds. An image mapped into sRGB has more muted reds than an image mapped into Adobe RGB (**Figure 2.30**).

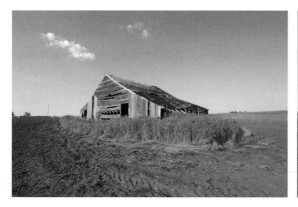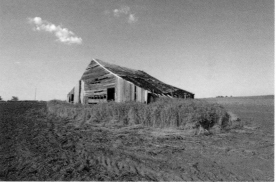

Figure 2.30 The left image has been mapped into sRGB, whereas the right image has been mapped into the larger Adobe RGB, resulting in some colors being slightly more saturated.

Many digital cameras offer a menu option that lets you select sRGB or Adobe RGB (**Figure 2.31**). The sRGB specification was designed with the hope that it would become the standard color space used on the Web. As you've probably already discovered if you've posted any images on the Web, Web pages don't look the same from one monitor to the next. However, because of its smaller color space, if you tag your images as sRGB, there's a better chance that they'll look good on a greater number of monitors. The smaller color palette of sRGB means you'll stand less chance of pushing older or less advanced monitors beyond their capabilities.

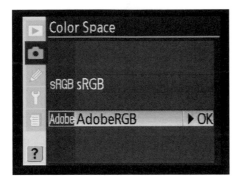

Figure 2.31 Your camera probably includes a menu option for selecting a color space, usually sRGB or Adobe RGB.

Most quality desktop photo printers have a gamut that's larger than sRGB. So if you are shooting with the intent of printing, or if you plan on doing a lot of image editing, tagging your images with the larger Adobe RGB color space is a better option. If you're shooting raw your camera setting is not as critical because you can always select a different color space later. But even though you can always retag your images later, having them come out of the camera properly tagged will save you a step during your postproduction phase (we'll discuss this in more detail in Chapter 4).

Color Management in Capture NX

Once you've acquired and installed the requisite monitor and printer profiles, you might want to make a few preference changes in Capture NX.

1. Open Capture NX's Preferences and click the Color Management tab.

2. Change the Default RGB color space pop-up menu to the color space that you'd like to use for your images. You'll probably want to set this to sRGB or Adobe RGB or to keep it at its default of Nikon Adobe RGB. This is the same as the Adobe RGB color space and is provided for those users who don't have an Adobe RGB profile already installed on their system.

If you want, you can change the Printer Profile pop-up menu to a specific printer profile, but you'll also have the opportunity to set a printer profile when you print. I'll discuss printing and the color management issues related to printing in detail in Chapter 7, "Output." There you will learn how to make a more educated color space choice.

Basic Image Editing

There are several reasons that you will decide to edit your images. Sometimes you employ an image editor to fix mistakes, such as exposure or color problems, or to remove sensor dust or optical artifacts. At other times, you edit your images because your camera has a limited dynamic range, and it's not possible to achieve in-camera the image that you had in mind while shooting. You might also choose to edit your images because the result you're trying to create requires special effects such as compositing.

Image editing can occur at many different places within your workflow. In Chapter 2, we outlined a plan for how to take your images through postproduction and we placed the image-editing step after your sorting and selecting stage to ensure that you don't waste time editing and correcting images that you don't ultimately want to use. However, you might have your own workflow, and on a very small shoot—perhaps you spied a beautiful sunset out the window and quickly ran out to shoot half a dozen images—you might simply transfer all of the images you shot and run each one through your image editor.

Capture NX can facilitate all of the edits and corrections that you'll need to make to most of your images. Tone and color corrections can be applied globally or locally, providing you with a tremendous amount of editing power.

In this chapter, after reviewing the correct way to open your images, you'll learn how to use all of NX's global tone and color correction controls. (By "global" I mean the tools that affect your entire image rather than just one part of it.) In addition, I'll discuss how to save your images. Saving is a simple process, but because Capture NX is a nondestructive editing system, it's important to understand how it stores edits and images.

While you're probably itching to get editing, there's just a little bit of theory that needs to be discussed first. Capture NX uses a *nondestructive* image-editing architecture, which makes it very different from many other image-editing programs that you might use. Offering extreme flexibility, nondestructive editing is not hard to learn, but you'll need to know a few concepts to better understand how to make the most of it.

UNDERSTANDING NONDESTRUCTIVE EDITING

When you open an image in most image-editing or painting programs, the image data is read into the computer's memory. The color of each pixel in the image is represented by a number, and when you edit any of the pixels in the image, their color values—and corresponding underlying numbers—are altered. When you save the image, the new numbers are written back to the original file. This type of editing is called *destructive editing* because the original pixel values are destroyed when you make editing changes (**Figure 3.1**). Later, undoing or altering an edit that you've already made can be very difficult or even impossible. For this reason, when using a destructive editor you want to always save a copy of your original file so that you can return to the original image if you need to.

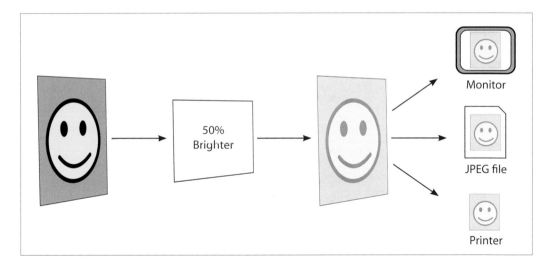

Figure 3.1 In a destructive editing process, when you make an edit (such as the brightening edit shown here), the pixels in your image are changed. When you output to a screen, printer, or file, those new, changed pixels are sent to the relevant device.

In a *nondestructive editing* process, your original image data is read into memory, but when you make an edit the original pixel values are *not* altered. Instead, each edit is added to a list of all of the edits that you have specified for that image. Any time the computer needs to display or output the image, the list of edits is applied to the original data. These edits are applied on the fly, whether you're displaying the images onscreen, printing to a printer, or saving to a file (**Figure 3.2**). Because your original pixel data is never altered, you can remove or alter any edit at any time and in any order.

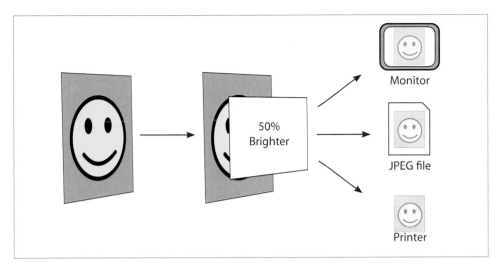

Figure 3.2 In a nondestructive editing process, any edit is simply added to a list of edits to be applied to the original image data. When you output to a screen, printer, or file, those edits are applied in real time as the image data is moved to the relevant device.

Some programs provide both destructive and nondestructive editing. Photoshop's Brush tool, for example, performs destructive changes to your image—it alters the original pixels; however, Photoshop's adjustment layers are completely nondestructive—their effects are applied in real time.

Capture NX, by contrast, provides only nondestructive editing tools. All of the edits that you make in Capture NX are stored in the Edit List palette (**Figure 3.3**).

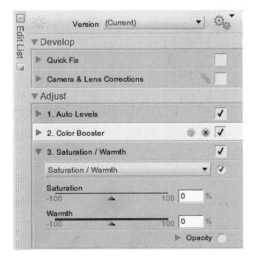

Figure 3.3 Capture NX's Edit List palette stores every edit that you make to your image. You can deactivate or alter any edit at any time, and if you save in NEF format, your edit list will still be there the next time you open the file. This is the advantage of nondestructive editing.

At any time, you can view and alter any of these edits by simply clicking the reveal arrow to the left of the edit name. You can also completely remove an edit by unchecking the edit's check box. This edit list is applied on the fly to your image data as the image is written to the screen or printed.

You have two options when you save your image. If you want to preserve your edit list (so that you can return to it later to refine or alter your edits), you'll need to save your image in NEF format. Although many people think that a NEF file means that the image is a raw file, the NEF format can actually hold far more than just raw data. NEF files can hold normal processed-image data—just like you would save in a TIFF or JPEG file—along with the list of edits that you create in Capture NX. NEF is an all-purpose container that can hold all of the data that Capture NX needs to store, from raw files captured by your Nikon camera to processed TIFF or JPEG images, as well as the Edit List you've used to alter your original file.

If you want to view your image in an application other than Capture NX, save it as a JPEG or TIFF file. These are standard raster file formats that are compatible with almost any image-editing program. However, JPEG and TIFF files *cannot* preserve your edit list. If you save an image out of Capture NX as a JPEG or TIFF file, when you open the image again, the Capture NX Edit List palette will be empty. Consequently, you should save both NEF *and* JPEG or TIFF files of your image. You'll use the NEF file as your master, editable image, and your JPEG or TIFF file for distribution or for editing your image in another application.

We'll explore saving and editing in more detail later in this chapter.

Very often, you'll want to perform the same edits to entire batches of images. If you've shot a series of images in the same lighting setup, for example, the same Tone, Color, and White Balance adjustments will probably be relevant to all of the images. For this reason, Capture NX includes powerful batch processing capabilities that make short work out of applying edits to large groups of images. These features are all detailed in Chapter 6, "Version Control and Batch Processing."

When your images are finished, you'll be ready to output them. While Capture NX is a completely nondestructive editing environment, you'll have no problem moving your finished images into other applications that can read TIFF or JPEG files. All of these details are covered in Chapter 7, "Output," along with an explanation of how to print your images using Capture NX's fully color-managed printing architecture.

TIP: *In addition to Capture NX's nondestructive architecture, the program also offers unlimited undoing, meaning you can simply keep hitting Undo to back up through your edits. As with any program, any Undo you make is not saved with your document. Between these two features, you should never have any concerns about exploring new edits.*

OPENING IMAGES

You can open your images in Capture NX in many ways, and which one is right for you is largely a matter of personal preference. (I'm assuming you've already transferred your images to your computer, a topic covered in detail in Chapter 1.)

Capture NX can open TIFF files, JPEG files, or Nikon NEF files.

Opening with the Browser

In the last chapter, you saw how the Capture NX Browser lets you see thumbnail views of all of the images in a folder and how it lets you add ratings and metadata to your images so that you can easily sort out the ones that you want to edit. Once you find an image in the Browser that you'd like to begin editing, simply double-click on it to open it in Capture NX, or drag it into the Edit window.

The Open Image Command

The Open Image command (File > Open Image) works just like the Open command in any other application. Choose it and you'll be presented with your operating system's standard Open dialog box, which lets you navigate to the file that you want to open. Select the file and click the Open button to open it in Capture NX.

Open Recent

Under the File menu you'll also find an Open Recent command, which lists the last ten documents that you've opened. You can simply select one of these items to reopen the document.

The Welcome Dialog Box

When you launch Capture NX, the program displays a dialog box that lists the last ten images you've opened. Click one of these images and Capture NX opens it. The Open Recent Browser section of the dialog box shows the last ten folders and documents that you've viewed in the Browser palette. You can click on a folder to automatically browse that folder or on an image to open that image in the Editor (**Figure 3.4**).

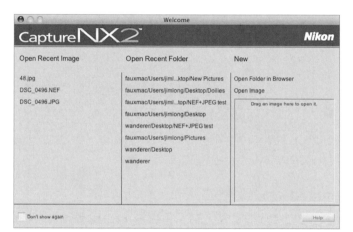

Figure 3.4 Capture NX's Welcome screen provides single-click shortcuts to recently opened documents and folders. You can deactivate this screen by checking the Don't Show Again check box and reopen it later by choosing Help > Show Welcome Screen.

In the New section, you'll find options for invoking the program's Open dialog box and Open Folder in Browser dialog box. On the Mac, you can drag an image from your desktop into the "Drag an image here to open it" portion of the dialog box to open it immediately. On Windows, you can simply drag it into the Edit window.

If you'd rather not be presented with the Welcome dialog box, click the "Don't show again" check box.

Opening from Your OS

Of course, you can also open images in Capture NX using all of the normal mechanisms provided by your operating system.

> **NOTE:** There are color differences between the Browser and the editor. When you open an image from the NX Browser, you may find that the color looks slightly different in the editor. The NX Browser is not color managed, meaning it doesn't pay any attention to any profiles that you may configure using NX's color management tools. So, if you see a slight color shift, don't worry; the editor color is the color that will be used for your final output.

Opening Raw Files

Capture NX can open the raw files that are produced by almost any raw-capable Nikon camera. It *cannot* open raw files produced by non-Nikon cameras. If you're working with non-Nikon raw files, you'll need to perform your initial raw conversion using a different program and save the resulting images as TIFF files. You can then bring those TIFF images into Capture NX. (See Chapter 2 for more on these types of workflow concerns.)

Some raw-capable image editors require you to first perform a raw conversion step before passing the results on to the rest of your image-editing process. In Capture NX, there is no separate raw conversion step. Simply open a Nikon raw file just as you would a TIFF or JPEG and start editing. All of your image-editing controls will look the same no matter what type of image you're editing, although you may find some extra functionality in some controls when working with raw files. I'll cover all of these differences throughout the next two chapters.

IMAGE-EDITING WORKFLOW

Once you've opened your image, you're ready to start editing. However, before diving into the editing controls, it's a good idea to make a plan of attack—that is, to take a critical look at your image and determine which edits you think it might need. Certain edits are best performed in a specific order, so developing an editing plan can help you work more efficiently and prevent you from having to backtrack later.

In general, you should proceed through your edits in the following order:

Make geometric corrections. You can't always frame your image precisely as you want it in the camera. Sometimes, the proper framing isn't possible (maybe you want a very skinny image, for example), and sometimes you'll simply discover later that a crop allows you to recompose your image to bring better focus to your subject (**Figure 3.5**).

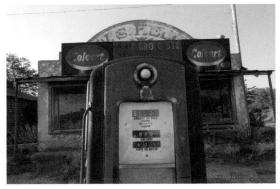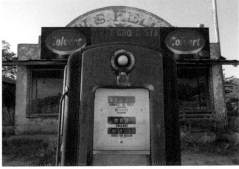

Figure 3.5 For this image, the editing workflow began with straightening and cropping the image.

Similarly, if you didn't shoot your image straight, you may want to straighten it. If your image suffers from extreme distortion problems—like you might get when using a very wide-angle lens—you might want to employ some kind of distortion correction.

All of these edits can result in a cropping of your image, which is why it's best to perform them first. After all, you don't want to waste time adjusting the color and tone of part of an image that will ultimately be cropped away by another edit.

> **TIP:** Cropping out things you don't want will make the Capture NX histogram more accurate (since it won't be including irrelevant data in its reading) and will help you make color and tonal decisions that are correct for your final image composition. You'll learn about the histogram in more detail shortly.

Remove color casts. If you did your camera work right, you won't need to worry about this step. Sometimes, especially in low-light situations, there's no way to shoot without acquiring a color cast. For a number of reasons, it's best to correct color casts early in your editing workflow. First off, if the color cast is very bad you'll want to see if it's even possible to get rid of it. If it's not possible, then you might decide that you don't want to edit any further. Second, once you've corrected the color cast, you'll have a better idea of what other edits the image might need. And finally, if you're working with a non-raw file, correcting the color cast might "use up" some of your editing latitude. With the cast corrected (**Figure 3.6**), you'll have a better idea of how far you can push your additional edits. (You'll learn about this concept of editing "latitude" in Chapter 5.)

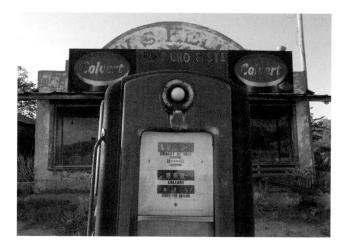

Figure 3.6 Because the image had a slightly cool cast, it was corrected to a more neutral color tone.

Do initial retouching. Retouching can occur in several places in your workflow. You might, for example, want to get all of your tonal and color corrections done before you begin retouching. However, if your image has some especially bad troubles—red eye problems, sensor dust, or other problems that will make the image unusable if they can't be corrected—then you should fix these troubles early in your workflow. If they can't be corrected, then you'll know that this image probably isn't worth continuing with. So, for this early retouching step you'll aim to correct red eye, chromatic aberration (color fringe around high-contrast details that can occur in certain types of images), sensor dust problem, and any other issue that would be a deal-breaker if corrections won't work (stray hairs, skin blemishes, etc.).

Adjust tone and contrast. Next, you'll attack any basic tone and contrast problems. If the image is overexposed or underexposed, or has too little or too much contrast, you should fix those problems in this step. Because altering tone and contrast usually has an impact on the color in your image, you want tone and contrast adjustments out of the way before you turn to color correction. The tone and contrast corrections might be global corrections, or they might be corrections and adjustments that are applied to isolated parts of the image (**Figure 3.7**).

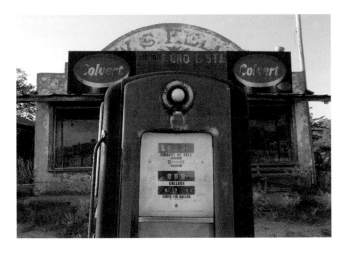

Figure 3.7 Adjusting the image's contrast and tone restored some of the blacks and improved the overall contrast.

Perform color correction. Any additional color corrections that weren't repaired by your tone and contrast adjustments can be applied now. These might include hue adjustments and shifts or saturation changes (**Figure 3.8**). As with tone and contrast corrections, these adjustments might be either global or local.

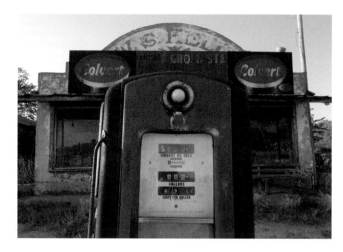

Figure 3.8 A saturation adjustment was applied to give the colors more punch.

Make final tweaks. Color corrections might affect your previous tone and contrast adjustments, so you might need to make minor corrections to those adjustments. Those, in turn, might mess up your color. Usually, you'll go back and forth between adjusting tone and contrast and making color corrections until your image is complete. Also, as you work more on the image, you might get other ideas about what you want to do to it.

Sharpen and output the image. With your image corrected, you're ready to apply sharpening (**Figure 3.9**), and then to output your final result, either as a print or an electronic file. Depending on your output needs, you might also need to resize the file. For example, if you want to email a copy to a friend, you might want to create a small version for output, that's more reasonable for emailing. Conversely, if you're going to print the image on a large-format printer, you might need to greatly enlarge the image.

You won't need to perform all of the preceding steps on every image, and some images might require a very different workflow. For example, an image shot in extremely low light might need an initial brightening before you can see it well enough to crop it or make any other edits. Fortunately, thanks to Capture NX's nondestructive editing architecture, it's very easy to adjust your workflow on the fly.

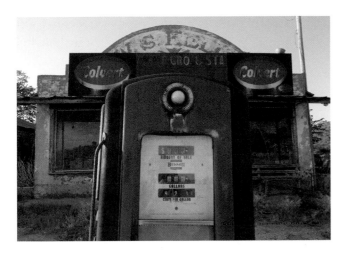

Figure 3.9 The final step, an Unsharp Mask adjustment, was applied to sharpen the image for output.

You'll learn the details of each category of edit as you work through this chapter.

ZOOMING AND PANNING YOUR IMAGE

When you open a landscape-oriented image in Capture NX, it opens to the largest size that will fit within the confines of your screen and NX's palettes. On an image with a high pixel-count, this will usually mean that you're looking at a reduced view of your image. Portrait-oriented images seem to open at various sizes, so you'll probably need to zoom in or out to get the view that you want. Capture NX shows the level of current magnification as a percentage in the title bar of the image (**Figure 3.10**). There are a few ways that you can zoom and pan around your image.

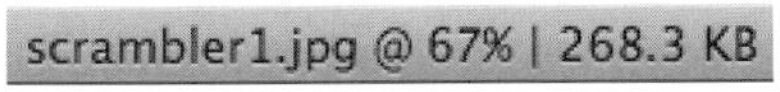

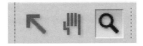

Figure 3.10 Capture NX always shows the current zoom percentage in the title bar of the image.

The Zoom tool lets you zoom in and out of your image. To use the Zoom tool:

1. In the toolbar, click on the Zoom tool to select it, or press Z (**Figure 3.11**).

Figure 3.11 The Zoom tool lets you zoom in and out of your image.

2. Click on the area you want centered as you zoom.

Capture NX will zoom into your image, with the point you clicked on in the center of the window. When you reach 100 percent, you're looking at individual pixels in the image. When you go beyond 100 percent, you're looking at an enlarged view of those individual pixels.

3. To zoom out, hold down Alt/Option while clicking in the image.

4. To pan about your image while zoomed in, you can click on the scroll bars on the right side and the bottom of the image. An easier way to pan is to press and hold the spacebar, which turns your cursor into a grabber hand. With the spacebar down, click and drag in your image to pan about.

The Bird's Eye palette provides another way to zoom and navigate about your image.

1. If the Bird's Eye palette is not visible, choose Window > Bird's Eye to activate it (**Figure 3.12**).

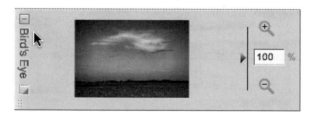

Figure 3.12 The Bird's Eye palette provides another way to zoom in and out of your image.

2. To zoom in and out of your image using the Bird's Eye palette, click the + (plus) and – (minus) icons in the palette, or use the zoom slider, or enter a percentage into the zoom field.

As you zoom in, the Bird's Eye palette will gray out anything that's not visible at the current magnification level, letting you see exactly which part of your image you're currently viewing (**Figure 3.13**).

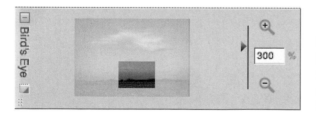

Figure 3.13 When you zoom in, the Bird's Eye palette presents a small navigation box that you can drag around to see a different part of your image.

3. To pan about your image, click and drag in the Bird's Eye palette to another part of your image, which will move the box that indicates what's visible.

Zooming and Panning with the Keyboard

By far, the easiest way to zoom and pan your image is to use the keyboard. With keyboard controls, you don't have to change tools or interrupt other edits that you're currently working on.

To zoom in and out using the keyboard:

1. Press Control/Command + to zoom in. That's the plus sign up on the top row of keys, where the numbers are. Note that you don't have to press Shift.

2. Press Control/Command – to zoom out. That's the minus sign right next to the plus. Again, you don't have to shift.

3. Press Control/Command-0 (that's a zero) to zoom out to a size that will fit the entire image on your screen. This is the same zoom level that the image will open up to by default.

4. Press Control/Command-Alt/Option-0 to view your image at 100 percent. You'll do this regularly when sharpening your image.

As with the Zoom tool, when you zoom in with the keyboard, you can press and hold the spacebar and then click and drag in the image to pan about.

THE CAPTURE NX EDIT LIST

As discussed earlier, Capture NX never alters any of the pixels in your original image file. Instead, it simply keeps a list of the edits that you want to make. These edits are applied to your original image file in real-time, and the results are written to the screen (or to a file if you're exporting, or to a printer if you're printing). The practical upshot of this process is that you can change or remove any edit at any time. The change simply alters the list, and a new image is created by applying the new list of edits to the original master file.

By default, the Edit List is visible on the right side of your display. You can toggle it on and off by choosing Window > Edit List. You'll most likely never turn off the Edit List, as you'll use it to manage and alter all of the edits you make to your image.

Anatomy of the Edit List

The Edit List palette is divided into two panes, *Develop* and *Adjust*. By default, the Develop pane has two main edit groups, *Quick Fix* and *Camera & Lens Corrections*. If you're working on a raw file, then you'll also see a *Camera Settings* edit in the Develop pane. You can open and close each of these sections, just as you can open and close the Develop and Adjust panes, to free up more space (**Figure 3.14**).

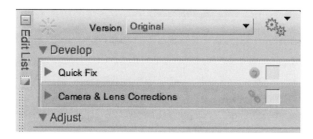

Figure 3.14 The Edit List is divided into two areas, Quick Fix and Adjust. Both can be opened and closed.

The Develop pane

Quick Fix provides all of the controls you'll want for 90 percent of the tone and color corrections you'll need to make. The tools in the Camera & Lens Control section are used to control problems resulting from lens issues such as distortion and chromatic aberration, or camera troubles such as red eye.

As you can see, everything the Develop pane contains is analogous to a traditional film development process. With these tools, you can tweak and adjust your image into an excellent product.

Note that both Quick Fix and Camera & Lens Corrections have a big check box next to their names. With this check box, you can activate or deactivate the effects of these controls. Every edit that appears in the Edit List will have a check box like this (**Figure 3.15**).

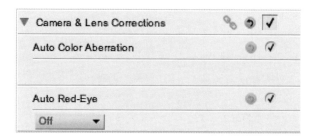

Figure 3.15 Each edit in the Edit List has a check box in its title bar, which lets you turn the effects of the edit on and off.

Quick Fix and Camera & Lens Correction each contain a few different operations. For example, Camera & Lens Correction includes Auto Color Aberration, and Auto Red Eye. Each of these edits has a smaller check box next to it, which you can use to turn these individual effects on and off. When you uncheck an edit, its settings do not alter. Instead, it simply ceases to have an effect on your image, thus providing you with a quick way to see the before and after effects of an edit.

As long as you save your image as a NEF file, all of these parameters will be stored with your image. So, at any time you can open an image and alter the parameters of an edit, or you can deactivate an edit altogether. This is the power of nondestructive editing.

Note that you won't see any other edits in the Develop pane. Quick Fix, Camera & Lens Correction, and Camera Settings are the only edits that appear in this part of the edit list.

> **NOTE:** I'll be covering Camera Settings in detail in Chapter 4, where you'll learn about working with raw files.

The Adjust pane

The Adjust pane is where all other edits that you make are listed. If you crop an image, straighten it, or use any of Capture NX's localized editing tools, the controls for each of those tools will appear in the Adjust pane (**Figure 3.16**).

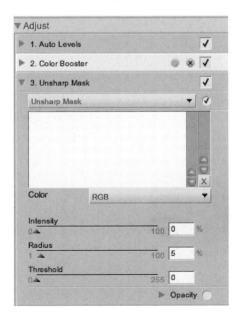

Figure 3.16 After some typical editing, the Adjust pane will fill up with edits.

As with the Develop pane, everything that gets listed in the Adjust pane is an individual edit that can be turned on and off and whose parameters can be adjusted at any time.

> **NOTE:** *The edits in the Develop pane are intended to get you to a good base image. For some images, the Develop pane edits will be all you need. For other images, you'll need to apply some additional edits. You'll find that some of the other edits you can add do duplicate some of the functionality of the Develop pane. However, this is one important difference between the Develop controls and the other edits you can add: The Develop edits do not work with any of the selective editing tools that you'll learn about in Chapter 5.*

Edit Steps get added to the Adjust pane in the following ways.

- When you select an adjustment from the Adjust or Filter menu, an Edit Step is added for that specific adjustment.

- When you use one of Capture NX's tools—Crop, Straighten, Rotate, Control Points, and the Red Eye tool—an Edit Step is added.

- You can also click the New Step button at the bottom of the Edit List to add a new edit. Then select the type of edit you want from the Select Adjustment pull-down menu at the top of the new edit (**Figure 3.17**).

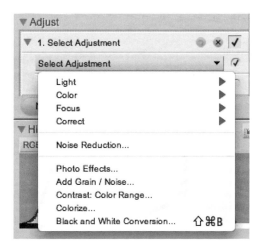

Figure 3.17 At the top of each edit is a pull-down menu that lets you specify exactly what type of edit you want.

As with the edits in the Develop pane, edits in the Adjust pane have a check box that enables you to activate and deactivate the effect. Most also have a reveal arrow that opens the edit so that you can see its parameters.

Additional controls

The Edit List contains some other controls. At the very top of the Edit List you'll see a Version pop-up menu, which allows you to create different versions of your image (**Figure 3.18**);

that is, different copies of the image, each with different edits. To the right of the pop-up menu is an Action menu, which gives you controls for copying edits from one image to another. You'll learn about both of these menus in Chapter 6.

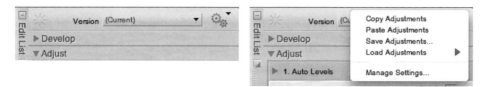

Figure 3.18 The Version and Action menus let you create multiple versions of an image, and perform sophisticated batch processing operations.

Opening Images Saved with Previous Versions of Nikon Capture

If you've used previous versions of Nikon Capture (versions 1 through 4, before it became NX) or Capture NX, then you won't have any trouble opening up your old files, even though NX 2's Edit List looks so different. Capture NX 2 is fully compatible with NEF files produced by all previous versions of Capture and Capture NX.

Obviously, Capture NX 2's Edit List varies in many ways from its predecessor, the biggest difference being the lack of Base Adjustments. However, all of the Base Adjustments edits that you might have made with Capture NX (or previous versions of Capture) are still in there, they just now get added to the appropriate edits in the Edit List. Some will be added as edits in the Adjust section, while others will be added to the edits in the Develop section.

One nice improvement in NX 2 is that you can now apply edits in *any* order. You're no longer constrained to having Base Adjustments sit, well, at the base.

Since TIFF and JPEG files don't include edit information, there's no concern about compatibility with previous versions.

Deleting an Edit step

You can delete any edit in the Adjust portion of the Edit List by clicking on the small X that appears in the Edit's title bar, next to the check box. You can also delete an edit by clicking the edit's title bar to select it and then pressing the Delete key. You can delete multiple Edit Steps at once by clicking to select the first one, and then Shift-clicking to select additional sequential edits. If you want to select noncontiguous edits, click to select the first one and then Command/Control-click additional edits to add them to the selection.

> **TIP:** If you right-click (Command-click on the Macintosh) on any edit, you can choose to Expand, Collapse, or Select all of the edits in the Edit List. If you want to quickly unclutter the list, collapsing all can be a great way to do it.

Changing the type of edit

The name of each edit in the Adjust pane is listed in the title bar of the edit controls. As you saw earlier, each edit also contains a pop-up menu that displays the edit type (**Figure 3.19**).

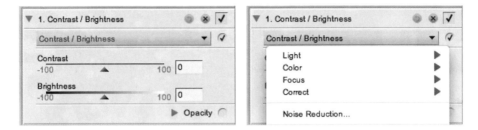

Figure 3.19 Every edit in the Adjust panel contains a pop-up menu that lets you change the edit to another type.

Open this menu and you'll see a list of *all* of the different types of edits that can be applied to an image. So, at any time you can change an edit from one type to another. This can be handy if you realize that the edit that you've applied isn't doing what you want and that you need to switch to a different type of edit. Rather than delete the first edit and apply a second, you can simply change the edit from one type to another.

Opacity

Many edits have an Opacity control at the bottom. For example, Hue/Saturation and the Distortion Control both have an Opacity option at the bottom of their controls.

Click the reveal arrow next to the Opacity title to view the Opacity controls (**Figure 3.20**).

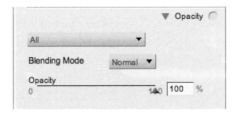

Figure 3.20 Every edit includes Opacity controls that let you attenuate the effect of that edit without changing the edit's parameters.

Adjusting the opacity lets you attenuate the degree of effect that your edit is having. For example, if you apply a really strong Saturation/Warmth adjustment, and then decide later that you might want to dial it back, you can lower its opacity. Why not just dial in less adjustment? Because if you've made an especially finicky adjustment that requires the alteration of many parameters, it can be complicated to simply "dial it down." Also, if you later decide that you want to dial it back up, you'll have to remember what you did. By lowering the opacity, you can scale back the effect with a single slider, and easily restore it later.

The opacity edit works by essentially laying a copy of your image on top of itself. The upper layer includes the edit whose opacity you're adjusting, while the lower one doesn't. When you lower the opacity slider, you're simply changing the opacity of that upper layer, so that the two images are composited together. Changing the parameter in the Blending Mode pop-up will further alter the way the two images are composited. We'll be looking at these controls in more detail in the next chapter.

Resetting an edit to its default parameters

There might be times when you want to clear an edit's settings and start over. In the Edit's title bar, clicking the default arrow (which doesn't appear until you've adjusted some parameters in the edit) will reset the edit to its default settings (**Figure 3.21**).

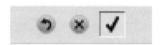

Figure 3.21 The left-most button on an Edit List's title bar resets the parameters of the edit to their defaults.

Now that you understand the workings of the Edit List, you're ready to dive into some actual editing. As mentioned in the editing workflow discussion earlier in this chapter, your first task will be to perform any geometric adjustments that might result in a crop of your image.

GEOMETRIC ADJUSTMENTS

Capture NX provides several tools for performing geometric corrections to your images, for those times when you couldn't frame your image the way you wanted or didn't have your camera quite level. Some are available from the toolbar, and others are implemented as menu commands.

> **TIP:** You might need a quick brightening. If you've been shooting in low light, then your image might be so underexposed that you can't see its details well enough to make any kind of adjustments. You'll want to use the Quick Fix controls to apply a brightening to your image so that you can see well enough to start on your workflow. This adjustment doesn't have to be at all accurate—just enough to let you see what you're doing. Because Capture NX is nondestructive, you can easily remove the edit or dial it back when you get to your tone and contrast adjustments later.

Rotate

Most digital cameras these days include a rotation sensor that lets them determine if you are shooting in vertical or horizontal orientation (sometimes referred to as *portrait* or *landscape*). When the camera saves an image, it stores a flag in the image metadata that indicates the orientation of the image.

Capture NX, like many other image editors, can read this orientation flag and automatically display your image appropriately. There will be times, though, when the flag won't get set or will get set incorrectly, and your image will be oriented wrong. Or, you might be working with scans or with a camera that lacks an orientation sensor. For all of these instances, Capture NX provides a Rotate tool that rotates your image in 90-degree increments.

To rotate an image 90 degrees clockwise:

1. Click the Rotate 90 degrees Clockwise tool on the toolbar (**Figure 3.22**) once.

     Figure 3.22 The Rotate tool on Capture NX's toolbar lets you rotate your images in 90 degree increments.

2. Note that a Rotate Edit Step is added to your Edit List.

To rotate an image 90 degrees counterclockwise:

1. Click and hold the Rotate 90 degrees Clockwise tool.

2. From the resulting pop-up menu (**Figure 3.23**), select the Rotate 90 degrees CCW tool. Your image will be rotated accordingly.

    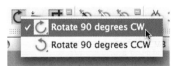 **Figure 3.23** If you click and hold the Rotate button, a pop-up menu appears and allows you to select between clockwise and counterclockwise rotation.

3. Note that a Rotate Edit Step is added to your Edit List.

As you continue to click the Rotate tools, additional Rotate Edits are added to your list. So, for example, if you click twice to rotate an image 180 degrees, you'll see two Rotate Edits in your Edit List.

> **TIP:** Use Option/Alt to rotate the other way. If the Rotate tool is set for clockwise rotation, clicking on it while holding down Option/Alt will rotate counterclockwise. The opposite will happen if the tool is set for counterclockwise rotation.

Straighten

You can use Capture NX's Straighten tool to level out those images that might have been shot a little off-kilter. Be aware, however, that straightening an image also results in your image being cropped. When you rotate an image to straighten it, it goes "out of true" with the rectangular canvas that contains it (**Figure 3.24**). Capture NX automatically crops the image to eliminate this extra space.

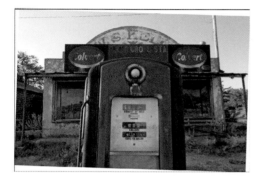

Figure 3.24 When you rotate an image to straighten it, it goes out of true with its original rectangular canvas and requires cropping to restore it to a rectangular shape. Capture NX's Straighten tool rotates and crops at the same time.

To straighten an image:

1. Click the Straighten tool on the Capture NX toolbar, or select Edit > Rotate > Straighten. A Straighten edit is added to your Edit List, and the Straighten settings automatically open.

2. Click in your image at one end of something in the scene that should be horizontal, (such as the horizon) and drag to the other end of the object, and then release the mouse (**Figure 3.25**).

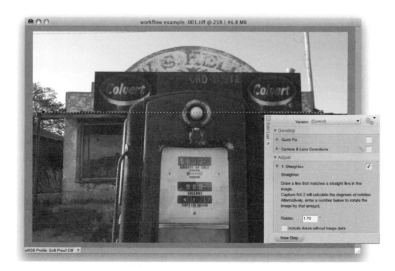

Figure 3.25
To straighten an image, use the Straighten tool to drag a line across something in your image that should be horizontal. Capture NX automatically calculates the amount of rotation necessary to straighten your image.

Capture NX automatically calculates the amount of image rotation required to straighten the line. That value is automatically entered in the Straighten Settings palette, and your image is rotated and cropped.

> **TIP:** *If it's easier to spot a line in your image that should be vertical, you can use the same technique on a vertical line rather than a horizontal line.*

If you hold the Straighten tool over the image, you'll see that the original line that you drew now has control handles on either end. If the straightening you specified isn't correct, drag the handles to redefine the line. As you move them, the image will automatically be restraightened and cropped. You can also adjust the straightening numerically by altering the Rotate value that appears in the Straighten edit in the Edit List.

> **TIP:** *If you'd rather not let Capture NX automatically crop your image after straightening, check the Include Areas without image data check box in the Straighten Settings palette.*

Crop

The Capture NX Crop tool lets you crop your image by dragging a rectangle to define the crop that you want.

To crop an image:

1. Click the Crop tool on the toolbar, or press C.

2. Drag in your image to define the cropping rectangle that you want (**Figure 3.26**).

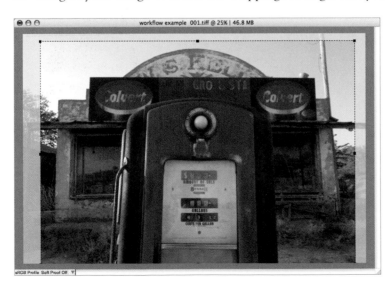

Figure 3.26 You can use the Crop tool to drag a cropping rectangle around your image. Adjust the crop by dragging on the crop handles. Accept the crop by pressing Return or double-clicking within the crop area.

3. If your crop needs any adjustment, click and drag on the control handles on the border of the crop rectangle.

4. When your crop is adjusted to your liking, double-click within the crop rectangle or press Return.

Like all other edits, cropping in Capture NX is nondestructive. If you later decide that you don't like the crop, click the Crop entry in the Edit List, and press Delete to remove the crop, then re-crop.

> **TIP:** *If you hold down the Alt or Option key with the Crop tool selected, Capture NX superimposes a grid of horizontal and vertical guidelines over your image. You can also activate the grid by checking Show crop assistance grid in the Crop tool options bar.*

Crop options

When you select the Crop tool, the Options bar beneath the toolbar displays Crop tool parameters. With these options, you can constrain your crops to a specific aspect ratio. Change the Free Crop menu to Fixed Aspect Ratio, and then enter the aspect ratio that you want in the text fields (**Figure 3.27**).

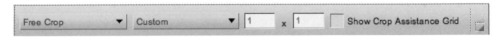

Figure 3.27 The Crop Options bar lets you specify a fixed aspect ratio that you want to crop to.

Flipping

You can flip your image vertically or horizontally (or both) by using the Flip commands (Edit > Flip). A Flip edit will be added to your Edit List. The Flip adjustment provides no additional parameters.

> **The Grid**
>
> Some geometric corrections will be easier to make if you activate Capture NX's grid. Choose View > Show Grid to superimpose a reference grid over your image. The grid provides a reference for true horizontal and vertical.
>
> You can change the color of the grid lines as well as their frequency and number of subdivisions by choosing Preferences > Display and then editing the Grid parameters.
>
> To deactivate the grid, choose View > Show Grid again.

Distortion Control

If you're shooting with a wide-angle lens (or a really low-quality lens of any focal length), you might notice distortion in the corners of your image; that is, straight lines that begin to curve as they near the edge of the frame. You can correct for this distortion using Capture NX's Distortion Control.

To correct distortion in an image:

1. Open the image (**Figure 3.28**).

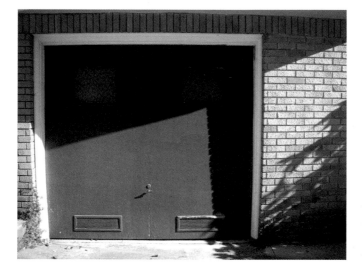

Figure 3.28 Because this image was shot with a wide-angle lens, it has distortion problems. The horizontal lines bow near the edges of the frame.

2. Select Adjust > Correct > Distortion Control. A Distortion Control edit is added to the Adjust portion of the Edit List, and you'll see a slight correction applied to the image. This is the result of the Distortion Control's default setting of 10 percent.

3. Slide the Correction slider back and forth to correct the corner distortion of your image. As you can see, the Distortion Control works by applying a spherical distortion to your image. The corners of your image bow in and out, allowing you to correct for the bowing introduced by your lens (**Figure 3.29**).

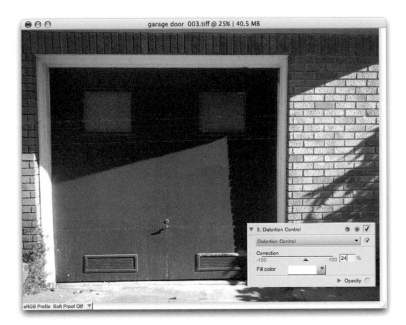

Figure 3.29 Using the Distortion Control adjustment, you can easily correct the bowed distortion at the edges of the frame.

Note that if your image has been cropped, you may have to apply a fairly high amount of distortion before you start to see the correction in the cropped portion of your image.

In an uncropped image, the corner correction results in empty space being left on the edges and corners of your image—it's as if the picture has been peeled back off the canvas, revealing the white material beneath. The Distortion Control Settings palette lets you pick a color for the revealed underlying pixels.

Keeping All Edit Steps Active

By default, when you adjust an edit, all edits that occur *after* that edit in the Edit List are temporarily deactivated. This can make it difficult to see the cumulative effects of all of your edits. If you'd prefer for all of your edits to remain active at all times, go to the Capture NX Preferences and, in the General section, check the *Keep All Steps Active in Edit List* check box.

This can slow down the overall processing of your images, so if you find that Capture NX runs too slowly with this option checked, you might want to turn it off.

INITIAL RETOUCHING

With your geometric corrections out of the way, you're ready to move on to the initial retouching steps. These are the edits that you'll make to correct specific troubles that will otherwise make the image unusable.

Correcting Color Aberrations

When you take a picture, your camera's lens focuses the light that bounces off your scene onto the sensor in your camera. However, some lenses—especially wide-angle lenses—sometimes have trouble focusing all wavelengths of light onto the exact same point on your sensor. The result can be weird color fringes. Very often these fringes occur around high-contrast areas in your image. This is usually referred to as a *chromatic aberration.*

At other times, especially when shooting very bright scenes, the individual pixels on your camera's image sensor can "overflow" with photons. When this happens, excess photons can spill over into adjacent pixels, creating a phenomenon called *sensor blooming.* Sensor blooming also manifests in your image as colored fringes.

Capture NX provides two controls for tackling these problems. The first is Auto Color Aberration, which appears in the Camera & Lens Correction Edit in the Quick Fix pane. By default, this edit is turned on if you're editing a NEF file. For JPEGs and TIFFs, you'll need to manually activate it. There are no parameters for this control, you simply turn it on or off by clicking on its check box (**Figure 3.30**).

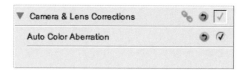

Figure 3.30 Activating Auto Color Aberration in the Camera & Lens Correction edit can often fix chromatic aberration troubles.

Auto Color Aberration is a subtle correction that will work for some color aberrations. If you don't see an effect, turn it off. It's time to switch to a more powerful control.

In the image crop shown in **Figure 3.31**, you can see both cyan and magenta fringing around the power pole. This is an extreme magnification of the image, and whether or not this problem would show up in print depends on the quality of your printer and the size at which you choose to print. For the 8 x 10s I was printing, it was visible, so I decided to remove the fringe.

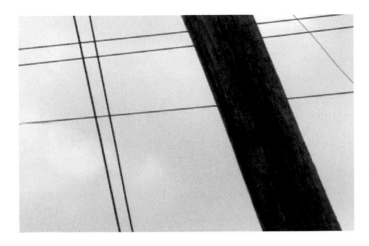

Figure 3.31 This image has trouble with magenta and cyan fringing along the edge of the pole. Capture NX easily removes color fringes.

To remove color fringing:

1. Select Adjust > Correct > Color Aberration Control. A Color Aberration Control edit is added to your Edit List, and the Color Aberration Settings palette appears.

2. If the fringe you're trying to remove is red or purple, drag the Red–Cyan slider to the left. The fringe should disappear (**Figure 3.32**). If the fringe is blue or yellowish, use the Blue–Yellow slider.

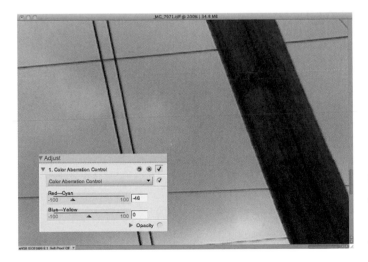

Figure 3.32 The Color Aberration Correction edit lets you use a simple slider interface to remove color fringing.

TIP: *When adjusting the Color Aberration Control sliders, it's best to view your image at 100 percent. Individual pixels can matter when you're making this edit, so you want a clear view of your image data.*

If you push a correction too far, a different colored fringe might appear. Fortunately, it's easy enough to redo your adjustment if you need to. While this is technically a color correction, removing color fringing is often something you do at the beginning of your workflow so you can assess whether the image is useful. If you can't completely remove the color fringing, you may decide not to use the image.

Red Eye Correction

Red eye isn't actually a geometric problem, but like color aberrations, it's one of those edits that you want to be sure you can pull off before you bother with any other edits. If you can't get your subject's eyes looking right, then you'll probably want to dump the image.

In the Camera & Lens Correction edit of the Develop pane, there's an Auto Red Eye option. Open its reveal arrow, and change the Off pop-up menu to Automatic. Capture NX will attempt to automatically detect red eye troubles and then remove them. Note that Auto Red Eye must know the orientation of your image. If your camera didn't accurately record orientation, then Auto Red Eye won't work.

If, for whatever reason, the Auto Red Eye doesn't work, then you'll need to move on to the Red Eye Control Point.

To use the Red Eye Control Point:

1. Click the Red Eye Control Point tool to select it.

2. Click with the tool in the center of a red eye.

3. A handle will appear next to the Red Eye Control Point. Drag this handle left and right to change the size of the red eye adjustment area.

Capture NX will automatically correct the area inside the circle.

The Auto Retouch Brush

The Auto Retouch Brush is used to remove things from your images. It's analogous to airbrushing in the film world, and you can use it to tackle the same sorts of problems that were traditionally airbrushed. With it, you can eliminate sensor dust, stray hairs, wrinkles—anything that you don't want in your image.

You don't have to know much to use the Auto Retouch Brush. We'll use it to remove the stray hair that's going to this woman's mouth (**Figure 3.33**).

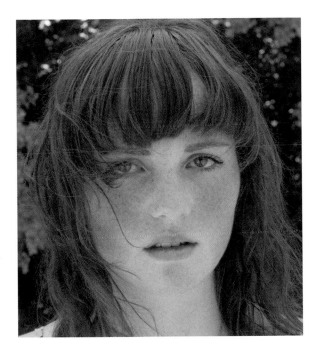

Figure 3.33 We're going to use the Auto Retouch Brush to remove the hair going to this woman's mouth.

To use the Auto Retouch Brush:

1. Select the brush from the toolbar.

2. Set the brush size to the width of the thing you want to remove. You can make the brush bigger by pressing] (right bracket) and smaller by pressing [(left bracket). It's a good idea to zoom in to get a better look (**Figure 3.34**). The Auto Retouch Brush cursor is a circle that shows you the exact size of the brush.

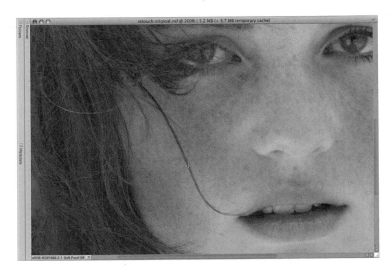

Figure 3.34 Zoom in to get a good look, then set the brush size to be just a little wider than what you want to remove.

3. Using very small strokes, brush out the item you want to eliminate. When you brush with the Auto Retouch Brush, you'll see a semitransparent red paint on your image. When you release the mouse button, the retouch effect will be applied (**Figure 3.35**).

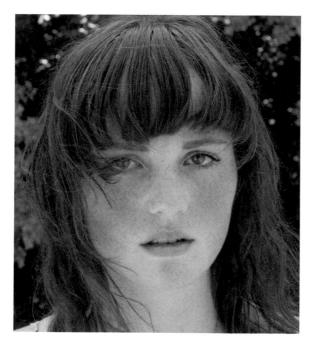

Figure 3.35 After using the Auto Retouch Brush, the intrusive hair is gone.

Note that as you use the retouch brush, Auto Retouch Brush edits appear in the Edit list (**Figure 3.36**). As with any other type of edit, you can uncheck the check boxes to deactivate any Auto Retouch Brush edit.

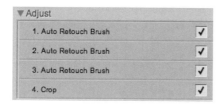

Figure 3.36 As you use the Auto Retouch Brush, new edits will appear in the Edit List.

The Auto Retouch Brush works by copying pixels from the area surrounding where you brushed. It then pastes those into the brushed area, and does some complex blending and feathering to make for a smooth touch-up. Small strokes work better than large strokes because it means the brush will be copying from a smaller area, and so stands a better chance of copying relevant pixels.

There will be times when you'll find that the brush copies data from the object you're trying to paint out. If this happens, try reducing the size of the brush, and using even smaller strokes. Consider using individual clicks of the mouse.

The Auto Retouch Brush is ideal for sensor dust, skin blemishes, and other issues that are usually a small area on top of a mostly uniform field of color or texture. The Auto Retouch Brush won't work so well working in areas with lots of detail or repeating texture. But, between the nondestructive nature of the Auto Retouch Brush, and Capture NX's unlimited undo feature, there's no risk in experimenting with the brush.

Moving On to Tone and Color

As mentioned in our editing workflow discussion, after geometric and color cast corrections, your next edits will be to tone and contrast, and then to color. Before we dive in to those edits and adjustments, though, it's essential that you understand one additional tool.

HISTOGRAM 101

If you're not already familiar with an image-editing histogram, read this section very thoroughly. Although it may seem to veer dangerously close to something math-like, understanding a histogram is actually very simple, and as you'll see, a histogram can be an essential editing *and* shooting tool.

A histogram is nothing more than a bar chart that graphs the distribution of tones in an image, with black at the left edge, white at the right, and one vertical bar for every tone in between. In other words, for every gray value in the image—from 0 gray at the left to 255 gray at the right—the histogram shows a bar representing the number of pixels in your image with that value. For a very simple image like the one in **Figure 3.37**, the histogram contains only four lines: one at the extreme left edge, representing the black swatch; two in the middle for the two gray swatches; and one at the extreme right edge for the white swatch.

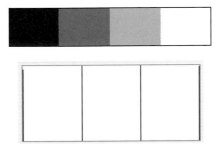

Figure 3.37 This simple four-tone image (top) yields a histogram (bottom) with four bars: one for each tone.

That's really all there is to a histogram. As an image becomes more complex, containing more tones, the histogram fills with more bars. **Figure 3.38** shows a simple grayscale ramp and its corresponding histogram.

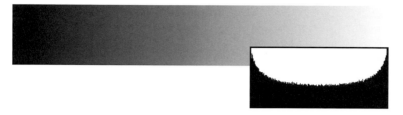

Figure 3.38 A histogram is simply a graph of the distribution of tones in an image. The histogram for this gray ramp (top) shows a smooth distribution, from black on the left of the histogram to white on the right.

Now consider some real-world examples. **Figure 3.39** shows a well-exposed image and its corresponding histogram. (The gray ramp beneath the histogram is provided to help you see that the histogram charts black to white.) The histogram shows that this image has a fairly complete range of tones from black to white. The vertical shape of the histogram is irrelevant—*there's no "correct" shape that we're trying to achieve.* Every image will have a uniquely shaped histogram because every image has a unique amount of varying tones. One of the important points we can learn from the histogram is that this image has a good range of contrast, from complete black to complete white.

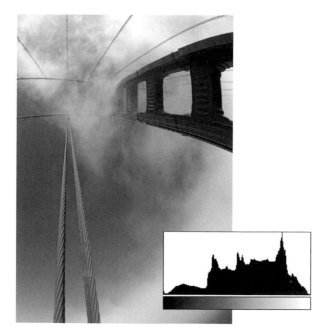

Figure 3.39 This figure is well exposed and so has a histogram that contains a lot of data, ranging from black to white. However, neither end of the histogram is clipped at the edge. Instead, both the shadows and highlights make smooth transitions to complete black and white.

Figure 3.40 shows an overexposed image. On the left side of the histogram the data tapers off, dwindling to nothing by the time it reaches the leftmost, black end. On the other side, the image data slams into the right edge of the histogram, creating a spike, and indicating overexposure, a situation referred to as *clipping*. Remember: Where there's pure white, there is no contrast and no information—no image data—and therefore no detail. Because the histogram shows a preponderance of pure white, it's safe to say that the image is over-exposed and, therefore, has lost detail.

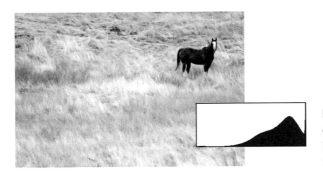

Figure 3.40 This image is plainly overexposed. Its histogram lacks data in the shadows and midtones, and the highlights are heavily clipped.

Figure 3.41 shows an underexposed image, and as you would expect, the results are pretty much the opposite of **Figure 3.40**. The histogram's data is piled up at the left side of the graph, indicating an undue number of pixels that have been reduced to featureless blobs of black. Although this image may not look so bad underexposed, there's no way to pull any detail back out of those solid-black shadow areas if you want to. Ideally, it's better to have a well-exposed image that you can darken later than to have a dark image (or an overly exposed bright image) with less editing flexibility.

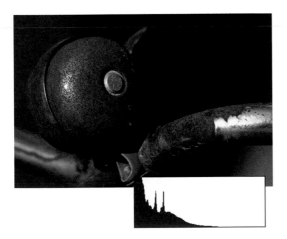

Figure 3.41 This underexposed image sports a histogram with the majority of its data crammed against the left, black side. Because the blacks are clipped, the shadows in this image are solid black, making it impossible to pull out any usable detail.

In addition to helping you spot overexposure and underexposure, your histogram can help you analyze other image troubles.

Contrasty Histograms

The human eye is much more sensitive to changes in luminance, or brightness, than it is to changes in color. Because of this, images that have more contrast are often more appealing (**Figure 3.42**).

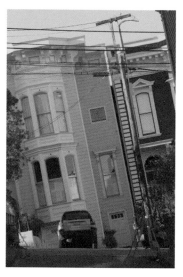 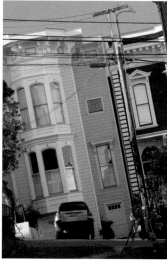

Figure 3.42 In general, images with greater contrast, such as the image on the right here, are more pleasing to the eye.

Because an image with greater contrast usually has more tones and gradations, it delivers better detail and subtlety. I say "usually" because an image *can* have great contrast between its darkest and lightest tones without having a lot of other tones in between (consider a black-and-white checkerboard). The histogram makes it simple to determine how much contrast your image has and how much data there is between your lightest and darkest tones.

Figure 3.43 shows the histogram for the low contrast image shown in Figure 3.42. You can see that the image data extends neither all the way down to black nor all the way up to white—it's collected in the middle. In other words, there's not a lot of contrast between the darkest and lightest tones (Figure 3.43).

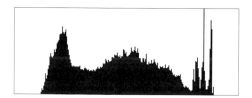

Figure 3.43 Capture NX's histogram of the left image in Figure 3.42 shows that the image has no black or white tones. The distance from the darkest to the lightest tone is very short, showing low contrast.

By contrast (sorry!), **Figure 3.44** shows a well-exposed image. Its histogram shows data that extends all the way to both ends, yielding an image with a good range of detail from black to white.

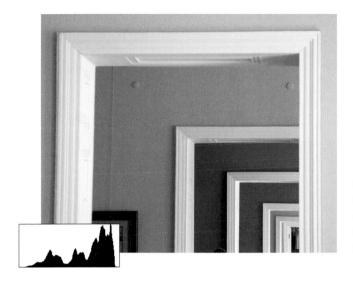

Figure 3.44 This image was well exposed and has a good range of contrast. The histogram shows that the tonal range goes from black to white without clipping on either end.

Another way of thinking about the histogram is to describe it as showing how much information you've captured. The histogram in Figure 3.39 showed an image with a tremendous range of information (that is, tonal levels), whereas the histogram in Figure 3.41 showed a much smaller quantity of information. But again, there will be times when your subject simply doesn't possess a lot of image data. Think of a picture of a zebra.

Capture NX's Histogram Displays

Capture NX displays the histogram for your image in two different locations. The Quick Fix edit displays a histogram as part of its Levels & Curves control. We'll explore this in detail in a bit. The Photo Info palette also always shows the histogram for the currently open image (**Figure 3.45**). Unlike the histogram in the Quick Fix pane, the Photo Info histogram displays a histogram that's been updated to show the effects of all of your current edits.

There are a number of handy histogram controls in the Photo Info palette, and we'll look at each of them later.

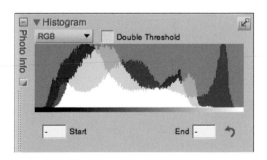

Figure 3.45 The Photo Info palette displays a continuously updated histogram of your image, showing the effects of every edit that you've made.

In-the-field Histograms

As you start editing with Capture NX, you're going to quickly understand the power of the histogram. Your camera most likely also has a histogram display that you can view after you take a shot (some cameras even have a live histogram feature that can superimpose a histogram over your image while you're shooting). Using an in-camera histogram, you can take a shot and then quickly assess whether it's over- or under-exposed and also see how much contrast it has (**Figure 3.46**).

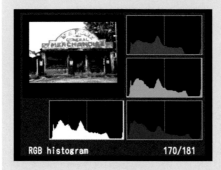

Figure 3.46 Your camera probably includes an option to display a histogram of any image stored on its card. Taking the time to look at the histogram can help you spot exposure problems.

You might think, "But I can tell if the image is over- or underexposed simply by looking at the LCD screen." Bear in mind, however, that the image on the LCD screen is often inaccurate. To ensure that the screen is visible in bright light, most cameras apply a liberal boost in contrast and saturation to the images on their LCD screen. So, as far as evaluating an image goes, the LCD screen is really only good for judging composition.

However, the in-camera histogram *is* an accurate way of assessing exposure in an image. Consult your camera's manual to find out how to access the histogram.

ADJUSTING TONE AND CONTRAST

There's no right or wrong order in which to make tone, contrast, and color adjustments, and all three affect each other. However, as we discussed earlier, you'll usually want to adjust tone and contrast first, because these adjustments often resolve some of the color issues in your image. In addition, if you've been shooting in low light, you'll need to adjust tone and contrast simply to get the image up to a brightness level that lets you see the details and specifics of your picture. In this section, we'll look at each of Capture NX's tone and contrast adjustments.

Quick Fix

As mentioned earlier, if you simply follow the controls in the Edit List from top to bottom, you'll be following a fairly good workflow for adjusting tone, contrast, and color. Quick Fix is the first edit you'll see, and the Quick Fix edit starts with a levels and curves control—the big histogram at the top of the Quick Fix section and it's the editing tool you'll probably use more than any other.

Let's consider a low-contrast image like the one shown in **Figure 3.47**, which shows an image, along with the Quick Fix edit.

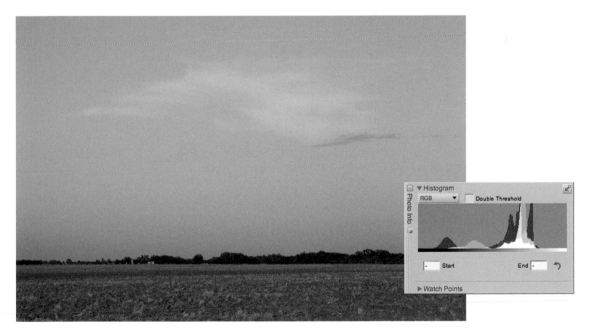

Figure 3.47 This image suffers from low contrast, which you can determine by looking at the image but also by examining the histogram.

The image is plainly lacking in contrast, and the histogram confirms this. The data in the image neither goes all the way to black nor all the way to white. The camera's histogram would have revealed the same thing, and if I'd been paying attention to it, I would have known that I probably needed to try a slightly different exposure. Fortunately, with the Quick Fix levels and curves control, this is an easy problem to fix.

> **TIP:** You'll use the levels and curves control for doing more than just correcting low contrast images. I'm using a low contrast example here because it's a good way of exploring all of the tool's controls.

The problem with this image is that the whitest thing in it is not actually white, but only about 75 percent white. I can tell this by looking at the histogram, where I see that the right-most edge of the image data falls at about the three-quarter mark.

Similarly, the blackest thing in the image is not true black, which would be 0 percent, but closer to around 15 percent. I can tell this by looking at the left edge of the data in the histogram (**Figure 3.48**).

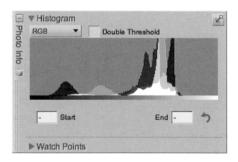

Figure 3.48 By looking at the position of the right-most and left-most data in the histogram, I can determine how white and how black the lightest and darkest things in the image are.

Overall, there's not a lot of distance between the darkest and lightest points. In other words, there's not a huge contrast between the darkest thing in the image, and the lightest. Fortunately, we can easily change that.

Adjusting black point and white point

Just beneath the histogram in the Quick Fix palette are three small triangles, one at the extreme left (or black) edge, one at the right, and one in the middle. These denote the current black, mid-, and white points in your image (**Figure 3.49**). The black point arrow tells us that, currently, black in our image is represented by any pixel with a value of 0—we can tell because it's pointed to the left-most point on the histogram, the point with a value of 0. However, since we have no pixels with a value of 0 percent, there's no actual black in the picture. Similarly, white is represented by a value of 100 percent, and we have no pixels with that value, so there's no white.

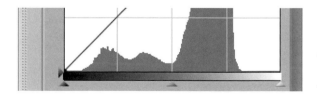

Figure 3.49 The levels sliders in the Quick Fix tool give us control over, respectively, the black, mid-, and white points in our image.

TIP: You can think of black and white values as percentages or integers, that is, black as having a value of 0 and white as having a value of 255. Whichever way you choose to look at it, the concept of the levels controls remains the same.

These arrows are not just indicators, they're also controls—you can slide them back and forth. So, if we slide the black point until it sits over the left-most data in our image, we indicate that those tones should be black. All of the other tones to the right of the black point are remapped, so that the tonal relationships remain the same (**Figure 3.50**).

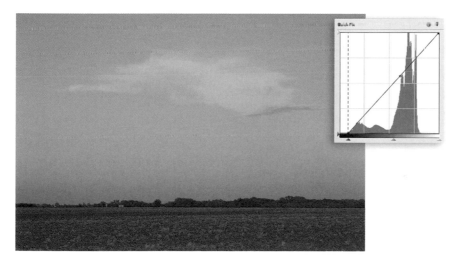

Figure 3.50 After I adjust the black point, contrast in the image is already improved.

The blacks in the image are now much better, but the image is dark overall, and the whites are still weak. If you drag the white point slider from its current location (where there's no data) to the brightest data in the image, you remap that brightest data to white (**Figure 3.51**).

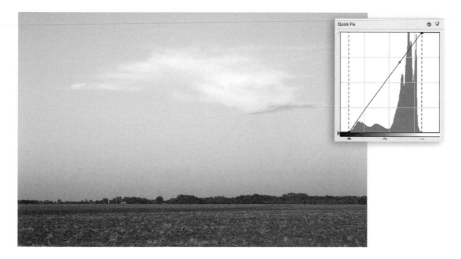

Figure 3.51 A white-point adjustment restores some brightness and improves contrast further.

After resetting our black and white points, our image now has much better contrast. Notice, though, that the levels controls are smart. When we brightened the white point, our blacks did not get brighter and wash out. Think of the data in the histogram as being rubbery. We can hold down one end and stretch or squish the other. When we do this, the middle values get expanded or contracted, but the opposite end doesn't move. This allows us to adjust either black or white without worrying about screwing up the other.

Adjusting the midpoint

The middle slider, the midpoint (which is sometimes referred to as the *gamma* slider) allows you to alter the brightness of the middle tones in the image without changing the value of the white or black points. Note in the histogram that the majority of the tones are still on the bright side. So, while the image has better contrast, it's still a little washed out. What we'd like to do is redistribute the tones so that a bunch of those bright tones are further to the left, so that the midtones will be a little darker overall.

If you move the midpoint slider to the left, the image gets brighter—to the right it gets darker (**Figure 3.52**). However, the brightest and darkest parts of the image don't change.

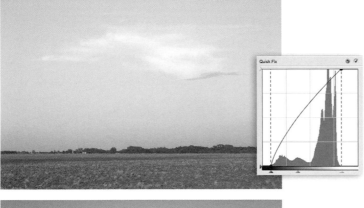

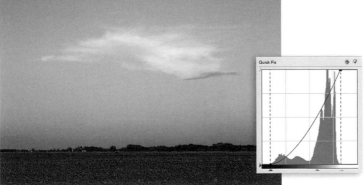

Figure 3.52 Moving the midpoint slider lets me brighten and darken the middle tones in the image without affecting black or white.

To get the effect that I want, I move the midtone slider to the right, which darkens those bright areas on the right side of the histogram without messing up white or black (**Figure 3.53**). Now the sky looks less "hot" and has more detail in it.

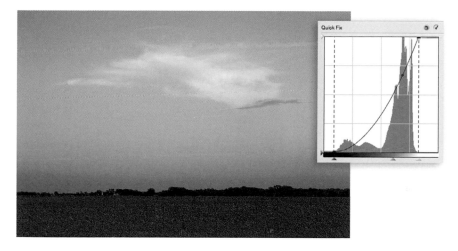

Figure 3.53 Ultimately, I've decided on this adjustment for the midtones.

At the moment, I'm mostly paying attention to the exposure in the sky. As I'm darkening it, some of the shadow tones on the ground are getting too dark, but I'm not worrying too much about those, as I know I can fix those later.

Take a look at the histogram in the Photo Info palette. It has been updated to show the new distribution of tones in our image. If you uncheck the Quick Fix edit, you can easily see a before and after (**Figure 3.54**).

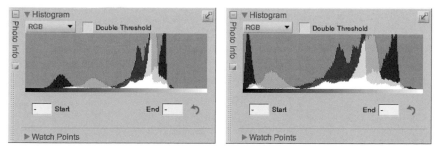

Figure 3.54 Here you can see before and after histograms. The left histogram shows our original image, the right reflects our white, black, and midpoint adjustments.

What you can see here is that the tones in our image are now more evenly distributed across the entire range of the histogram. An even distribution will not always be appropriate, but for this image it is. And how do you know? By seeing that with the adjustment, more of the image has good detail.

When you move the midpoint slider to the left, Capture NX expands the tones between the midpoint and the white point. Because there are now more bright tones in your image, your image appears, overall, brighter. At the same time, this move compresses the tones between the midpoint slider and the black point (**Figure 3.55**). When you move the slider to the right, the opposite happens.

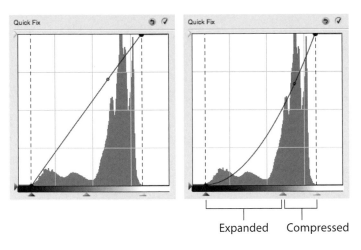

Expanded   Compressed

Figure 3.55 When you move the midpoint slider, the tones to one side of the slider are expanded so that there are more of them, whereas the tones to the other side are compressed.

If all of this is confusing, don't worry—you can simply move the slider and immediately see the results. I'm just including the theory for those who want a better understanding of how to read the levels and curves display.

> **TIP:** *Unchecking an edit in the Edit List does not undo the settings for that edit, meaning you can easily turn an edit on and off to view its effects.*

Reading the curve

You've probably already noticed the diagonal black line that Capture NX draws when you move the Levels slider. This line is actually a curve; it just happens to be a straight curve when you first start moving the sliders. The curve is simply a graph of how the tones in your image are being altered. It shows how the original input colors are remapped into new output colors (**Figure 3.56**). Where part of the curve goes down, those tones get darker. Where the curve bends upward, the corresponding tones are brightened.

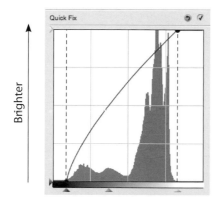

Brighter

Figure 3.56 Where the curve curves upward, the tones in your image get brighter. A downward curve results in a darkening of that part of the curve.

Like the histogram, the left end of the curve corresponds to black, and the right end represents white. The histogram behind the curve makes it easy to understand which part of the curve corresponds to specific tones in your image.

The important thing to notice about the curve is that it's, well, curvy. Rather than a specific tone being simply brightened or darkened, tones across a broad area are adjusted along the curve so that the brightening and darkening in your image is attenuated across the tonal range. This makes for a much more natural, realistic adjustment, and the curve provides another way to see how the amount of adjustment made by the levels controls varies across the tonal range.

In Figure 3.56 you can see that the darker tones in the image have received more brightening than the lighter tones; the curve is more pronounced at the low end of the graph.

> **TIP:** *If you want to know where a specific tone in your image is reflected in the histogram, choose the Direct Select tool (the one that looks like an arrow) and mouse over your image. A small dot will appear on the curve to indicate the exact point on the curve that corresponds to that tone. Sometimes this feature is a little buggy and only works if you first make an adjustment to the curve. You can then undo that adjustment and this should work fine.*

Decreasing contrast

While you'll spend most of your time as a photographer trying to achieve contrast, there are times when an image can look a little harsh if it's too contrasty. Dark tones can be too dark, light tones too intense. In these instances, you might want to *de*crease contrast in your image, which is another thing you can do with Quick Fix.

To decrease contrast in an image:

1. In the Quick Fix edit, note the arrows on the left side of the levels and curves display. These are the Output arrows. Slide the bottom output arrow on the left side of the histogram toward the top. This will shift the black point of your image toward the center of the histogram.

2. Slide the top output arrow on the left side of the histogram toward the bottom. This will move the white point toward the center of the histogram (**Figure 3.57**).

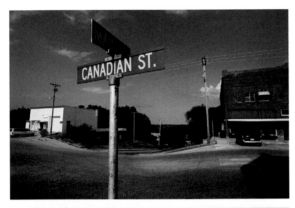

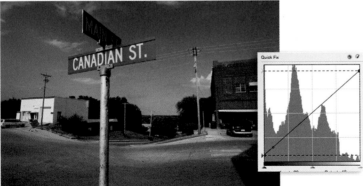

Figure 3.57 You can lower the contrast an image by using the controls on the left side of the histogram display in the Quick Fix edit.

If you look at the resulting histogram, it will have the characteristic "low-contrast" look. Obviously, you can easily push this edit too far. Also, note that this is not the best way to brighten up dark shadows, because as you adjust the black slider, *every* dark tone in your image will get lighter, not just the shadow tones. We'll learn how to brighten dark shadows later.

What Does a Combed Histogram Mean?

As you edit your images, your histogram begins to show *combing*, areas where there are no tones or where there are big single-pixel spikes (**Figure 3.58**). I've already discussed how the Levels control stretches and squashes the tones in your images, expanding some areas to make them brighter and compressing others to make them darker. When an area is expanded, the tonal information that it contains must be stretched out to fill the wider tonal range. Because there is a finite amount of tonal information in your image, Capture NX cannot magically fill a wider tonal range with a limited amount of data, so it must leave some tones empty. These are the blank spots in the histogram.

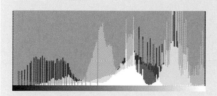

Figure 3.58 Your histogram will show combing and spiking as your edits cause data loss.

When a tonal range is compressed, Capture NX must throw out some tones to fit the data into the smaller space. These discarded tones appear as spikes.

Except for White Balance adjustments to raw images, *all* image adjustments will usually result in some data loss, so don't panic if you start to see combing in your histogram. It's a normal part of image editing. There is a misconception that if you're ever seeing data loss in your histogram, that means your image will always be visibly degraded. This simply isn't true. However, too much data loss can appear as visible artifacts in your image. We'll explore this problem in more detail in the next chapter.

There is also sometimes a misunderstanding of the term *nondestructive editing*. Some people believe that this term refers to a type of editing that doesn't result in data loss, but this is wrong. All edits result in data loss. Nondestructive editing simply means an editing architecture that doesn't alter any of the data in your original image file. See the discussion of nondestructive editing earlier in this chapter for more details.

Adjusting curves

In the Levels discussion, you saw how the black curve represents your Levels adjustment changes as you move the Levels sliders around. If you prefer, you can also edit this curve directly by clicking on it and dragging to reshape it. The advantage of manipulating the curve directly is that you can add as many control points as you want to create a curve shape that can't be achieved with the Levels sliders. Direct curve manipulation lets you create very isolated tonal adjustments; that is, tonal adjustments that affect a very specific part of the image's tonal range.

Consider the image in **Figure 3.59**.

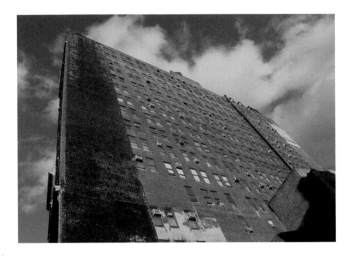

Figure 3.59 This image needs a little brightening. However, we'd like the black stripe on the side of the building to remain black.

It's a little dull in the midtones and could use a contrast boost. However, you want to be very careful that you don't brighten the black stripe on the side of the building. You want to keep it very black as you manipulate the other tones in the image.

Instead of using Levels, manipulate the curve directly. To reshape the curve, simply click somewhere on it and drag. The curve is a bit like a rubber band—as you pull one part of it, the rest of it changes. You'll often need to add more points to "lock down" part of your curve so that you can isolate the specific tonal range that you want.

With a few simple control points, you can improve the contrast in the image while preserving the darkness of the black stripe (**Figure 3.60**).

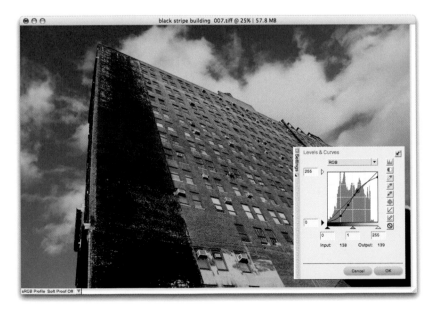

Figure 3.60 To correct this image, we defined a curve that darkened some shadow tones, brightened some midtones, and darkened some of the brightest whites in the image.

Remember, each part of the curve represents a different range of tones. Where the curve goes downward, those tones are darkened. Where it bends upward, tones are lightened.

More Levels & Curves   Capture NX has an additional Levels & Curves edit that you can apply, one that provides some more advanced controls. We'll look at it later in this chapter.

Highlight and Shadow Clipping Displays

Capture NX can show clipping displays that indicate exactly which highlights and shadow tones in your image are clipped (that is, overexposed or underexposed). If you choose View > Show Lost Highlights (or press Shift-H), any clipped highlights in your image will appear colored (**Figure 3.61**).

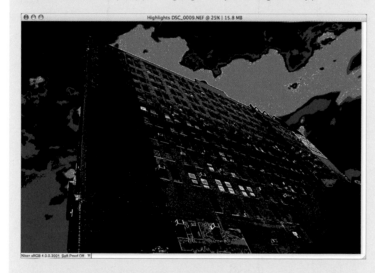

Figure 3.61 Show Lost Highlights indicates any clipped pixels by coloring them. Different colors indicate clipping in specific channels, or combinations of channels.

Pixels that are clipped in all three channels appear white. Areas that are clipped in only the red, green, and blue channels appear in those colors. Pixels clipped in only two channels are displayed in the appropriate secondary color. Pixels that aren't clipped at all appear black.

Choose View > Show Lost Shadows (or press Shift-S) to see a similar display that shows clipped shadow tones.

Exposure Compensation

Beneath the levels and curves control in the Quick Fix box is an Exposure Compensation slider. This control works only on raw files, and we'll cover it in detail in Chapter 4, "Working with Raw Files."

Contrast

Next is the Contrast slider, which does exactly the same thing that you've been doing with the Levels controls, but with a single slider. When you slide the Contrast slider to the right, contrast in your image is increased (**Figure 3.62**). This is exactly the same as moving both the white and black levels adjustments toward the middle.

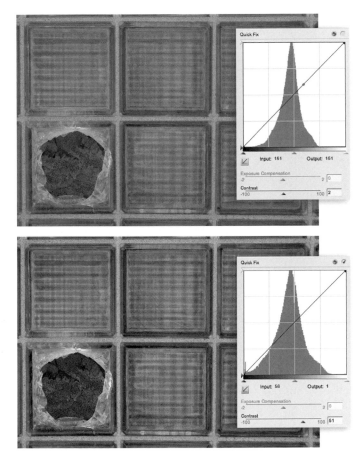

Figure 3.62 You can increase or decrease contrast in an image by moving the Contrast slider in the Quick Fix edit.

When you slide the Contrast slider to the left, contrast in your image is decreased. This is the same as adjusting the Output sliders in the Levels control.

Highlight Protection

Sometimes you'll want to darken only the highlights in an image. While you can use the white point levels slider to alter the bright tones of your image, adjusting the white point will alter *all* of the white tones that appear in your scene. While some of these tones will be highlights, others might simply be things that are white—a rose petal, or a white T-shirt. Ideally, you want a way to adjust *only* the white tones that are highlights. The Highlight Protection slider will do this.

When you slide the Highlight Protection slider to the right, Capture NX identifies all of the areas in your image that are highlights, and then darkens them (**Figure 3.63**).

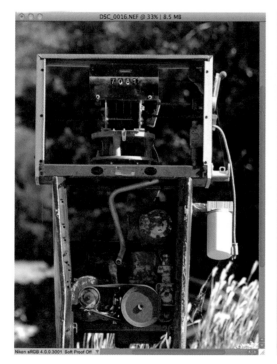 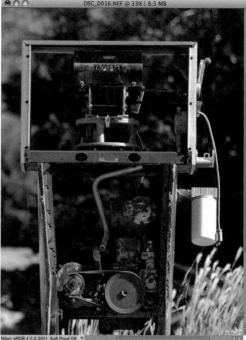

Figure 3.63 By dialing the Highlight Protection slider up, we've managed to pull down the overblown highlights in this image. Notice the improved detail on the chrome and on the white bottle on the right side of the gas pump.

As you can see, it applies its darkening in an intelligent way, gradually altering it to make a smooth transition between the affected and unaffected areas.

Shadow Protection

Shadow Protection works like the Highlight Protection slider, except that when you drag it to the right, Capture NX automatically identifies areas in your image that are shadows, and brightens them.

Returning to the image we worked on earlier, we'll use the Shadow Protection slider to brighten the dark areas that were left too dark by our Levels adjustment. By simply sliding Shadow Protection to the right, the shadowy areas on the ground brighten up (**Figure 3.64**).

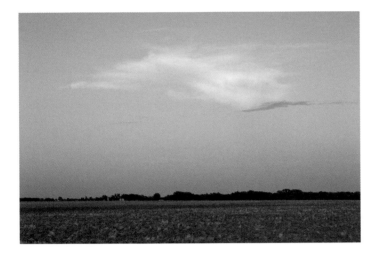

Figure 3.64 Here we used Shadow Protection to brighten up the shadowed areas at the bottom of the image.

Saturation

With the Saturation slider, you can increase or decrease the saturation in your image simply by moving the slider to the right or left. By sliding the Saturation slider to the left, we can render the red dirt in the previous image a little less garish (**Figure 3.65**).

Figure 3.65 Sliding the Saturation slider to the left lets us pull some saturation out of the somewhat garish colors that were introduced by our Levels adjustment.

As you probably already noticed, when you adjust contrast with the Levels controls or the Contrast slider, the saturation in your image changes. So, you'll want to make any necessary contrast and tone changes before you use the Saturation slider.

> **TIP:** The Shadow Protection slider can sometimes result in a loss of saturation in your image. You should be able to bump the color back up by moving the Saturation slider to the right.

Adjustments

So far, all of the controls we've been looking at sit in the Quick Fix area of the Edit List. But Capture NX has a number of other tone and contrast adjustments, which you can add to the Adjust area of the Edit List.

Auto Levels

Auto Levels attempts to automatically set the white point and black point in your image, and often does a very good job. It can be a good edit to start with, even before Quick Fix. Consider the low-contrast image in **Figure 3.66**.

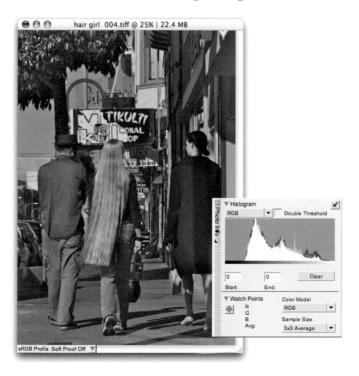

Figure 3.66 As you can see from this low-contrast image and its histogram, there's no black or white in the image. The tones cover a very small range; there's little contrast from the darkest to the lightest tones.

If you were to try to correct this with the Levels controls, you would drag the white and black sliders to the edge of the image data. If you add an Auto Levels edit to your Edit List, this adjustment will be made for you.

To add an Auto Levels edit:

1. Select Adjust > Light > Auto Levels.

2. An Auto Levels adjustment is added to your Edit List, and your image is adjusted (**Figure 3.67**).

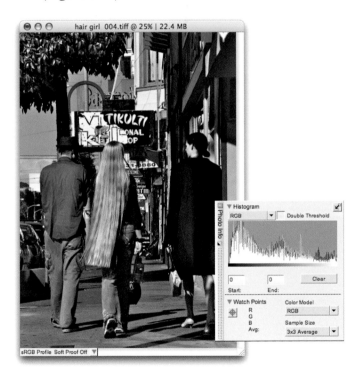

Figure 3.67 After adding an Auto Levels adjustment, the blacks and whites in the image are restored to true black and white. Intermediate tones are adjusted to preserve their original relationships.

3. Click OK in the Auto Levels Settings palette to accept the edit and close the palette.

If you look at the image's histogram now, you can see that Auto Levels successfully stretched the data in the image to better span a full range of black to white. However, some of the midtones in the image went a little dark in the process and could use a little fine-tuning. Fortunately, Auto Levels provides some additional manual controls.

To alter an Auto Levels edit:

1. In the Auto Levels Settings palette, choose Advanced from the Auto pop-up menu. Two new sliders appear (**Figure 3.68**).

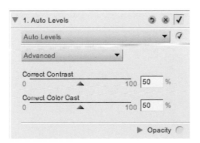

Figure 3.68 The Advanced Auto Levels option has two Auto Levels parameters for fine-tuning your adjustment.

2. Adjust the Correct Contrast slider to attenuate the amount of correction the Auto Levels adjustment applies. By default, Auto Levels applies a contrast adjustment of 100. If the result is too contrasty, you can dial it back by setting the slider to a lower value (**Figure 3.69**).

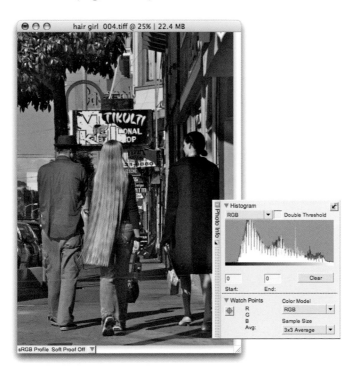

Figure 3.69 Using the Correct Contrast slider in the Auto Levels Settings palette, you can reduce the amount of contrast applied by the Auto Levels adjustment.

Correcting color casts

In addition to adjusting the white point and black point in an image, the Auto Levels adjustment also attempts to correct any color cast problems. A color cast usually stems from one color channel (red, green, or blue) being more or less pronounced than another (**Figure 3.70**).

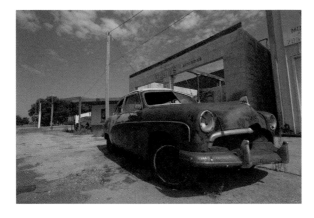

Figure 3.70 In addition to being too dark, this image is too yellow.

By adjusting the white and black points of individual color channels and thereby shifting the tones within those channels, color casts can be eliminated. On its own, Auto Levels does a good job of correcting color casts. For more control, you can use the Correct Color Cast slider.

To manually correct color casts using Auto Levels:

1. In the Auto Levels Settings palette, choose Advanced from the Auto pop-up menu.

2. Adjust the Correct Color Cast slider to eliminate the color cast in your image (**Figure 3.71**).

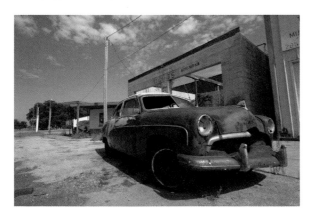

Figure 3.71 Auto Levels brightened up the image nicely, and adjustments made with the Correct Color Cast slider removed the yellow color cast.

Color casts can be somewhat subjective. It's often difficult to tell what "correct" color is in an image. Keep an eye on the histogram while adjusting the slider. As the three color channels fall more into registration with each other, you should approach more accurate color. (Obviously, if there's a large part of your image that is red, green, or blue, your histogram will be skewed.) Or, try to find a white object in your image. If you can render the object a true white, you'll have correct color throughout your image.

Getting Help from the Histogram

The Capture NX histogram provides some special utility functions that make it easy to identify exactly where certain tones lie in your image. If you click the Double Threshold check box, two sliders appear beneath the histogram display and your image changes to a *threshold* display. The darkest tones in your image will appear black, and the lightest will appear white. The rest will be represented as gray. If your image doesn't have any black or white, you can drag the two sliders inward until the darkest and lightest pixels are revealed (**Figure 3.72**).

Double Threshold view makes it simple to see what's white and black in your image, which is very handy when you start using the levels and curves eyedroppers that you'll learn about in the next section.

You can also highlight a range of tones in the Capture NX histogram by simply clicking and dragging across the histogram. Capture NX highlights the pixels in your image using colored pixels, allowing you to easily see where those particular tones appear (**Figure 3.73**). Click the Clear button—which appears as a curved arrow next to the End box—to return to a normal view of your image.

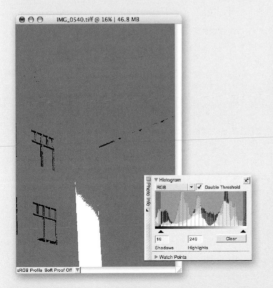

Figure 3.72 The Double Threshold view in the Histogram palette lets you see exactly where the brightest and darkest pixels are in your image.

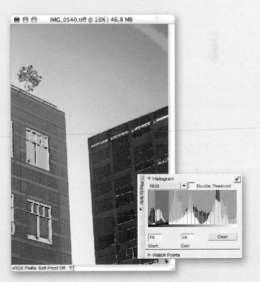

Figure 3.73 If you click and drag across the histogram, Capture NX highlights the pixels in your image that correspond to the selected tonal values.

continues on next page

Getting Help from the Histogram *continued*

The Watch Points section of the Histogram palette lets you monitor the RGB values of up to four specific points in your image. Click the Watch Points arrow, choose Add Watch Points, and then click somewhere in your image. Capture NX adds a watch point readout to the Histogram palette (**Figure 3.74**).

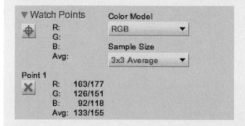

Figure 3.74 Watch Points allow you to keep an eye on the color values of specific pixels in your image.

Sometimes, an area in your image might be composed of slightly varying hues of pixels. If you choose another option from the Sample Size pop-up menu, the Watch Points you define will average a small area around the point you click on. This can often make for a more reliable color reading.

Auto Levels doesn't provide anything close to the fine level of control that you saw with the Quick Fix Levels & Curves adjustment, but for many images it will be all you need. For other images, it might create a good starting point, which you can then refine with additional edits.

Contrast/Brightness

Capture NX's Contrast/Brightness adjustment offers a different control for manipulating the contrast in your image. Operating like the controls that you might find on a TV set, Contrast/Brightness provides two simple sliders for making adjustments. Contrast/Brightness is somewhat of a blunt tool—it doesn't provide near the finesse and power of Levels & Curves—but keeping a careful eye on your histogram will help you keep the Contrast/Brightness adjustment under control.

You add a Contrast/Brightness adjustment by selecting Adjust > Light > Contrast/Brightness. The adjustment appears in your Edit List, and the Contrast/Brightness Parameters palette reveals your controls, which include two simple sliders, one for Contrast and the other for Brightness.

The Contrast slider is akin to simultaneously adjusting the white and black points in the Levels & Curves adjustment. The Brightness slider shifts the entire tonal range up or down to brighten or darken your image. Capture NX's Contrast/Brightness adjustment is fairly smart about the way that it makes its adjustments, so you shouldn't see color shifts or casts developing as you move the sliders.

To use the feature, you'll probably need to go back and forth between the two sliders. For example, **Figure 3.75** shows a low-contrast image to which we'll add a Contrast/ Brightness edit by selecting Adjust > Light > Contrast/Brightness.

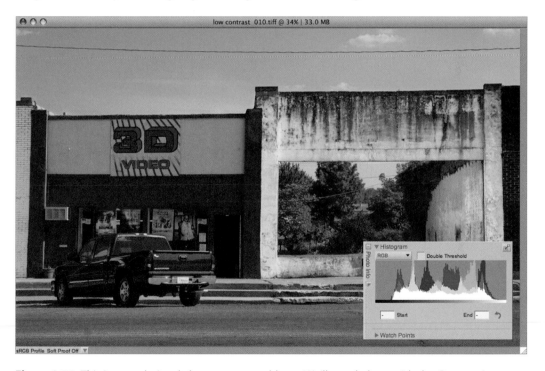

Figure 3.75 This image obviously has contrast problems. We'll attack them with the Contrast/ Brightness edit.

Since the problem is lack of contrast, begin by moving the Contrast slider to the right to increase the contrast (**Figure 3.76**).

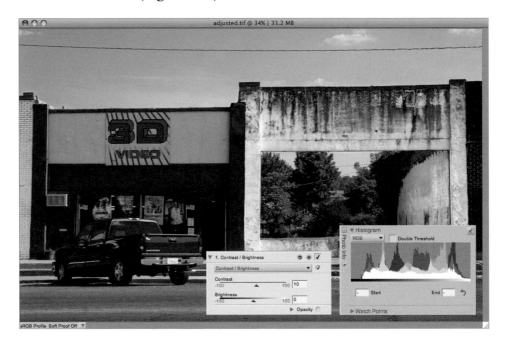

Figure 3.76 Begin by increasing the contrast by sliding the Contrast slider to the right.

However, you can't increase the contrast too far before you begin to clip the whites. Also, note that there still isn't any true black. Use the Brightness slider to shift the entire tonal range down a bit (**Figure 3.77**).

With the extra headroom that was created by darkening the image, you can make another Contrast move to further expand the contrast in the image (**Figure 3.78**).

As you can see, Contrast/Brightness doesn't provide the fine degree of control that Levels & Curves provides, but if you keep an eye on your histogram while you're working, you can make good use of the tool.

> **TIP:** If you audition Contrast/Brightness but can't quite get the image the way you want it, just change the Contrast/Brightness edit into a Levels edit, and redo your adjustment there. You learned how to change one type of edit into another earlier in this chapter.

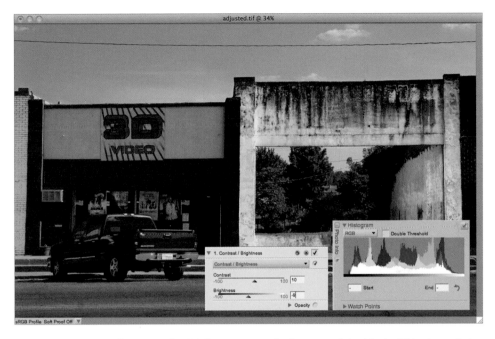

Figure 3.77 By next lowering the Brightness, not only do some of the blacks fill in, but a little headroom frees up above the whites.

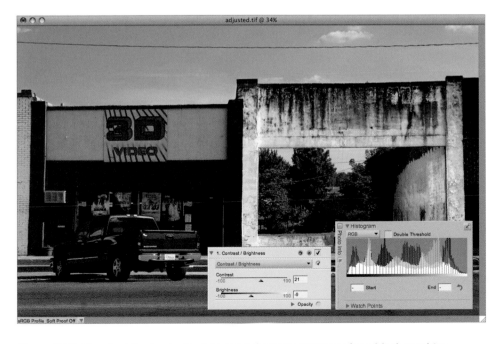

Figure 3.78 One final Contrast adjustment produces strong tones from black to white.

D-Lighting

D-Lighting is a tonal adjustment tool that's kind of like the Protect Highlights and Protect Shadows edits but is a little more automated. D-Lighting will automatically brighten shadow areas and/or darken highlights, as it sees necessary. When you brighten a shadow using D-Lighting, Capture NX automatically analyzes your image to determine which dark pixels are shadows, and brightens only those. Dark pixels that are simply dark objects are left unaffected.

To use D-Lighting to brighten shadows:

1. Open an image that needs its shadows brightened. In this example, we'll use a portrait that really should have been shot using a fill flash. The shadow on the right half of the man's face is too dark (**Figure 3.79**).

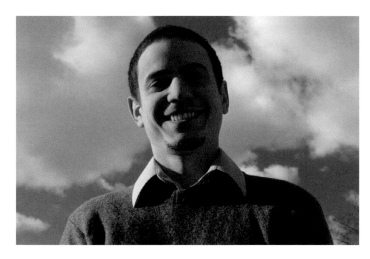

Figure 3.79 This image should have been shot with a fill flash. We'll use the D-Lighting edit to brighten the shadow on the man's face.

2. Add a D-Lighting edit to the image by choosing Adjust > Light > D-Lighting. A D-Lighting edit is added to the Edit List.

3. Drag the Adjustment slider to the right. Your shadows will brighten (**Figure 3.80**).

That's all there is to it. D-Lighting does the rest. It analyzes the image to determine which tones are shadow tones and automatically brightens them. Notice that it rolls off the brightening around the shadow to produce a more realistic effect.

If you choose the Better Quality option, the Adjustment slider will have more sensitivity, allowing for a subtler, higher-quality effect (**Figure 3.81**). In this mode, the adjustment is more computationally intensive, but on a reasonably fast computer you shouldn't notice a significant difference in performance.

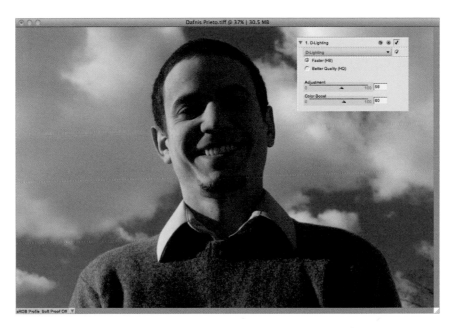

Figure 3.80 You can brighten the shadows by simply dragging the Adjustment slider to the right.

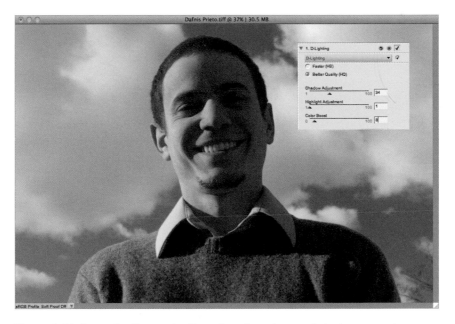

Figure 3.81 Better Quality mode allows for a finer degree of shadow control, allowing you to create more subtle, realistic improvements.

The Color Boost slider that is available in both Better Quality and Faster modes allows you to increase the color saturation in the shadow areas. Sometimes, as you brighten a shadow it becomes slightly washed out. Color Boost allows you to restore some of the color that's lost in the brightening process (**Figure 3.82**).

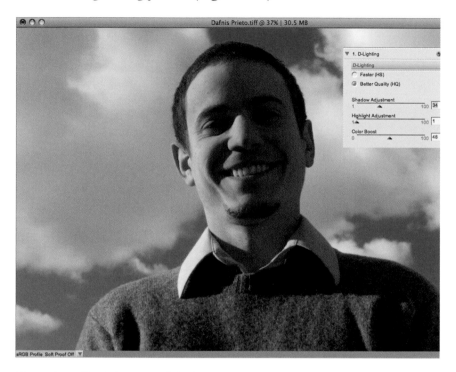

Figure 3.82 The Color Boost slider lets you restore some of the color saturation that gets lost in the shadow brightening.

Levels & Curves

While the Quick Fix edit in the Develop pane offers a very capable Levels & curves control, Capture NX provides an additional separate Levels & Curves edit that offers some additional power.

You add a Levels & Curves adjustment like any other type of adjustment. Choose Adjust > Light > Levels & Curves, or press Command/Control-L, and a Levels & Curves adjustment is added to the Adjust section of your Edit List.

The Levels & Curves edit provides an interface just like the Levels & Curves section of the Quick Fix edit, but with some additional buttons (**Figure 3.83**).

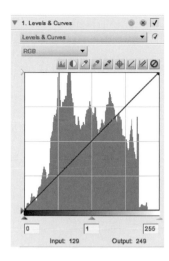

Figure 3.83 Capture NX's Levels & Curves dialog box gives you access to traditional levels and curves controls in a single interface.

I'm going to use Levels & Curves to fix the image shown in **Figure 3.84**. As you can see it's a typical low-contrast image. However, if you notice, it has a slight red cast to it. This cast is going to get stronger as I increase the contrast in the image. So, we'll use some additional Levels controls to address this issue.

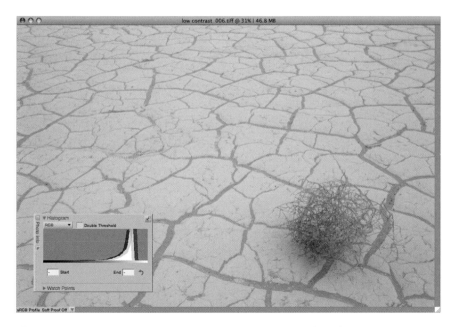

Figure 3.84 This image suffers from contrast problems, and a color cast issue. We'll correct all of these with the Levels & Curves edit.

First, let's set the black, white, and midpoint sliders to get some more contrast into the image (**Figure 3.85**).

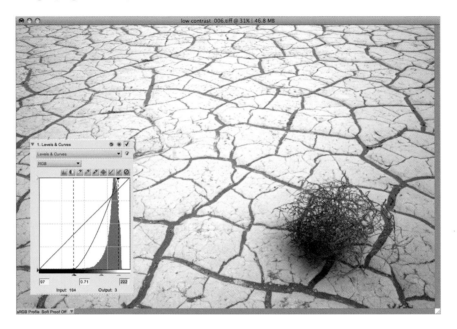

Figure 3.85 Fixing the contrast with Levels & Curves is easy, but now we have a color cast problem.

Again, I haven't done anything here that you couldn't do with the levels and curves control in Quick Fix. I set the black, white, and midpoints to yield an image with better detail throughout its tonal range. But now the image's red cast is far more noticeable. Fortunately, Levels & Curves has some controls that will help us with that.

Adjusting individual channels

All digital images are a combination of three different *color channels*, one containing all of the red information in the image, one containing all of the green, and the third holding all of the blue. When these channels mix together, you see a full-color image.

Directly above the histogram in the Levels & Curves Settings, you'll see an RGB pop-up menu. This indicates that the changes you make with the Levels & Curves control are applied to the full, composite RGB image. But Levels & Curves also lets you operate on individual color channels. If you click the RGB menu, you can select a specific color channel to edit (**Figure 3.86**).

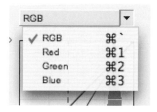

Figure 3.86 The pop-up menu above the histogram in the Levels & Curves dialog box lets you elect to operate on individual color channels.

Because this image has a red cast, let's select the Red channel, and then perform a gamma adjustment on that channel to darken, or reduce, the amount of red in the image (**Figure 3.87**).

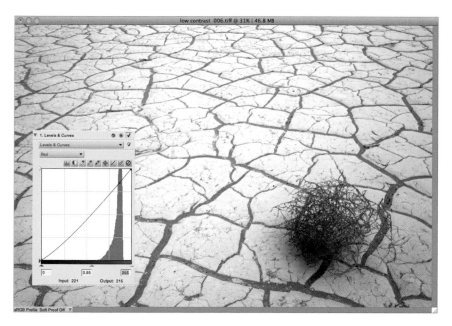

Figure 3.87 Here we made a very slight midpoint adjustment to the red channel to reduce the amount of red in the image. This lessens the reddish cast.

The Red channel adjustment does not eliminate the RGB adjustment you made earlier. You can make separate adjustments for each channel within the same Levels & Curves adjustment.

Channel adjustments are often the easiest way to deal with specific color problems. However, Capture NX provides some additional, easier tools that often solve many color problems.

> **TIP:** *In the Levels & Curves dialog box, you can automatically switch to the red, green, or blue channel editor by pressing Command/Control-1, 2, or 3. To switch back to RGB view, press Command/Control-~.*

Levels & Curves eyedroppers

Above the levels and curves histogram are a series of buttons that provide very simple mechanisms for defining the white, black, and midpoints in your image (**Figure 3.88**).

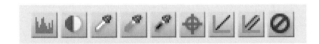

Figure 3.88 From left to right, the Levels & Curves buttons are Show Before/After Histogram, Auto Contrast, Set White Point, Set Neutral Point, Set Black Point, Add Anchor Point, Reset Current Channel, Reset All Channels, and Reset this Effect.

Show Before/After Histogram gives you a quick way to see how your histogram has changed. Click and hold the button to see what your histogram will look like after the Levels & Curves adjustment is applied. This is a good way to see if your histogram is getting too "combed" (see the sidebar "What Does a Combed Histogram Mean?").

Auto Contrast automatically sets the white point and black point of each color channel. Basically, it moves the edges of the data, just like you did manually. Auto Contrast aims for a fairly contrasty look. By default, it discards half a percent of the brightest and darkest pixels in your image, but you can change this behavior using Capture NX's Preferences.

To change the amount of white and black clipping that Auto Contrast performs:

1. Open the Capture NX Preferences and click Levels and Sampling.

2. Change the percentage values in the Black auto-contrast clip and White auto-contrast clip fields. Higher numbers cause the function to clip more data, resulting in a more contrasty image.

Auto Contrast works well on some images, but often yields bad color casts and too much contrast.

Reset Current Channel, Reset All Channels undoes any adjustments you have made.

Reset This Effect lets you see a before and an after version. Click and hold to see your original, unadjusted image.

Perhaps the most useful of these tools are the **Set White Point**, **Set Neutral Point**, and **Set Black Point** eyedroppers, which allow you to automatically define points by clicking in your image.

With the White Point eyedropper, click on something in your image that is supposed to be white, and Capture NX sets the white point in the image to the value of the tone you clicked on (**Figure 3.89**).

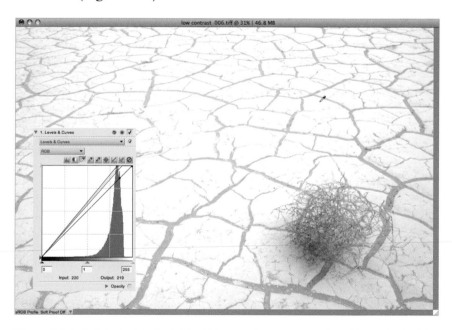

Figure 3.89 I clicked with the White Point eyedropper to set the white point in this image. Notice that the histogram now shows separate red, green, and blue curves, indicating that it adjusted each channel separately.

Notice that the levels and curves histogram is now showing separate red, green, and blue curves, in addition to the composite curve (which is represented by black). Each of these component curves is in a slightly different place, because Levels & Curves has automatically adjusted the white point in each separate channel. It determined the degree of adjustment based on the value of the point you clicked on.

The Black Point eyedropper works the same way, but sets the black point (**Figure 3.90**).

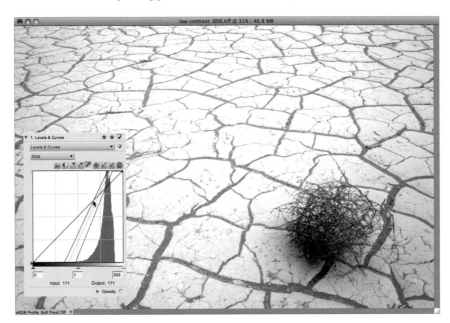

Figure 3.90 I clicked with the black point dropper on something black in the image, and now the contrast is much improved.

> **TIP:** If you're not sure where the whitest and blackest points are in your image, press Shift-H to toggle the clipped highlight display, and Shift-S to toggle the clipped shadow display. If the brightest and darkest points in your image aren't over- or underexposed, then this won't help. Note that you can click with the droppers while these displays are active.

With these eyedroppers, why would you ever set Levels by hand? Because there will be times when there is no white or black in your images. In these instances, you'll want to set the white and black points manually.

The Set Neutral Point eyedropper lets you easily neutralize color casts. To use it, click on something in your image that should be *gray*. Capture NX automatically adjusts the individual color channels to render the tone gray, thus neutralizing the color cast in your image (**Figure 3.91**).

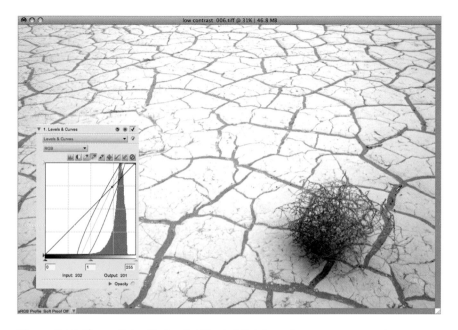

Figure 3.91 If you click with the Set Neutral Point eyedropper on an area in your image that should be gray, Capture NX neutralizes any color casts. Again, you can tell from the histogram that changes have been made to each color channel.

> **TIP:** If you're working with an individual channel, you can hold down the Option/Alt key while clicking with either the White Point or Black Point eyedropper to constrain your edit to the current channel.

LCH

As you'll see in the next section, the LCH edit provides some very sophisticated color manipulation controls. However, it can also be used to great effect for your tonal corrections.

LCH stands for Lightness, Chroma, and Hue. With the LCH editor, you can manipulate any one of these parameters without affecting the other. The practical upshot for tonal corrections is that you can change the lightness in an image without affecting any of the color.

When you first add an LCH adjustment (Adjust > Color > LCH), you'll see the Master Lightness editor (**Figure 3.92**). The controls in this editor work just like the Levels & Curves controls that you've already learned about.

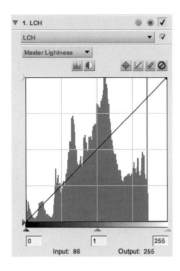

Figure 3.92 The Master Lightness controls in the LCH adjustment provide controls similar to the Levels & Curves adjustment, but with some important under-the-hood differences.

The Levels & Curves edit makes its changes by manipulating the red, green, and blue channels in your document. Because it is directly affecting individual color channels, there are times when heavy adjustments can produce color shifts in your image.

For example, if you look closely at the building image that was edited earlier, you'll see a pronounced red shift along the boundaries of some of the shadows after using the Levels & Curves edit (**Figure 3.93**).

The Master Lightness control in the LCH edit lets you make the same types of tonal adjustments but without any hue shift (**Figure 3.94**).

So why wouldn't you use LCH for all of your tonal corrections? Because as you've seen, there are times when you need to neutralize color casts in your image or perform other single-channel edits. Also, you may simply prefer the look of a Levels & Curves adjustment. Sometimes, the hue and saturation boost provided by Levels & Curves is very pleasing.

We'll look at the rest of the LCH controls in the next section.

> **TIP:** If you're not sure how to use the controls in the Master Lightness section of the LCH edit, consult the explanation in the "Quick Fix" section earlier in this chapter.

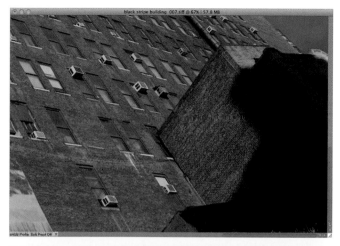

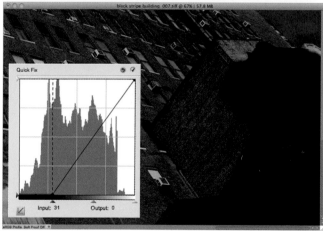

Figure 3.93 In this before and after, you can see how a strong Levels adjustment can introduce color shifts in your image. Note how the bricks picked up a strong red cast, especially in the shadow transition area.

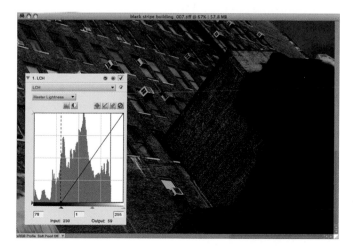

Figure 3.94 Making the same edit with the LCH adjustment lets you improve the tone of the image without picking up any hue shift.

COLOR CORRECTION

As outlined in our editing workflow discussion, you begin your edits by first making any tone and contrast adjustments. Because these adjustments can affect saturation and color in your image, you want them out of the way before you begin tweaking and adjusting specific color problems.

In looking at the tonal controls in the last section, you probably already noticed how they can affect the color in your image, but Capture NX also has plenty of controls specifically designed for color correction.

LCH Revisited

You've already seen how you can use the Master Lightness control in the LCH edit to adjust the brightness tones without affecting their hue. LCH provides some additional controls for affecting the color values in your image.

You can add an LCH edit to your image by selecting Adjust > Color > LCH. At the top of the LCH controls is a pop-up menu that lets you choose which of the LCH editors you want to work with (**Figure 3.95**).

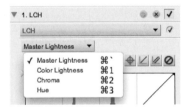

Figure 3.95 The pop-up menu at the top of the LCH Settings palette lets you select which LCH editor you want to use.

Color Lightness controls

The Color Lightness controls let you alter the brightness of a color without changing its hue. With Color Lightness, you can zero in on specific hues in your image and lighten or darken them.

To use the Color Lightness controls to brighten a hue:

1. Add an LCH edit to your image by selecting Adjust > Color > LCH.

2. Choose Color Lightness from the Channel pop-up menu.

3. Without clicking, drag your mouse to the color in your image that you want to change. A small circle appears on the curve in the Color Lightness display (**Figure 3.96**). This circle indicates which part of the curve corresponds to the color you're pointing at.

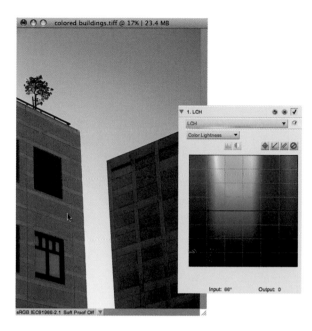

Figure 3.96 The small circle on the Color Lightness curve shows you the location of the color value that your mouse is currently pointing at.

4. Click on the indicated part of the curve and drag upward. A small spike appears in the curve.

5. Notice the small slider control directly beneath the Color Lightness color ramp. Drag it to the right (**Figure 3.97**).

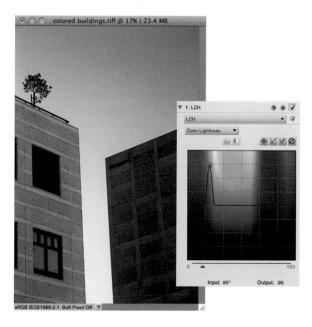

Figure 3.97 We used the Color Lightness controls to lighten the yellow tones of this building.

When you click a point on the curve, you select the color you want to adjust. The farther you drag up or down, the more the color will be altered. Dragging up brightens, whereas dragging down darkens. The hue of the color doesn't change.

The slider control lets you specify how many neighboring tones are adjusted. By moving the slider back and forth, you can create more realistic transitions around your edit.

Chroma

The LCH Chroma editor lets you change the saturation of your image—or just a part of your image—without changing the hue or lightness. The Chroma controls work just like the Color Lightness controls. You can click on the curve to indicate which hues you want to adjust and then drag up or down to add or remove saturation (**Figure 3.98**).

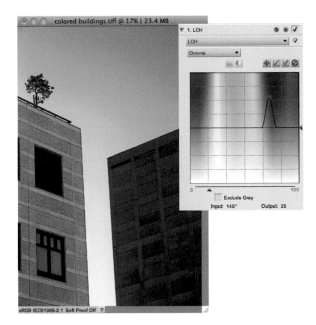

Figure 3.98 Here we increased the saturation of the blues in the image without affecting the yellow building at all.

Note that the Chroma curve has an additional control on the right side: This slider lets you drag the entire curve up or down to change the saturation of the entire image.

The Exclude Gray option lets you protect the grays in your image from any adjustment.

Hue

The Hue adjustment lets you change hues without affecting saturation (chroma) or brightness (**Figure 3.99**).

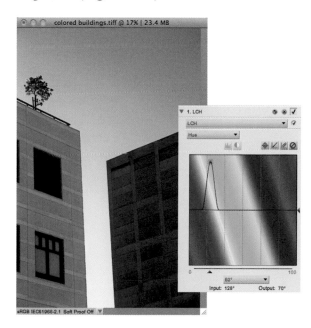

Figure 3.99 We used the LCH Hue adjustment to change the hue of the yellow building to a truly ugly shade of green. Note that none of the other hues in the image were affected, and the overall brightness and saturation of the affected area has remained unchanged.

The controls work the same as Color Lightness: Select the point on the curve that you want to edit, and then drag it up or down. Use the slider to control the width of the edited part of the curve. Choosing options from the pop-up menu beneath the curve display lets you increase the amount of hue change that the edit applies.

Color Balance

The Color Balance edit lets you adjust the amount of red, green, and blue in your image, as well as the contrast and brightness. Unlike the LCH adjustment, Color Balance makes no effort to preserve the hue, saturation, or lightness; it simply allows you to add more or less of each color.

To use Color Balance:

1. Select Adjust > Color > Color Balance, or press Command/Control-B to add a Color Balance edit to your document's Edit List.

2. Move the Red slider to shift the color in your image from cyan to red. Move the Green slider to shift the color from magenta to green, and move the Blue slider to shift from Yellow to Blue. You can use the Contrast and Brightness sliders to perform the same edit you'd make with the Contrast/Brightness edit.

Color Balance is something of a brute force tool, but you can use it to attack color casts or change the overall color tone of an image (**Figure 3.100**).

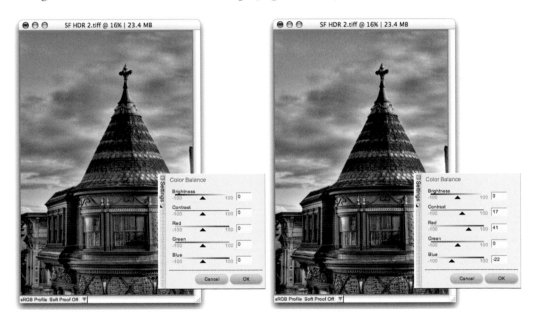

Figure 3.100 We used the Color Balance edit to increase the contrast and add warmth to this image.

Color Booster

The Color Booster edit (Adjust > Color > Color Booster) lets you increase the saturation of an image, but offers the option of protecting skin tones. Usually, increasing the saturation of skin tones turns people weird colors. With the Color Booster, you can simply check the Protect Skin Tones check box to protect skin tones from the effect of the edit (**Figure 3.101**).

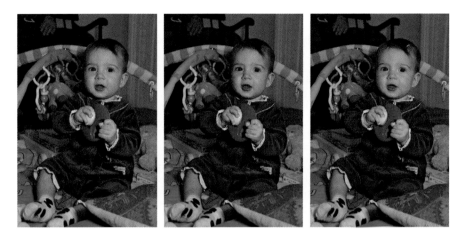

Figure 3.101 We took the original image shown on the left, applied a Color Booster edit to produce the more saturated image shown in the middle, and then activated the Protect Skin Tones option to produce the image on the right. The result is a nicely saturated image with good skin tones.

Saturation/Warmth

With the Saturation/Warmth edit (Adjust > Color > Saturation/Warmth) you can increase or decrease the saturation in an image by simply sliding the saturation slider (**Figure 3.102**).

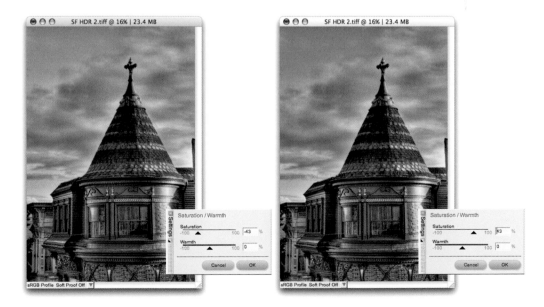

Figure 3.102 Using the Saturation slider in the Saturation/Warmth edit, you can increase or decrease the saturation in an image.

The Saturation adjustment in the Saturation/Warmth edit is a little more aggressive than the adjustment in the Quick Fix edit.

The Warmth slider lets you warm or cool the colors in your image (**Figure 3.103**). The Warmth slider produces an effect similar to what you can achieve with the White Balance adjustment when working with raw files.

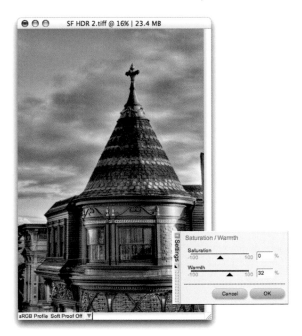

Figure 3.103 With the Warmth slider you can easily warm or cool the colors in an image.

SAVING FILES

After you've edited an image, you have several options for saving it. Because of its non-destructive nature, saving in Capture NX is a little more complex than in a normal image-editing program. You need to decide if you want to save a finished "baked" image that has all of your edits applied, or if you want to save a version of the image that you can return to later to alter and adjust your edits.

Working on a JPEG or TIFF File

If the file you opened was originally a JPEG or TIFF and you choose File > Save, the edits that you've made will be applied to the image and then be written out in its original format, overwriting the original, and recompressing it if it was a JPEG. However, if you later open the image in Capture NX, you won't have access to any of the edits that you made—your Edit List will be empty.

If you want to preserve your edits for later adjustment, choose File > Save As and choose NEF from the File Format pop-up menu.

While many people think that NEF is simply Nikon's raw file format, it's actually much more. NEF files can contain normal bitmap data such as TIFF and JPEG data, along with XML data such as the Edit List that you create in Capture NX. When you open this file later, all of your edits will be preserved.

You'll probably end up saving two versions of your edited image: a NEF version containing all of your edits and a TIFF or JPEG version that you deliver to your client or send to another editing program for additional edits.

> **TIP:** To maintain the most quality, save your TIFF files as 16-bit TIFFs. Capture NX provides both 8-bit and 16-bit TIFF options.

Working on a Raw File

If you're working with a raw file, your file is already stored in NEF format. Executing a simple Save command writes your Edit List into the file. When you next open the file, all of your edits appear in the Edit List. However, if you want to give the file to others, they will have to have Capture NX to be able to read and view it. If you'd rather deliver a "normal" file to them, choose Save As to export a TIFF or JPEG file.

NEF Options

When you save a NEF file, Capture NX presents you with a Save Options Dialog that contains some simple options. If your camera was not set to shoot compressed NEF files, then you'll have two compression options available.

Compressed applies a compression algorithm that reduces file size by 40 percent to 50 percent. There's some debate amongst nitpickers as to whether this compression is lossless or not. If there is data loss, it appears to be impossible to see. If you're skeptical of such technology, simply skip compression, or use the Lossless compressed. However, if disk space is a premium, you might want to consider making some comparisons of your own to determine if you find compressed NEF files acceptable.

Lossless compressed reduces your file sizes by 20 percent to 40 percent with no loss of quality.

Embed ICC Profile lets you embed a custom color profile in the resulting files.

JPEG Options

When you save a file as a JPEG, the Save Options Dialog includes a check box for embedding an ICC profile and also has as a Quality slider that lets you select how much compression you want applied to the file. The Quality menu provides preset compression levels labeled with simple descriptions of quality versus balance.

TIFF Options

When TIFF is selected for saving, the Save Options Dialog provides the standard set of TIFF options, including Bit Depth, Color Mode, Compression settings, and Embed an ICC Profile.

CHAPTER FOUR

Working with Raw Files

If you have a Nikon camera that can shoot raw files, then Capture NX provides you with some important additional tools that will allow you to perform edits on your raw files and to maintain a level of quality, that simply can't be achieved when shooting in JPEG or TIFF mode.

In this chapter we're going to look at Capture NX's raw processing capabilities. Unfortunately, Capture NX does not support raw formats from other cameras, so as mentioned earlier, if you're using a non-Nikon camera and are shooting raw, you'll have to do your raw conversion elsewhere. However, while Capture NX may not be able to handle your non-Nikon raw files, you still might want to read the first few sections of this chapter to get a better understanding of how your camera works and of why you might want to consider shooting raw. The concepts presented in this first section are true for any camera that shoots raw, and for any raw conversion software. In the second half of this chapter, we'll get to Capture NX's specific raw controls.

WHAT IS RAW, AND WHY SHOULD YOU USE IT?

There are a number of reasons to shoot raw instead of JPEG—in fact, I've shot exclusively raw with my digital cameras for years, because I find the advantages that it provides are worth the few annoyances that raw can introduce to your workflow. In this section, we're going to look at why you might want to make the switch to raw. To better understand how raw and JPEG differ, you need to know some of the details of how your camera works.

How Your Digital Camera Creates an Image

A piece of film is a remarkably self-contained apparatus. Nothing more than a piece of celluloid with a thin layer of chemical emulsion, film works without any power source, and with no mechanical apparatus. (The battery and mechanics in your film camera are there just to make photography easier—they're not actually essential.) Despite its simplicity, a piece of film is both an imaging technology *and* a storage device. By comparison, your digital camera requires a large number of sophisticated technologies. Packed with everything from light-sensitive imaging chips to custom amplifiers to onboard computers and removable storage technologies, there's a lot going on in even the smallest digital camera.

Just as film photographers of old had an in-depth understanding of the imaging properties of their films and chemistries, digital photographers can benefit from a deeper knowledge of how their camera works.

How a digital camera sees

From one perspective, there's very little difference between a digital camera and a film camera. They both use a lens to focus light through an aperture and a shutter onto a focal plane. The only detail that makes a camera a *digital* camera is that the focal plane holds a digital image sensor rather than a piece of film.

The quality of your final image is determined by many factors, from the sophistication of your lens to your (or your light meter's) decision as to which shutter speed and aperture size to use. One downside to digital photography is that the actual imaging technology is a static, unchangeable part of your camera. You can't change the image sensor if you don't like the quality of its output.

Just like a piece of film, an image sensor is light sensitive, be it a CCD (charge-coupled device) or CMOS (complementary metal oxide semiconductor) chip. The surface of the chip is divided into a grid of *photosites*, one for each pixel in the final image. Each photosite has a diode that is sensitive to light (a *photodiode*). The photodiode produces an electric charge proportional to the amount of light it receives during an exposure. To interpret the image captured by the sensor, the voltage of each photosite is measured and then converted to a digital value, thus producing a digital representation of the pattern of light that fell on the sensor's surface.

Measuring the varying amounts of light that were focused onto the surface of the sensor (a process called *sampling*) yields a big batch of numbers, which in turn can be processed into a final image.

However, knowing how *much* light there is in a particular photosite doesn't tell you anything about the *color* of the resulting pixel. Rather, all you have is a record of the varying brightness, or *luminance*, values that have struck the image sensor. This is fine if you're interested in black-and-white photography. If you want to shoot full color, though, things get a little more complex.

Mixing a batch of color

If you've ever bought paint at a hardware store, or if you learned about the color wheel in grade school, you might already know that you can mix together a few primary colors of ink pigments to create every other color. Light works the same way, but the primary colors of ink are cyan, magenta, and yellow, whereas the primary colors of light are red, green, and blue. What's more, ink pigments mix together in a subtractive process. As you mix more ink colors, your result gets darker until the ink turns black. Light mixes together in an additive process; as you mix more light, the light gets brighter until it ultimately turns white.

In 1869, James Clerk Maxwell and Thomas Sutton performed an experiment to test a theory about a way of creating color photographs. They shot three black-and-white photographs of a tartan ribbon. For each photo they fixed their camera with a separate colored filter: one red, one blue, and one green. Later, they projected the images using three separate projectors, each fitted with the appropriate red, green, or blue filter. When the projected images were superimposed over each other, they yielded a full-color picture.

Your digital camera uses a similar technique—and a lot of math—to calculate the correct color of each pixel. Every photosite on your camera's sensor is covered with a colored filter—red, green, or blue. Red and green filters alternate in one row, and blue and green alternate in the following row (**Figure 4.1**). There are twice as many green photosites because your eyes are much more sensitive to green than to any other color.

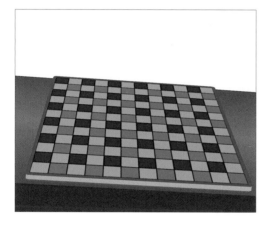

Figure 4.1 In a typical digital camera, each pixel on the image sensor is covered with a colored filter: red, green, or blue. Although your camera doesn't capture full color for each pixel, it can interpolate the correct color of any pixel by analyzing the color of the surrounding pixels. This array of colors is called a Bayer pattern after Dr. Bryce Bayer, the Kodak scientist who devised it in the early 1970s.

As you've probably already surmised, this scheme still doesn't produce a color image. For that, the filtered pixel data must be run through an interpolation algorithm, which calculates the correct color for each pixel by analyzing the color of its filtered neighbors.

Say that you want to determine the color of a particular pixel that has a green filter and a value of 100 percent. If you look at the surrounding pixels with their mix of red, blue, and green filters and find each of those pixels also has a value of 100 percent, it's a pretty safe bet that the correct color of the pixel in question is white, since 100 percent each of red, green, and blue yields white (**Figure 4.2**).

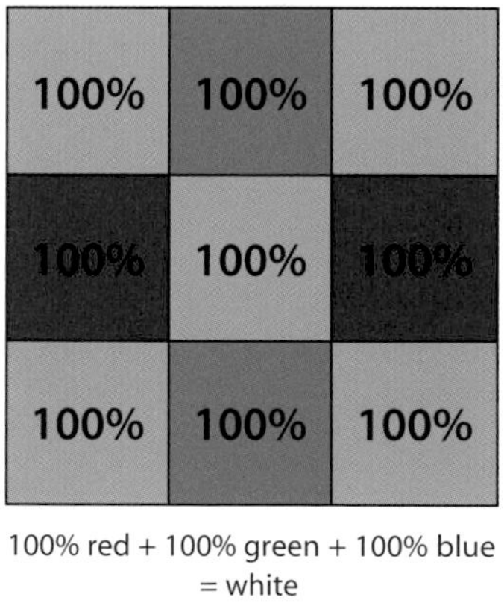

100%	100%	100%
100%	100%	100%
100%	100%	100%

100% red + 100% green + 100% blue
= white

Figure 4.2 To calculate the true color of the 100 percent green pixel in the middle of this grid, you examine the surrounding pixels. Because they're all 100 percent, it's a good chance that the target pixel is pure white, since 100 percent of red, green, and blue combines to produce white.

Of course, the pixel may be some other color—a single dot of color in a field of white. However, pixels are *extremely* tiny (in the case of a typical consumer digital camera, 26 million pixels could fit on a dime), so odds are small that the pixel is a color other than white. Nevertheless, there can be sudden changes of color in an image—as is the case, for example, in an object with a sharply defined edge. To help average out the colors from pixel to pixel and therefore improve the chances of an accurate calculation, digital cameras contain a special filter that blurs the image slightly, thus gently smearing the color. Although blurring an image may seem antithetical to good photography, the amount of blur introduced is not so great that it can't be corrected for later in software.

This process of interpolation is called *demosaicing,* a cumbersome word derived from the idea of breaking down the chip's mosaic of RGB-filtered pixels into a full-color image. There are many different demosaicing algorithms. Because the camera's ability to accurately demosaic has a tremendous bearing on the overall color quality and accuracy of the camera's images, demosaicing algorithms are closely guarded trade secrets.

The Bayer pattern is an example of a *color filter array (CFA)*. Not all cameras use an array of red, green, and blue filters. For example, some cameras use cyan, yellow, green, and magenta arrays. In the end, a vendor's choice of CFA doesn't really matter as long as the camera yields color that you like.

A final image from a digital camera consists of three separate *color channels*, one each for red, green, and blue information. Just as in Maxwell's and Sutton's experiment, when these three channels are combined, you get a full-color image (**Figure 4.3**).

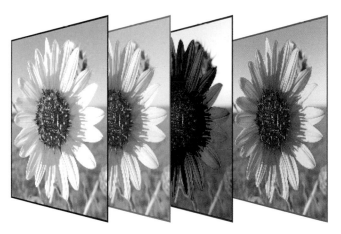

Figure 4.3 Your camera creates a full-color image by combining three separate red, green, and blue channels. If you're confused by the fact that an individual channel appears in grayscale, remember that each channel contains only one color component—so the red channel contains just the red information for the image; brighter tones represent more red, darker tones, less.

Digital Image Composition

A final image from your digital camera is composed of a grid of tiny pixels that correspond to the photosites on your camera's image sensor. The color of each pixel in an image is usually specified using three numbers: one for the red component, one for the blue, and one for the green. If your final image is an *8-bit image,* then 8-bit numbers are used to represent each component. This means that any pixel in any individual channel can have a value between 0 and 255. When three 8-bit channels are combined, you have a composite 24-bit image that is capable of displaying any of approximately 16 million colors. Although this is a far greater number of colors than the eye can perceive, bear in mind that a lot of these colors are essentially redundant. RGB values of 1, 0, 0 (1 red, 0 green, 0 blue) and 1, 1, 0 are not significantly different. Therefore, the number of *significant* colors in that 16-million color assortment is actually much smaller.

In a *16-bit image*, 16-bit numbers are used for each channel, resulting in an image that can have trillions of unique colors. Although the difference between 1, 0, 0 and 1, 1, 0, will be the same as in an 8-bit image because each pixel of each channel can have a value between 0 and 65,535, 16-bit images have a greater number of significant colors. You won't necessarily see more colors, but these extra values will give you more latitude when editing.

The concept of color channels is important to understand because some edits and corrections can be achieved only by manipulating the individual color channels of an image. What's more, some problems are easier to identify and solve if you are in the habit of thinking in terms of individual channels.

How Your Camera Makes a JPEG Image

By default, your camera probably shoots in JPEG mode. In fact, depending on your camera, JPEG images might be your only option. More advanced cameras will also offer a raw mode. When a camera is shooting JPEG images, a lot of things happen after the sensor makes its capture.

The camera first reads the data off of the sensor and then amplifies it. As you learned earlier, each pixel on your image sensor produces a voltage that is proportional to the amount of light that struck that site. When you increase the ISO setting on your camera, all you're doing is increasing the amount of amplification that is applied to the original data. Unfortunately, just as turning up the volume on your stereo produces more noise and hiss, turning up the amount of amplification in your camera increases the amount of noise (ugly grainy patterns) in your image (**Figure 4.4**).

After being amplified, the data is passed to your camera's onboard computer, where a number of important image processing steps occur.

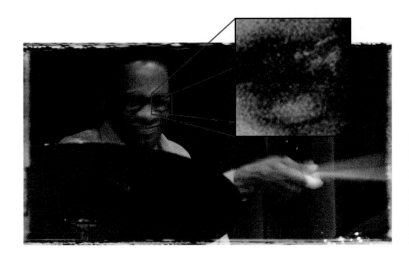

Figure 4.4 As you increase the ISO setting of your camera (often done when shooting in low light), you increase the amount of noise in your image.

Demosaicing

The raw image data is first passed through the camera's demosaicing algorithms to determine the actual color of each pixel. Although the computing power in your digital camera would make a desktop computer user of a dozen years ago green with envy, demosaicing is so complicated that camera vendors sometimes have to take shortcuts with their demosaicing algorithms to keep the camera from getting bogged down with processing. After all, a computer can sit there and work for as long as it needs, but the camera has to be ready to shoot again in a fraction of a second. The ability to make the most of the camera's processing resources is one reason that some cameras are better at demosaicing than others.

Colorimetric interpretation

Earlier it was noted that each photosite has a red, green, or blue filter over it, but "red," "green," and "blue" were never defined. Your camera is programmed with colorimetric information about the exact color of these filters and so can adjust the overall color information of the image to compensate for the fact that its red filters, for example, may actually have a bit of yellow in them.

Color space

After all this computation, your camera's computer will have a set of color values for each pixel in your image. For example, a particular pixel may have measured as 100 percent red, 0 percent green, and 0 percent blue, meaning it should be a bright red pixel. But what does 100 percent red mean—100 percent of what?

To ensure that different devices and pieces of software understand what "100 percent red" means, your image is mapped to a *color space*. Color spaces are simply specifications that define exactly what color a particular color value—such as 100 percent red—corresponds to.

Most cameras provide a choice of a couple of color spaces, usually sRGB and Adobe RGB. Your choice of color space can affect the appearance of your final image because the same color values might map to different actual colors in different spaces. For example, 100 percent red in the Adobe RGB color space is defined as a much brighter color than 100 percent red in the sRGB space.

All of these color spaces are smaller than the full range of colors that your eyes can see, and some of them may be smaller than the full range of colors that your camera can capture. If you tell your camera to use sRGB, but your camera is capable of capturing, say, brighter blues than provided for in the sRGB color space, the blue tones in your image will be squeezed down to fit in the sRGB space. Your image may still look fine, but if the image were mapped to a larger color space, there's a chance that more of the colors your camera captured would be visible.

After demosaicing your image, the camera converts the resulting color values to the color space you've selected. (Most cameras default to sRGB.) Note that if you're shooting raw, you can change this color space later using Capture NX.

White balance

Different types of light shine at different intensities, measured as a temperature using the Kelvin (K) scale. To properly interpret the color in your image, your digital camera needs to know what type of light is illuminating your scene.

White balancing is the process of calibrating your camera to match the current lighting situation. Because white contains all colors, calibrating your camera to properly represent white automatically calibrates it for any color in your scene.

Your camera will likely provide many different white balance settings, from an Auto White Balance mode that tries to guess the proper white balance, to specific modes that let you choose the type of light you're shooting in, to preset modes that let you manually create custom white balance settings. These settings don't have any impact on the way the camera shoots or captures data. Instead, they affect how the camera processes the data after it's been demosaiced and mapped to a color space.

When you shoot in Auto White Balance mode, the camera employs special algorithms for identifying what the correct white balance setting should be. Although most auto white balance mechanisms these days are very sophisticated, even the best ones can confuse mixed lighting situations—for example, shooting in a tungsten-lit room with sunlight streaming through the windows, shooting into a building from outside, and so on.

If you're using a specific white balance or preset mode, the camera adjusts the color balance of the image according to those settings.

> **TIP:** As you'll see, one of the great advantages of shooting in raw mode is that you can adjust the white balance of an image after you shoot. This makes it much easier to deal with tricky lighting situations.

Gamma, contrast, and color adjustments

Suppose you expose a digital camera sensor to a light and it registers a brightness value of 50. If you expose the same camera to twice as much light, it will register a brightness value of 100. Although this makes perfect sense, it is, unfortunately, not the way your eyes work. Doubling the amount of light that hits your eyes does not result in a doubling of perceived brightness, because your eyes do not have a linear response to light.

Our eyes are much more sensitive to changes in illumination at very low levels and very high levels than they are to changes in moderate brightness. For this reason, we don't perceive changes in light in the same linear way that a digital camera does.

To compensate for this, a camera applies a mathematical curve to the image data to make the brightness levels in the image match what the eye would see. This *gamma correction* process redistributes the tones in an image so that there's more contrast at the extreme ends of the tonal spectrum. A gamma-corrected image has more subtle change in its darkest and lightest tones than does an uncorrected, linear image (**Figure 4.5**).

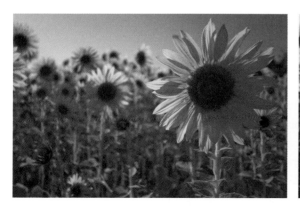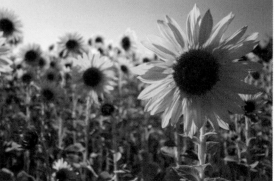

Figure 4.5 The left image shows what your camera captures—a linear image. The right image shows how your eyes perceive the same scene. Because your eyes have a nonlinear response to light, they perceive more contrast in the shadows and highlights.

Next, the camera adjusts the image's contrast and color. These alterations are usually fairly straightforward—an increase in contrast, perhaps a boost to the saturation of the image. Most cameras let you adjust these parameters using the built-in menuing system, and most cameras provide some variation on the options shown in **Figure 4.6**.

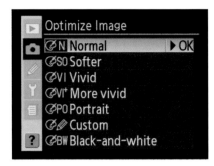

Figure 4.6 On most cameras, internal image processing can be controlled through a simple menu.

Noise reduction and sharpening

Many cameras employ some form of noise reduction. Some cameras also automatically switch on an additional, more aggressive noise reduction process when you shoot using a lengthy exposure.

All cameras also perform some sharpening of their images. How much varies from camera to camera, and the sharpening amount can usually be adjusted by the user. This sharpening is employed partly to compensate for the blurring that is applied to even out color variations during the demosaicing stage (**Figure 4.7**).

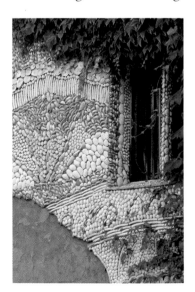 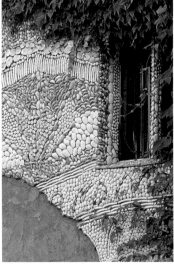

Figure 4.7 This figure shows the same image sharpened two different ways. The image on the left has been reasonably sharpened, but the one on the right has been aggressively oversharpened, resulting in a picture with harsher contrast.

Eight-bit conversion

Your camera's image sensor attempts to determine a numeric value that represents the amount of light that strikes a particular pixel. Most cameras capture 10 to 12 bits of data for each pixel on the sensor. In the binary counting scheme that all computers use, 12 bits allow you to count from 0 to 4095, which means that you can represent 4096 different shades that the sensor can capture, from the darkest to the lightest tones.

The JPEG format allows only 8-bit images. With 8 bits, you can count from 0 to 255. Obviously, converting to 8 bits from 12 means throwing out some data, which manifests in your final image as a loss of fine color transitions and details. Although this loss may not be perceptible (particularly if you're outputting to a monitor or printer that's not good enough to display those extra colors anyway), it can have a big impact on how far you can push your color corrections and adjustments.

JPEG compression

With your image data interpreted, corrected, and converted to 8-bit, it's ready to be compressed for storage on your camera's media card. JPEG compression exploits the fact that your eyes are more sensitive to changes in luminance than they are to changes in color.

With JPEG compression, your image will take up far less space, allowing you to fit more images onto your camera's storage card. However, JPEG is a lossy compressor, which means your image loses image quality. How much depends on the level of JPEG compression that you choose to apply.

On most cameras, the best level of JPEG compression is indistinguishable from an uncompressed image. However, you must be very careful to not recompress a JPEG image. JPEG compressing an image that has already been through a JPEG compression process can increase the image quality loss to a level that is perceptible (**Figure 4.8**). You must keep this in mind through your JPEG workflow.

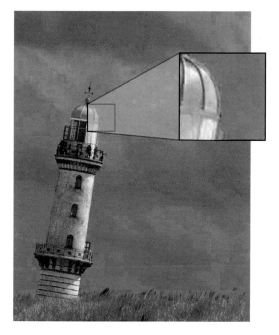

Figure 4.8 In this rather extreme example of JPEG compression, you can see the posterization effects that can occur from aggressive compression (or repeated recompression) as well as the blocky artifacts that JPEG compression can produce.

File storage

Finally, the image is written to your camera's memory card. These days, many cameras include sophisticated memory buffers that let them process images in an onboard RAM cache while simultaneously writing out other images to the storage card. Good buffer and writing performance is what allows some cameras to achieve high frame rates when shooting in burst mode.

Your camera also stores important *exchangeable image file (EXIF)* information in the header of the JPEG file. The EXIF header contains, among other things, all of the relevant exposure information for your shot. Everything from camera make and model to shutter speed, aperture setting, ISO speed, white balance setting, exposure compensation setting, and much more is included in the file, and you can reference all of this information from within Capture NX (**Figure 4.9**).

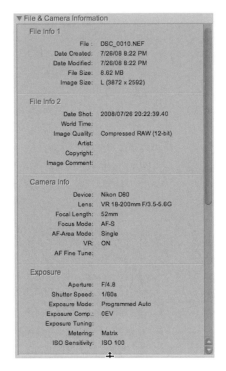

Figure 4.9 Capture NX allows you to look at the EXIF data of any image that you're browsing or editing.

How Your Camera Makes a Raw Image

It's much easier for your camera to make a raw file than a JPEG file for the simple reason that when shooting raw, your camera passes the hard work on to you, or rather, to you and your computer. When shooting in raw mode, the camera does nothing more than collect the data from the image sensor, amplify it, and then write it to the storage card along with the usual EXIF information. In addition, certain camera settings such as white balance and any image processing settings are stored. It's your job to take that raw file and run it through software to turn it into a usable image.

A raw converter, such as the one included in Capture NX, is just a stand-alone variation of the same type of software that's built into your camera. With it, you move all of the computation that's normally done in your camera onto your desktop, where you have more control and a few more options.

Why should you do it yourself when you can get your camera to do it for you? Let's take a look at each image processing step to see why raw is a better way to go for many images.

Demosaicing

As mentioned earlier, the quality of a demosaicing algorithm often has a lot to do with the final image quality that you get from your camera. Demosaicing is a complex process, and a poorly demosaiced image can yield artifacts such as magenta or green fringes along high-contrast edges, poor edge detail, weird moiré patterns, or blue halos around specular highlights. Today, most cameras employ special circuits or digital signal processors designed specifically to handle the hundreds of calculations per pixel that are required to demosaic an image. Even though your camera may have a lot of processing power, it doesn't always have a lot of processing time. If you're shooting a burst of images at five frames per second, the camera can't devote much time to its image processing. Therefore, because time is often short and the custom chips used for demosaicing are often battery hogs, in-camera demosaicing algorithms will sometimes take shortcuts for the sake of speed and battery power.

Your desktop computer can afford to take more time to crunch numbers. Consequently, most raw conversion applications use a more sophisticated demosaicing algorithm than what's in your camera. This often results in better color and quality than your camera can provide when shooting in JPEG mode.

Colorimetric interpretation

Just as your camera does when shooting in JPEG mode, stand-alone raw converters must adjust the image to compensate for the specific color of the filters on your camera's image sensor. This colorimetric information is usually contained in special camera profiles that are included with the raw software. If your software doesn't provide a profile for your camera, it can't process that camera's raw files.

Color space

As explained earlier, your image data must be mapped to a color space when your camera shoots a JPEG file, and raw processing software on your computer must do the same thing. Your raw converter lets you specify which color space you want to use, and probably offers more choices than you'll find in your camera. In addition to the sRGB and Adobe RGB color spaces, which your camera probably offers, most raw converters provide choices such as ProPhoto RGB.

White balance

Good white balance is a tricky process, both objectively and subjectively. Objectively, calculating accurate white balance in a difficult lighting situation—say, sunlight streaming into a room lit with fluorescent light—can trip up even a quality camera. When working with raw files, you can adjust the white balance as you see fit, which can often mean the difference between a usable and an unusable image.

Subjectively, accurate white balance is not always the best white balance. Although you may have set the white balance accurately and achieved extremely precise color, an image that's a little warmer or cooler may actually be more pleasing. Altering the white balance of the image in your raw converter is often the best way to make such a change.

Even though your camera doesn't perform any white balance adjustments when shooting in raw mode, it does store the white balance setting in the image's EXIF information. Your raw converter, in turn, reads this setting and uses it as the initial white balance setting. You can start adjusting the white balance from there.

Why Is White Balance Measured as a Temperature?

It may seem strange to measure the *color* of light as a temperature, but if you've ever sat around a campfire (or accidentally left a skillet on the stove) then you know that as something heats up, it changes color. Color temperature is calculated by heating a completely black object and then noting the temperature at which it becomes a specific color. Curiously, the colors that we consider "warm," such as red, actually occur at lower temperatures than colors we consider "cool," like blue.

Gamma, contrast, and color adjustments

As discussed earlier, when shooting JPEG, your camera performs a gamma adjustment to the image so that the brightness values are closer to what our eyes see when they look at a scene. When shooting JPEG, you can't control the amount of gamma correction that your camera applies, but when processing a raw image you have more control, as you can easily adjust and tweak the gamma correction.

Similarly, although your camera may provide contrast, saturation, and brightness controls for JPEG shooting, these controls probably offer only three to five different settings. Raw converters provide controls with tremendous range and far more settings.

What's more, when you're working with raw files, Capture NX provides highlight recovery tools that allow you to perform corrections that simply aren't possible when you work with non-raw formats.

Noise reduction and sharpening

Just as your camera performs noise reduction and sharpening, your raw converter also includes these capabilities. However, like the gamma, contrast, and color adjustment controls, the noise reduction and sharpening controls of a raw converter provide much finer degrees of precision.

Eight-bit conversion

Although your camera must convert its 12-bit color data to 8 bits before storing it in JPEG format (because the JPEG format doesn't support higher bit depths), raw files aren't as limited. With your raw converter, you can choose to compress the image down to 8 bits or to write it as a 16-bit file. Sixteen bits provides more number space than you need for a 12-bit file, but the extra space means that you don't have to toss out any of your color information. The ability to output 16-bit files is one of the main quality advantages of shooting in raw.

File storage

With a raw file, you can choose to save your final edited image in any of several formats. Obviously, you're free to save your image as an 8-bit JPEG file, just as if you had originally shot in JPEG mode, but most likely you'll want to save in a non-compressed format to preserve as much image quality as possible. And if you decide to work in 16-bit mode, you'll want to choose a format that can handle 16-bit images, such as TIFF.

One of the great advantages of shooting in raw mode is that you can process your original image in many different ways and save it in various formats. Thus, there might be times when you *do* want to save your raw files in JPEG format—as part of a Web production workflow, for instance. This doesn't mean that you've actually compromised any of your precious raw data, since you can always go back to your original raw file, process it again, and write it to a different format.

What's more, as raw conversion software improves, you can return to your original raw files, reprocess them, and possibly produce better results. Raw files truly represent the digital equivalent of a negative.

> **NOTE:** *If you're shooting raw files with a Nikon camera then you might have the option to save as a compressed raw file. This is different from JPEG compression, and we'll discuss it in more detail later, when we cover file saving in Capture NX 2.*

Why Not Shoot in TIFF Mode?

Before the development of raw, cameras worked around the problem of JPEG compression artifacts by offering an uncompressed TIFF mode. Many cameras still offer a TIFF option, but shooting in TIFF mode is a far cry from shooting in raw.

First, TIFF files don't offer the editing flexibility of raw files, and most cameras write 8-bit TIFF files, meaning that you don't get the high-bit advantage of raw. Second, TIFF files are typically much larger than raw files. Whereas a raw file stores only one 12-bit number for each pixel, TIFF files are demosaiced into a three-channel color image, meaning that they have to store three 8-bit numbers per pixel.

Third, the high-quality JPEG modes on most cameras are *very* good. In general, you probably won't be able to discern the difference between a minimally compressed JPEG image and a TIFF image, so the storage space sacrifice will be of little value.

Raw Concerns

When compared side by side, it's easy to see that shooting raw offers a number of important advantages over shooting JPEG: editable white balance, 16-bit color support, and no compression artifacts. But as you've probably already suspected, there is a price to pay for this additional power.

Storage

Raw files are *big*. Whereas a fine-quality JPEG file from a 10-megapixel camera might weigh in at 3 MB, the same image shot in raw will devour 7–9 MB of storage space. Fortunately, this is not as grievous an issue as it used to be thanks to falling memory prices.

Workflow

One of the great advantages of digital photography is that it makes shooting lots of pictures very inexpensive. Thus, you can much more freely experiment, bracket your shots, and shoot photos of subjects that you normally might not want to risk a frame of film on. Consequently, it's very easy to quickly start drowning in images, all of which have unhelpful names like DSC0549.JPG.

Managing image glut is pretty easy with JPEG files since there are so many programs that can read them. In fact, both the Mac OS and Windows include JPEG readers.

With raw files, your workflow is a bit more complicated because a raw file doesn't contain any comprehensible image data until it has been processed: It's a little more difficult to quickly glance through a collection of raw images. Fortunately, both the Mac OS and Windows provide simple image viewers that let you look at raw files. These programs work by performing a simple automatic raw conversion, just like your camera does when shooting in JPEG mode.

However, because there's no set standard for the formatting of raw files, different vendors encode their raw data in various ways. Also, as you learned earlier, to perform a raw conversion, your raw conversion software has to determine certain things about the type of camera that was used to shoot the image, such as the colorimetric data about the colored filters on the camera's image sensor.

For these reasons, your raw conversion software must be outfitted with a special profile that describes the type of camera that produced the files that you want to convert. Unfortunately, these profiles have to be created by the software manufacturer. If your raw converter of choice doesn't support your specific camera model, you'll be unable to view and process raw files in that program.

Capture NX can process raw files from any Nikon camera that outputs *NEF (Nikon Electronic Format)* files. NEF files can contain raw camera data as well as non-raw data, just like a TIFF or JPEG file.

If you're shooting with a different type of camera, you won't be able to process your raw files in Capture NX. You'll need to process them using a different converter, save them as TIFF or JPEG files, and then bring the results into Capture NX when you want to edit them. We'll cover this process in more detail in the next chapter.

Shooting performance

Because raw files are so big, the camera requires more time and memory to buffer and store them. Depending on the quality of your camera, choosing to shoot in raw mode may compromise your ability to capture bursts of images at a fast frame rate. In addition, your camera may take longer to recover from a burst of shooting, because its buffer will fill up quickly and take more time to flush.

If you want speedy burst shooting *and* the ability to shoot raw, you might have to consider upgrading to a camera with better burst performance.

Raw Advantages

Shooting raw will not get you images with a wider range of colors or tones, just many more gradations of tone and color within the range captured, or more sharpness and detail. The advantage of raw has to do with when you start to edit. If you *never* perform any image editing, then there's little reason to shoot raw. Learn to use the adjustment controls in your camera, and keep shooting JPEG.

But, if you like to perform the types of edits that we saw in the last chapter, then there are huge advantages to shooting in raw. In simplest terms, raw files score over JPEG files when editing because:

• With raw files, you can adjust white balance after you shoot, with far greater latitude and accuracy than you can with JPEG images. In addition, there's no way to introduce artifacts or problems into your edit when using a raw converter to adjust white balance.

• Raw files often allow you to recover highlights that have been overexposed, allowing you to restore detail to areas that initially appear completely white.

• Because of their greater bit depth, raw files allow you to perform more edits before you begin to see visible degradation in your image.

• Since they aren't JPEG compressed, raw files never suffer from all of the visible artifacts introduced by JPEG compression.

• Because you're in control of the raw conversion that's normally performed inside your camera, you can tweak the conversion settings to your particular tastes.

• A raw file is a true digital negative. Years from now, if a much-improved raw conversion technology becomes available, you can re-process your raw files and possibly get better results.

• Finally, raw allows more sophisticated workflows that make it simple to apply the same edits to multiple images, and to process the same raw file in many different ways to get several different results.

In the rest of this chapter, we'll look at all of the raw editing controls that you'll find in Capture NX.

PROCESSING RAW IMAGES

For the most part, there's little difference in workflow between working with Nikon raw files in Capture NX and working with non-raw files. As with non-raw files, you'll need to transfer your raw images from your camera's media card to your computer. You can use any of the methods discussed earlier to perform this transfer, and most of the browsers that I mentioned will be able to display thumbnails of your raw files. If your browser of choice can't display your raw images, it may simply be that your camera is too new and you need to wait for an update.

Once you've transferred your images, sorted them, organized them, and made your selections, you're ready to start editing. Open the raw file you want to edit using any of the normal file opening techniques.

What Happens When You Open a Raw File

Earlier in this chapter you learned about all of the steps that must be taken to produce a full-color image from the raw data that your camera collects. When you shoot in JPEG mode, your camera takes care of executing all of these steps.

When you open a raw file in Capture NX, the program goes through all of the steps that your camera would take if it were processing a JPEG file. It demosaics the data and performs colorimetric correction to compensate for the color filters on your camera's image sensor, it maps the image into a color space, adjusts the white balance of your image according to the camera setting you were using, applies gamma correction and a little bit of color adjustment, noise reduction, and sharpening. It does *not* convert the image to 8-bit data.

When it has done all of this, it presents the image to you on-screen, just as if it were a JPEG or TIFF image. However, if you look at the Edit List, you'll see a few new options. Above the Quick Fix edit, you'll now see a Camera Settings edit, and in the Quick Fix edit itself you'll see that the Exposure Compensation slider is now active. Finally, the Camera & Lens Correction edit will have two additional controls. With these added options, you'll be able to make edits that aren't possible with JPEG or TIFF files.

The Camera Settings Edit

With the Camera Settings edit you can control a few of the essential raw conversion parameters that Capture NX uses during its raw conversion. When you move any of the sliders in the Camera Settings edit, Capture NX goes back to the original raw file and *reprocesses it* with those new settings.

In the last chapter you saw how we performed fairly radical alterations to the color in an image by making adjustments to individual color channels. You also saw how these adjustments led to data loss, and you saw the resultant combing that appeared in the histogram. When you alter settings in the Camera Settings edit, there's no risk of data loss, because when you make a change, Capture NX does not actually push and pull data around. Instead, it goes back to the original raw data and reconverts your image based on your new settings. Basically, when you change the White Balance sliders, you're altering the program's fundamental understanding of what red, green, and blue are. With this new understanding, it's recalculating your raw conversion. This is why you'll never see a combed histogram after you make a change to the Camera Settings edit—after every alteration, you're getting brand new, unadulterated data.

In general, you can work through the Camera Settings edit in order and you'll have a good editing workflow.

White Balance

At the top of the Camera Settings edit is the White Balance section. You've already learned that you can alter the white balance of a raw file after the fact, and these are the controls you'll use to perform those changes (**Figure 4.10**).

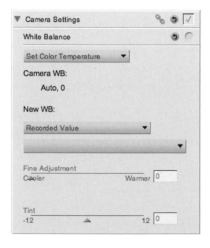

Figure 4.10 At the top of the Camera Settings edit are Capture NX's White Balance tools—essential controls for editing your raw files.

Initially, the White Balance edit shows you the white balance setting that was used by your camera when you took the picture. In the face of Figure 4.10, you can see that "Camera WB" was set to "Auto, 0" meaning the camera was set on Auto white balance. There are several ways you can change the white balance.

If the pop-up menu at the top of the White Balance controls is set to Set Color Temperature, then you can use the various sliders and controls to set the white balance of your image. If you choose Set Gray Point, then you can set white balance by using a special eyedropper tool.

Set Color Temperature. When Set Color Temperature is selected, you'll see a pop-up menu beneath New WB that says Recorded Value. This indicates that the white balance is currently set to the white balance setting that the camera recorded in the file. If you open that menu, you'll see a list of other white balance options (**Figure 4.11**).

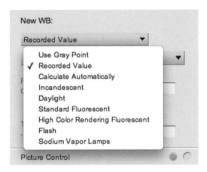

Figure 4.11 You can choose from the same white balance presets that you probably have in your Nikon camera.

You should recognize some of these. Incandescent, Daylight, Standard Fluorescent, High Color Rendering Fluorescent, Flash, and Sodium Vapor Lamps are the same types of white balance presets that you'll find in your camera. So, for example, if you choose Daylight, Capture NX will switch to a predefined white balance setting that Nikon has determined to be good for daylight shooting.

The Daylight setting, as well as the Fluorescent and Flash settings, includes a second menu with additional options. So, for example, if you choose Daylight, the secondary menu lets you choose between Direct sunlight, Shade, and Cloudy. Each of these will yield slightly different results (**Figure 4.12**)

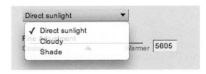

Figure 4.12 When you choose Daylight, a secondary pop-up menu lets you pick from direct, shady, or cloudy daylight, which can each have slightly different color temperatures.

Once you pick a preset, the Fine Adjustment and Tint sliders will become active. These let you refine the white balance manually. The Fine Adjustment slider lets you make the image cooler (more blue) or warmer (more red). The Tint slider lets you tint the image more magenta, or more green (**Figure 4.13**).

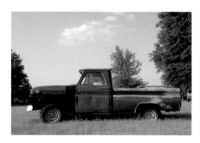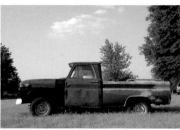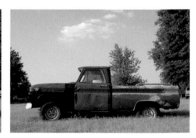

Figure 4.13 On the left is the original Daylight white balance. In the middle you can see the effects of dragging the Fine Adjustment slider toward Warmer, and on the right you can see the effects of dragging Fine Adjustment toward Cooler.

You can't use the Fine Adjustment and Tint sliders unless you choose a White Balance preset. So, if you shot with Auto White Balance and just want to warm up your image, you'll first need to pick the preset that most closely matches the lighting conditions in your image. For example, if you shot outside in daylight using Auto White Balance but you want to warm the image, first set New WB to Daylight. Then you can use the Fine Adjustment and Tint sliders.

If you were shooting with a Nikon flash using colored filters from the Nikon Color Filter set, then choose Flash from the New WB pop-up. From the secondary white balance menu, select the filter type that you used.

The Sodium Vapor setting is appropriate for shooting in sports venues or under streetlights.

If you choose Calculate Automatically, then Capture NX will employ its own auto white balance algorithm to determine a white balance. Sometimes, this can do a better job than your in-camera auto setting.

Set Gray Point. If you choose Set Gray Point (which you can select from the New WB pop-up menu or the pop-up menu at the top of the White Balance controls), you'll find the most accurate white balance control of all.

To correct white balance with a gray point eyedropper:

1. Make sure the Set Gray Point controls are showing (**Figure 4.14**).

2. Click the Start button.

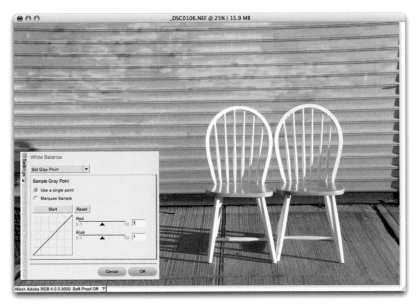

Figure 4.14 Using the Set Gray Point controls, you can set the white balance of your image by clicking within the image.

3. Click on something in your image that should be neutral gray. Capture NX automatically calculates a new White Balance setting (**Figure 4.15**).

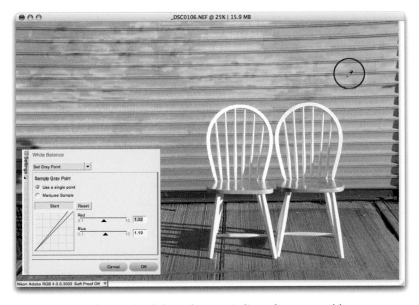

Figure 4.15 With a single click on the spot indicated, we were able to correct the white balance in this image.

4. If you want to refine your white balance—to warm it up or cool it down—adjust the Red and Blue sliders.

Capture NX will alter the curves in the curves swatch beneath the Start button (I know, they look like straight lines, but technically they're curves) to show how it has adjusted each primary color. Remember, like all other edits, white balance is nondestructive, so you can always go back and change it later if you want to. Either click Start again and click on a new point with the dropper, or click Reset to return to the original white balance that your camera recorded.

Sometimes, a gray pattern in your image is actually composed of a number of slightly varying pixels, so it can be difficult to know if you're clicking on the specific pixel that is the gray you want. This is especially true with noisier images. For these instances, click Marquee Selection. When you click Start, you'll be able to drag a selection around a group of pixels. Capture NX then averages the selection to come up with a single, more accurate gray value.

Picture Control

Picture Control is Nikon's proprietary scheme for sharing image processing settings between different cameras and pieces of software. If you have a Nikon camera that supports Picture Control, then you may have played with this feature. With Picture Control you can define different processing schemes that get applied to your images when you're shooting JPEG. If you choose a Picture Control when shooting raw, then your camera will note in the file that you selected that Picture Control. When you open the image in NX 2, the Picture Control will automatically be selected, and NX 2 will process your image accordingly.

The idea with Picture Control is that it provides a simple way to apply consistent edits to your images. If your workflow demands quick processing, then Picture Control might be a boon. For example, if you're a wedding photographer and you know that you always like to deliver images that have a certain level of warmth and saturation, then you can define a Picture Control with the characteristics that you like. Capture NX will automatically process those images according to the Picture Control setting you chose, just as if you'd been shooting JPEG images.

In Capture NX, you can change the Picture Control setting to a different Picture Control, disable it completely, or apply a Picture Control to an image that didn't originally have one.

To add a Picture Control to a raw image:

1. Scroll the Edit List until you can see the Picture Control portion of the Camera Settings edit.

2. Set the pop-up menu at the top of the Picture Control area to Picture Control (**Figure 4.16**).

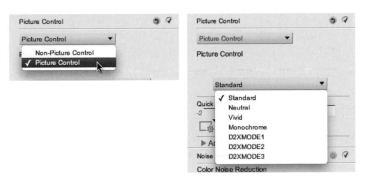

Figure 4.16 To add a Picture Control setting to a raw file, you must first select Picture Control, and then choose the Picture Control you want to apply.

3. Choose the Picture Control that you want to apply from the lower pop-up menu in the Picture Control area. Your image will change according to the settings in the Picture Control that you choose.

4. If you want to refine your image further, move the Quick Adjust slider, which alters the Sharpening, Contrast, and Saturation values according to parameters defined in the Picture Control that you have selected. Moving to the left decreases these values, while moving the slider to the right increases them.

5. If you click on the Advanced options, you'll gain access to individual sliders for each of the Quick Adjust parameters (**Figure 4.17**).

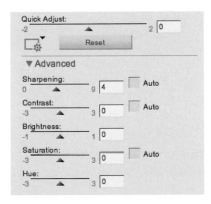

Figure 4.17 The Quick Adjust Advanced parameters let you fine tune the properties of a Picture Control that's been applied to an image.

NOTE: *You may wonder, what are those D2XMode options? Each one is a Picture Control: D2XMODE1, D2XMODE2, and D2XMODE3. They are configured to emulate the like-named "Color Mode" settings on the Nikon D2X and D2XS, and are provided for those who are used to working with those settings.*

Managing Picture Control

At the bottom of the Picture Control area is a Reset button, which resets any Quick Adjust parameters you might have changed.

To the left of the Reset button is the Manage Picture Control pop-up menu (**Figure 4.18**).

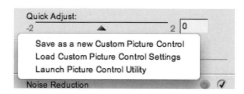

Figure 4.18 The Manage Picture Control pop-up menu lets you choose to save, load, or edit Picture Control settings.

If you've used the Quick Adjust controls to make changes to a Picture Control, you can save the results as an entirely *new* Picture Control, by choosing Save as a new Custom Picture Control from the Manage Picture Control menu.

You can choose Load Custom Picture Control Settings to load picture controls that you've gotten from someone else, or launch the Nikon Picture Control Editor to design a new Picture Control that you can add to Capture NX or download to your camera.

Picture Control and Raw

The great advantage of shooting in raw is that you have *more* editing control than you do when shooting JPEG. You've already seen the ability to change white balance on a raw file, and in a bit you'll see even more editing advantages. So with all this editing power, why fall back on a canned, boiler-plate editing function like Picture Control?

As discussed earlier, with Picture Control, you can ease the process of getting the same look from picture to picture and from shoot to shoot. If you know what type of edits work well for shots taken under a particular kind of light, then it might be that defining those edits once in a Picture Control is all you'll ever need to do to get your images looking the way that you want.

Of course, these same Picture Controls can be applied to JPEG images, and will yield the same results as if you applied them to a raw image. If you never expect to do any additional editing, then you might as well shoot in JPEG mode.

A lot of photographers, though, shoot in raw not because they want to edit every image, but just so that they have some protection against those one or two images that *do* need more extensive editing. If you're shooting in a situation where you might tend to overexpose, or where the auto white balance on your camera might fail, then having a raw file can allow you to salvage the image.

NOTE: Not all Nikon cameras offer Picture Control, so if you're working with an older model, you may not have a Picture Control option in-camera. You can still apply Picture Control after the fact and, as you'll see later, you can easily batch process entire folders full of images in order to add Picture Control to groups of files.

Non-Picture Control

If you change the Picture Control menu to Non-Picture Control (**Figure 4.19**), you'll gain access to the same Color Mode, Sharpening, Tone Compensation, and Saturation adjustments that you have in your Nikon camera. If you're used to using these sliders in your camera to get a look that you like, then you can make the same adjustments here and get the same results. Also, when you're shooting raw, these settings are stored with the raw file, and Capture NX will automatically read them and configure each of these options to match your in-camera configuration.

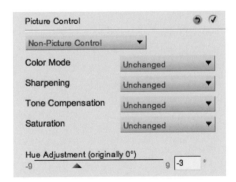

Figure 4.19 Choosing Non-Picture Control in the Camera Settings edit provides you with a different set of controls.

Noise Reduction

Earlier, you learned that after reading data off of the image sensor, the first thing your camera does is to amplify that data. Unfortunately, it's impossible to amplify a signal without introducing noise. But, these days most digital cameras, when used at low ISOs, shoot images with extremely low noise. However, as you crank up to higher ISO settings, there's a good chance that your images will get noisier.

As you saw earlier, noise is a speckled pattern that looks sort of like film grain, but isn't always as attractive. There are two types of noise, *luminance* noise, which appears as bright speckles, and *chrominance*, or *chroma* noise, which appears as colored blobs and artifacts.

When you shoot JPEG images, your camera applies some noise reduction when it sees fit. With a raw file, of course, this noise reduction process is left in your control, and you can use the Noise Reduction controls in the Camera Settings edit to reduce the noise in your image (**Figure 4.20**).

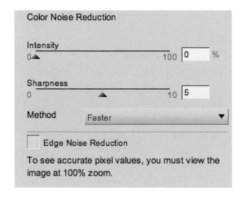

Figure 4.20 The Noise Reduction controls let you tackle noise problems in your raw images.

To apply noise reduction, simply move the Intensity and Sharpness sliders. Noise reduction algorithms tend to work by introducing controlled, localized amounts of blurring in your image in an attempt to smear noise artifacts until they can't be seen. As you drag the Intensity slider to the right, the amount of blurring will increase, and noise should be less visible.

Obviously, as you introduce blurring, you'll be sacrificing sharpness and detail. The Sharpness slider lets you try to restore some of this detail loss. Finding a balance between noise reduction and sharpness loss is your goal when applying noise reduction.

If you change the Faster pop-up menu to Better Quality, then image processing will take a little longer, but you might find better results.

If you see a pronounced level of noise along edges in your image, then check the Edge Noise Reduction button.

As recommended beneath the noise reduction controls, it's best to zoom in to 100 percent when performing your noise reduction corrections. This is mostly because any time you're concerned about sharpness, you should view your image at 100 percent.

That said, be aware that it's difficult to assess how bad a noise problem might be when you're viewing your image at 100 percent. At full magnification you're seeing individual pixels, and when you have an image with 8 million pixels—or more—an individual pixel is not actually significant if you're printing a 4 x 6 or 8 x 10. So, before you get too concerned about correcting noise, take a look at your image in its intended final form. You may find that the noise is not as bad as you feared.

Quick Fix and Raw

After you've adjusted the Camera Settings to your liking, you can move on to the rest of your editing workflow. As discussed in the last chapter, you'll first attack tonal corrections, and then move on to color. Whether you're working with a raw or JPEG image, you use the same techniques: Add the edit that you want to the Edit List and then adjust its parameters.

However, some controls in the Quick Fix edit work a little differently with raw files, and allow some extra power.

Exposure Compensation

When you open a raw file, the Exposure Compensation slider in the Quick Fix edit becomes available (**Figure 4.21**).

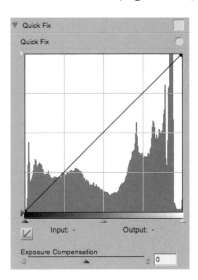

Figure 4.21 The Exposure Compensation slider in the Quick Fix edit only becomes active when you are working on a raw file.

The Exposure Compensation control does just what shooting with an exposure compensation adjustment would do—it increases or decreases the overall exposure in your image. The slider goes from –2 stops to +2 stops. So, if you move the Exposure Compensation slider to .5, then your image will be half a stop brighter (**Figure 4.22**).

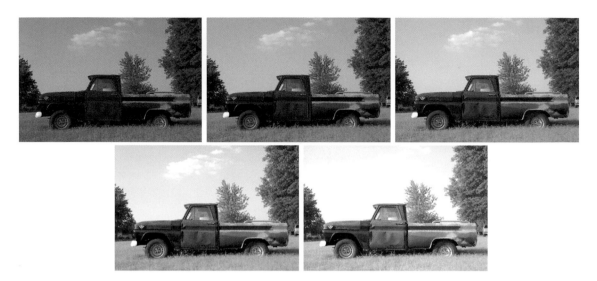

Figure 4.22 By moving the Exposure Compensation slider, we can dramatically change the exposure in an image. From left to right you can see –1, –.5, the original image, +.5, +1.

At first glance, Exposure Compensation seems to merely be brightening or darkening the image, just as you would do if you moved the white point in the Levels control (for brightening) or the black point (for darkening). But Exposure Compensation is more intelligent than that. Its algorithms mimic the way that an image brightens or darkens when exposure is changed. So, rather than just a straight white- or black-point change, when you move the Exposure Compensation slider, your image also gets a gamma adjustment so that the tonal relationships are correctly maintained.

So, if your first assessment of a raw file is that it's over- or underexposed, try correcting it with the Exposure Compensation slider first. You can then refine with the Levels & Curves and other tonal controls later.

Exposure Compensation has an additional, very important feature.

Highlight recovery

As you most likely already know, when you overexpose an image with your digital camera, highlight areas can blow out to detail-less areas of complete white. With JPEG images, these areas are simply lost. You might be able to change the white to a lighter shade of gray, but there's no way to restore detail to the area unless you clone or paint it in yourself.

With a raw file, though, there's a good chance that you'll be able to get some of that detail back. Consider the image in **Figure 4.23**.

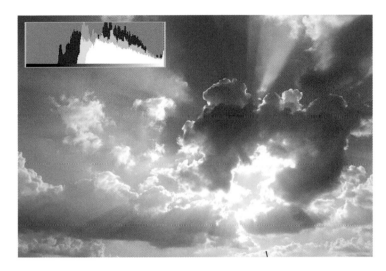

Figure 4.23 This image plainly has some overexposed highlights. You can see them in the bright areas around the edges of the clouds. Note the huge spike on the right side of the histogram.

The bright areas around the edges of the clouds are blown out to complete white. On the right side of the histogram, you can see a large spike, indicating that highlights have been clipped to complete white. If this were a JPEG or TIFF file and we tried to darken the image using the Levels control, we would end up with an image that was, overall, darker, but the overexposed highlights would still be complete white, as you can you can see in **Figure 4.24.**

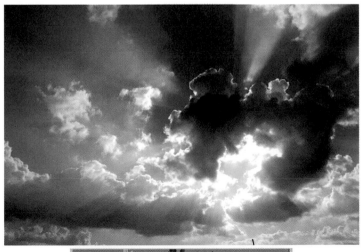

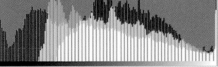

Figure 4.24 With a non-raw version of the clouds, we cannot recover the overexposed highlight areas of the clouds—they remain completely white.

With the raw file, though, we can move the Exposure Compensation slider to the left, which—as expected—darkens the image. But notice what happens to the highlights (**Figure 4.25**).

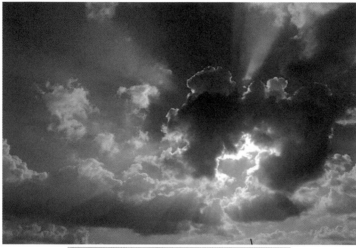

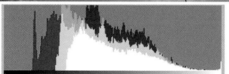

Figure 4.25 When we drag the Exposure Compensation slider to the left on a raw version of the clouds, something very different happens.

Many of the areas that were completely white now have detail in them. The image data and details that had been blown out to nothing but white pixels are back. Notice that, unlike with the image in Figure 4.25, when we lower Exposure Compensation on the raw image in Figure 4.24, the spike on the right side of the histogram gets much lower. Further, the resulting histogram is not combed. Plainly, something very different is going on here.

The first thing to understand is that when you overexpose an area, you don't always overexpose all three color channels. You might only overexpose one or two channels—say, just the blue, or just the blue and the green channels. If there's any data left over, Capture NX can analyze it and use that data to rebuild the missing channels. The result is what you see in Figure 4.25: image data where there previously did not appear to be any.

As Capture NX rebuilds these missing areas, their data is placed back within the normal bounds of the histogram, and so the spike begins to go away.

In many images, it's possible to eliminate the overexposure spike completely. In our example image, though, some areas are blown out so far that it doesn't matter how much we lower Exposure Compensation, there will still be a small spike on the right side. However, with this image it doesn't matter so much, because it's better to have the really bright part of the sun blown out to white.

Obviously, when you lower the Exposure Compensation slider to recover highlights, your entire image gets darker. However, you can then use the Levels & Curves controls in Quick Fix to brighten the rest of the image.

Many times, though, you'll be able to use an additional recovery tool.

Highlight Protection and raw images

In the last chapter you saw how the Highlight Protection slider allows you to darken highlight areas in an image. An *adaptive* tool, the Highlight Protection slider automatically figures out *what* in your image is a highlight and it applies an intelligent darkening that blends in well with surrounding tones. However, as you may have already discovered, when you're working with a non-raw file, Highlight Protection will never restore an area that's been blown out to complete white—it will only darken the white tone that's there.

When you're working with a raw file, though, Highlight Protection turns into a high-light recovery tool. Using Highlight Protection for recovery differs from using Exposure Compensation, though. It recovers clipped highlights, just like Exposure Compensation, but it restricts its effects to only the upper-quarter tones in your image so that as little extra darkening as possible is introduced (**Figure 4.26**).

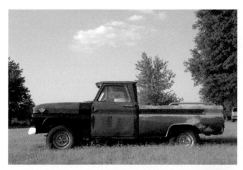
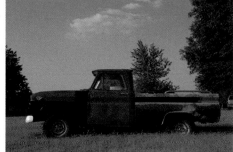
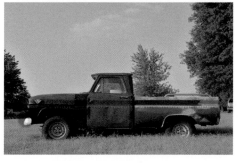

Figure 4.26 Clockwise from upper-left: the original image, which has some overexposed highlights in the clouds; the image after using Exposure Compensation to recover the highlights; finally, the image after recovering the clouds with the Highlight Protection slider. As you can see, Highlight Protection recovers highlights without darkening the entire image.

Highlight Protection can't recover as much highlight detail as Exposure Compensation can—it's only for slightly overexposed highlights. If you need to recover more, then you'll need to switch to the Exposure Compensation slider.

> **TIP:** On very rare occasions you'll run into a problem if you try to use both Exposure Compensation and Highlight Protection. If you start to see weird blotching in the highlights of your image, move the Highlight Protection slider all the way to the left, and perform your recovery using only the Exposure Compensation slider.

Highlight recovery and workflow

If you have a raw file that needs highlight recovery, then that will be the first step in your editing workflow. Partly because you'll want to see if it's possible to recover the highlights to your satisfaction; if it's not then you might want to abandon the image. But you'll also want to do highlight recovery first, because if you need to use the Exposure Compensation slider to recover highlights, then you won't be able to use it to perform any other brightening—you'll want to know this so that you can plan your edits.

So, perform highlight recovery first, then the rest of your tonal corrections, then move on to color correction.

Color Correction

Your color correction chores will pretty much be exactly the same for a raw file as they are for a JPEG or TIFF. However, you should try to achieve as much color correction as possible through white balance adjustments. As you've seen, changes in white balance on a raw file don't cause loss of data, so the more you can correct with White Balance, the better.

Camera & Lens Corrections

When you work with a raw file, the Camera and Lens Correction edit has two additional controls (**Figure 4.27**). Note that these two options are listed *before* the usual Camera & Lens Correction features. This is because these corrections are applied as the raw data is processed into an image. In other words, these are adjustments that your camera would normally perform on its own if you were shooting a JPEG image. As with all other raw adjustments, when you alter one of these parameters, Capture NX reconverts your raw image using your newly specified parameters.

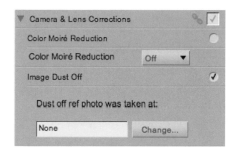

Figure 4.27 When you work with a raw file, the Camera & Lens Correction edit contains two additional controls.

Color moiré reduction

Sometimes, color images that have lots of detail will have moiré artifacts. Turning on Color Moiré Reduction activates special noise reduction algorithms that can reduce moiré artifacts in the colored parts of your image.

Image dust off

If you regularly change lenses in the field, there will come a time when you'll have images with visible sensor dust. Sensor dust appears as smudges or blotches in your image. If your Nikon camera supports it, you might be able to use a Dust Reference Image to automatically remove the dust from your image.

To automatically remove dust from an image:

1. Shoot a dust reference photo. Consult your camera's manual for details on how to do this. Dust reference photos have an extension of .NDF and can be transferred to your computer just like any other image.

2. Place the dust reference photo in the same folder as the image you want to edit.

3. Click the check box next to Image Dust Off in the Camera & Lens Correction edit. Capture NX should automatically locate the .NDF image and ask you if you want to use it. If it finds more than one image, it will ask you to choose the right one. Alternately, you can manually select an .NDF image by clicking the Change button in the Image Dust Off controls. Once you've selected an image, Capture NX automatically removes the dust from your image.

Dust can move and change, so it's best to shoot a dust reference image close to the time when you took the picture or before you change lenses.

> **An Ounce of Prevention Is Worth a Dust Off Edit**
>
> The best way to deal with dust is to make sure it never becomes a problem. Most sensor dust comes from camera and lens components. Keep the camera end of your lenses clean and use a blower brush to blow out the mirror chamber of your camera.
>
> *Never spray compressed air into the mirror chamber of your camera!* The liquid propellant used in compressed air canisters can leave residue on your sensor.
>
> If you end up with a sensor problem, consult your camera's manual for details on cleaning. Companies such as visibledust.com offer extremely effective sensor cleaning products.

Vignette control

A vignette is a darkening of the corners in your image. You most often see vignetting when shooting with a wide-angle lens. The Vignette Control slider lets you eliminate vignettes by applying a brightening to the corners of your image. Move the Vignette Control's Intensity slider to remove vignetting.

Note that you cannot add a vignette using this control—it is not a *creative* vignette tool, but rather a tool engineered to deal specifically with vignetting problems with particular Nikon lenses. Also, note that Vignette Control is always applied to the entire image. If you've cropped the image, you probably won't see any change in the corners of your image, as the effects of the control will most likely occur outside of your crop.

SAVING RAW FILES

For the most part, saving a raw file works just like saving a non-raw file. If you save the file as a NEF (its native format) then all of your editing controls will be preserved. If you save as a TIFF or JPEG then you'll get standard files that don't include your edit list. If you simply choose Save after opening and editing a raw file, your edits will be saved back into the NEF file that your camera generated. Don't worry, though, your original raw data remains untouched.

Note that if you open a raw file, edit it, then save it as a TIFF or JPEG, when the save is complete you'll *still* have all of your additional raw editing controls. In other words, after saving as a TIFF or JPEG, you're still editing a raw file. If you want to perform additional edits to the TIFF or JPEG that you saved, you'll have to explicitly open those files and then edit them.

As with non-raw files, you'll probably want to keep NEF versions as well as TIFFs or JPEGs.

CHAPTER FIVE
Advanced Image Editing

In the previous two chapters, you learned how to use Capture NX's tone- and color-correction controls to make adjustments to your entire image. But there will be many times when you'll want to make adjustments to just one part of an image. Sometimes only the foreground needs to be brightened, or some other part of the image needs to be edited completely independently of the rest. If you're coming from a wet darkroom background, you can think of Capture NX's localized editing tools as supercharged forms of dodging and burning. But where dodging and burning let you change localized exposure, Capture NX lets you make localized changes to *any* type of adjustment.

Before we get started with the selective editing tools, let's take a look at some ways you can use NX 2's interface to make your palette management easier.

WORKSPACES

So far you've seen how you can use the Browser palette to organize and manage your images, and you've seen the various editing palettes that you use to adjust your images. These are two very different workflow chores, though, and having extra tools cluttering up your work environment can be a hassle. To address this problem, Capture NX 2 lets you define Workspaces, which are predefined arrangements of palettes and controls that can be easily triggered and activated at any time.

To change to a different workspace, open the Window menu and choose Workspaces. From the Workspaces submenu, you can choose from four different predefined workspaces (**Figure 5.1**).

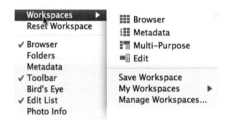 **Figure 5.1** You can use the Workspaces submenu to change from one workspace to another.

These are the four predefined Capture NX 2 workspaces that come with the program:

Browser workspace fills your screen with the Browser palette and also opens the Folders palette to give you ready access to your directory structure. This is a good workspace for the first part of your workflow—when you need to browse images to make selects and apply ratings—and is basically the configuration you saw in Chapter 1, "Installation, Interface, and Importing," when we talked about using the Browser.

Metadata opens the Browser palette but sets it to List view and opens the Metadata palette alongside. Browsing by metadata can be a convenient way of seeing all of the images with particular metadata characteristics (**Figure 5.2**).

When the Browser palette is set to List view, you can click on the name of any column to sort by that property. This makes it simple to automatically group images together that have the same metadata properties.

Multi-purpose gives you a Browser window and all of your image editing palettes (**Figure 5.3**).

If you need to be able to move quickly back and forth between browsing and looking at images in the Editor, this is a handy workspace. This workspace is ideal for really large monitors.

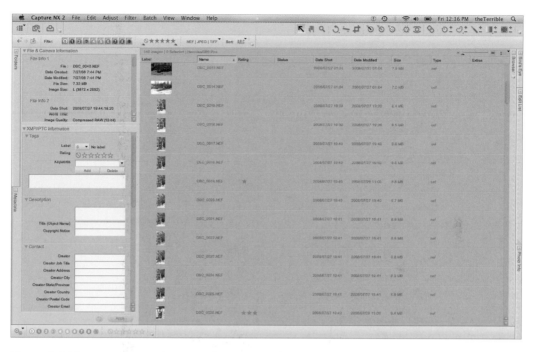

Figure 5.2 The metadata workspace makes it easy to browse and sort images by metadata.

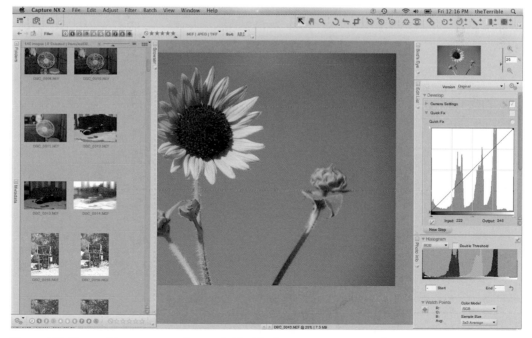

Figure 5.3 The multi-purpose workspace is ideal for large monitors, as it affords you both browsing and editing capabilities.

Edit closes the Browser and Folder palettes completely and leaves open the Edit List, Bird's Eye and Photo Info palettes—everything you need for serious editing. This is the workspace that you've seen in all of the previous editing examples.

You can also change workspaces by pressing Alt/Option-1 through 4 or use the drop-down menu on the far left of the toolbar.

Workspaces work independently of monitor resolution, meaning that if a palette is positioned on the right side of the screen, it will appear on the right side of the screen even if you later change to a higher or lower monitor resolution. For laptop users who move between their built-in screen, and a larger external monitor, this ensures that your palettes will always be where you expect them to be.

Defining Your Own Workspaces

You can easily define your own Workspaces so that you can quickly reconfigure Capture NX's palette layout to your own personal preference.

To create a custom workspace:

1. Configure the palettes the way you want them. Note that workspaces will also remember whether specific edits are opened or closed—except for the Quick Fix edit, which will always be open.

2. Choose Window > Workspaces > Save Workspace, then give your workspace a name.

To activate a workspace you've saved, choose Window > Workspaces > My Workspaces > *[workspace name]* (**Figure 5.4**).

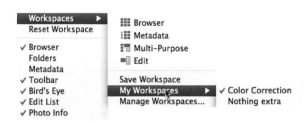

Figure 5.4 Workspaces that you've saved appear in the My Workspaces menu.

Managing workspaces you've created

If you choose Window > Workspaces > Manage Workspaces, you'll be taken to the Workspaces Preferences (**Figure 5.5**). You can also access these through the normal Preferences dialog.

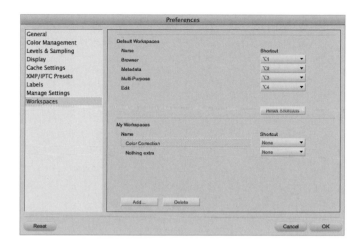

Figure 5.5 With the Workspaces Preferences dialog you can delete workspaces, or add or change workspace keyboard shortcuts.

From here you can delete workspaces or assign keyboard shortcuts to your custom workspaces. You can also alter the keyboard shortcuts for the stock workspaces.

If you want to modify the layout of an existing workspace, you'll need to delete it and redefine it the way you want.

> **TIP:** You can use custom workspaces to eliminate palettes. I never use the Bird's Eye palette, since it's so easy to zoom and pan using the keyboard. I've defined a workspace that has the Bird's Eye palette disabled, leaving me more room for the Edit List.

Screen Modes

So far, we've been using Capture NX 2 in its normal screen mode, where you can see all of the palettes and windows as well as your computer's desktop, menu bar, and other OS interface widgets. But Capture NX has two other screen modes.

Full Screen Mode

If you use a Mac, you can press F at any time to fill the area behind your NX windows with gray, hiding the desktop and giving you a less-cluttered view of your images.

When working with color, any other colors in your field of view can corrupt your perception of color accuracy. In fact, extreme color geeks will often paint the walls behind their computers gray, and they'll wear neutral colored smocks to keep the color of their clothing from reflecting onto the screen. While you probably don't need to go that far, switching to Full Screen mode will provide you with a better environment for making color adjustments.

Pressing F again returns you to normal Window mode. You can also activate Full Screen mode by choosing View > Full Screen.

> **TIP:** If you want to temporarily free up more screen space, perhaps so you can make the window larger, press Tab to hide all of Capture NX 2's palettes. Pressing Tab again will reactivate them.

> **TIP:** If your image appears off center or obscured by palettes when you enter full-screen mode, you can shift the image around by pressing the arrow keys when in Full Screen mode.

Presentation Mode

Pressing P at any time will put you in Presentation mode. All palettes will be hidden, along with your desktop, and the currently active image will be shown on a field of black.

When an image is displayed on black, it appears more contrasty and generally brighter, making this an ideal way to show off images to clients (**Figure 5.6**).

At the bottom of the screen are simple navigation arrows that let you cycle through all of the currently open windows.

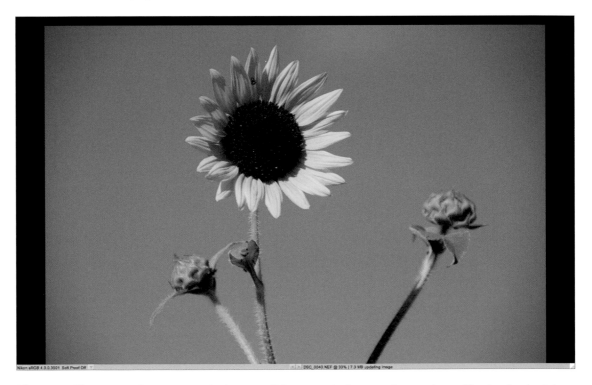

Figure 5.6 If you move the mouse to the bottom of the screen in Presentation mode, you'll get a simple status and navigation control.

Pressing P returns you to normal Window mode. You can also activate Presentation mode by choosing View > Presentation.

PHOTO FILTERS

Before we get to Capture NX 2's localized editing tools, let's take a look at some other adjustments that you can apply to your images. In Chapters 3 and 4, "Basic Image Editing" and "Working with Raw Files," you learned about geometric edits, tonal corrections, and color adjustments. Capture NX 2 also includes a plug-in architecture that lets you add even more editing effects, in the form of Photo Filters. NX 2 comes with several bundled filters, and you can easily add more.

Like all other edits, the filters in Capture NX are nondestructive, can be deactivated or altered at any time, and can be applied selectively using any of the Capture NX selection tools (which you'll learn about later in this chapter).

Photo Effects

The Photo Effects filter lets you apply simple tonal and color corrections to your image (**Figure 5.7**). The Photo Effects filter operates in several different modes, and you can switch among them using the pop-up menu.

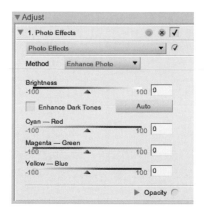

Figure 5.7 The Photo Effects edit lets you alter the luminosity and color balance of your image.

Enhance mode, the default, offers a Brightness slider, which lets you lighten or darken your image, and color sliders, which let you tone your image.

Black and White mode lets you adjust the Brightness slider and then adjust the mix of red, green, and blue color channels using the color sliders. Different channel mixes can yield very different results, as you can see in **Figure 5.8**. We'll discuss black-and-white conversion more in a later section.

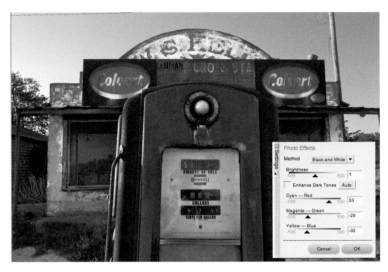

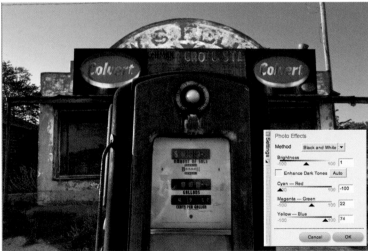

Figure 5.8 By mixing your color channels in different ways, you can create many different grayscale images from the same color source image.

Sepia mode lets you tone your image with a sepia tint. The Brightness slider controls the overall brightness of your image, and the color sliders are disabled.

Tinted performs a grayscale conversion on your image and then lets you tint the image with a color of your own mixing. Adjust the color sliders to choose your desired tint.

Add Grain/Noise

While digital photographers often spend time worrying about noise in their image, the fact is that sometimes grain and noise can add a nice texture to a photo. Capture NX's Grain/Noise filter lets you add grain of varying amounts and sizes. In addition, you can choose color or monochrome grain (**Figure 5.9**).

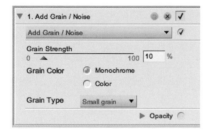

Figure 5.9 The Add Grain/Noise dialog box lets you add texture and grain to your images.

TIP: Sometimes, the best way to hide noise in your image is to add more. Adding noise to low-light, grainy images can often make them look better. This works particularly well with cell-phone images. The texture created by the noise often hides unsightly compression artifacts.

Contrast: Color Range

The Contrast: Color Range filter lets you adjust the brightness and contrast of specific colors in your image (**Figure 5.10**).

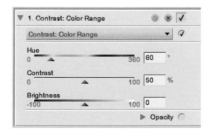

Figure 5.10 With Contrast: Color Range you can adjust the brightness and contrast of specific colors in your image.

The color that you select with the Hue slider will be lightened in your image, and its complementary color will be darkened. For example, in **Figure 5.11a** I selected a red color in the Hue slider, which brightens the flower. At the same time, the blue in the background is darkened (**Figure 5.11b**).

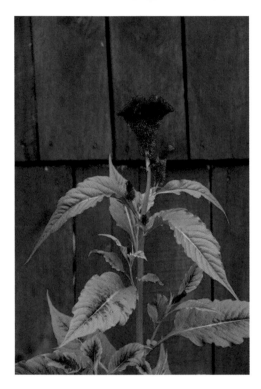

Figure 5.11a Here's the image before I applied a Contrast: Color Range adjustment.

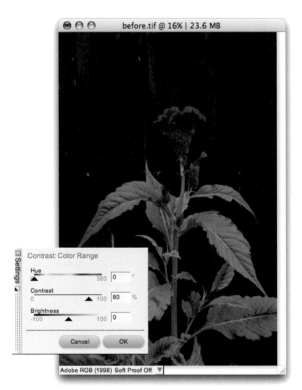

Figure 5.11b Here you can see the effect achieved after I targeted red, which increased the brightness of the red while simultaneously darkening the blue in the image.

The Contrast slider controls the amount of change that the filter produces, and the Brightness slider lets you adjust the overall luminosity of the image.

Note that unlike Color Balance controls, which affect the entire image, Contrast: Color Range has a very constrained effect.

Colorize

The Colorize filter lets you add a toning affect to your image (**Figure 5.12**).

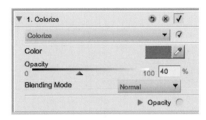

Figure 5.12 You can use the Colorize edit to add a color tone to your images.

The Colorize filter has three simple controls: a color swatch that lets you pick the color you want to tone with, an Opacity slider that lets you control the strength of the toning, and a Blending Mode pop-up menu that lets you select a method of blending the color into your image. Some methods will blend more color into the white areas, some will blend more into the dark, and some will yield fairly weird results. Just play with them until you find one you like (**Figure 5.13**).

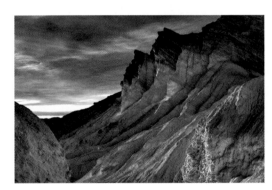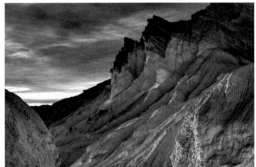

Figure 5.13 Before and after adding a Colorize edit.

Black and White Conversion

The Black and White Conversion filter provides another way to convert your images to grayscale. Unlike the Photo Effects filter, which lets you craft a custom channel mix, the Black and White Conversion filter lets you select a color filter, just like you might use when shooting black-and-white film (**Figure 5.14**).

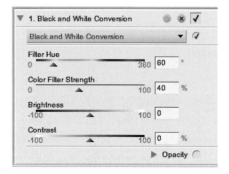

Figure 5.14 The Black and White Conversion filter provides a more traditional film-like approach to black-and-white conversion.

The Filter Hue slider lets you select the color of the filter you'd like to use for your black-and-white conversion. So, for example, you might choose a reddish filter for increased contrast in sky tones.

Color Filter Strength controls how strongly the filter color is applied during your conversion, and Brightness and Contrast let you control the overall luminosity and contrast of your image.

Installing Additional Filters

Capture NX 2 is compatible with several other plug-in collections, including Nik Color Efex Pro, which provides additional color manipulation edits. You can download a free trial from www.niksoftware.com.

KNOWING HOW FAR TO PUSH AN EDIT

Learning how to use Capture NX 2's editing tools is pretty simple, and you'll quickly get comfortable with them. Knowing *when* to use them is the part that takes practice, and often a degree of artistry. A capable image editor like Capture NX provides a limitless array of editing possibilities. This means a limitless array of choices, which can sometimes make for a frustrating array of options. When it's possible to do just about anything to an image, knowing what to do can be difficult. Equally confusing is when you have three or four different versions of an image and aren't sure which one you like best.

Very often, the best way to find your way out of such confusion is to limit your choices, and you can almost always limit your choices by using a technical measure. When you push an edit too far, your image quality will degrade, and image artifacts will begin to appear. Sometimes if you simply observe this boundary, your editing options will quickly narrow.

For example, in Chapter 3, "Basic Image Editing," we used the D-Lighting edit to brighten the shadowy side of a face in a portrait (see Figure 3.82, in Chapter 3). If you look closely at the shadow beneath the man's shirt color, you'll see *tone break* and *posterization* artifacts (**Figure 5.15**).

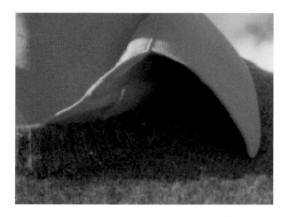

Figure 5.15 If you push an edit too far, so many tones will be discarded that you'll begin to see tone breaks and posterization in your image. This close-up of Figure 3.82, from Chapter 3, reveals bad artifacts underneath the shirt collar.

Chapter 3 also discussed how your image editor must throw out data as it redistributes tones when you edit. As it discards data, the gradients in your image become less smooth. You'll usually notice this in transitions from shadows to highlights, in skies, and chromed or other reflective surfaces (**Figure 5.16**).

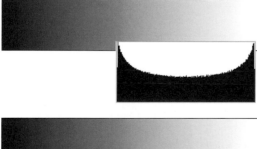

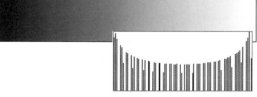

Figure 5.16 If we posterize this gray ramp, banding becomes visible because there are no longer enough tones to make a smooth transition from black to white. This same type of artifacting can appear in the gradients in your image if you push your edits too far.

So keep an eye on the gradients in your image while you're editing. If you start to see artifacts appear, you might want to back off of your edits. Of course, there will be times when you won't mind technical imperfection; for example, overexposed, noisy images can be very evocative. But for the most part keeping an eye on editing quality will help you make better decisions about which edits to make.

CHANGING COLOR SPACE

In Chapter 2, "Workflow, the Browser, and Color Management," I introduced the idea of *color spaces*—mathematical domains into which the colors in your image are mapped. Color spaces are necessary to know how to map real-world colors to the numeric values that your camera captures.

As explained earlier, your camera lets you specify the color space that you want your images mapped into—usually either sRGB or the larger Adobe RGB. If you're shooting JPEG or TIFF images, your color will be permanently altered to fit into these color spaces.

If you're shooting raw, you can select which color space you want to use in Capture NX. Because NX is nondestructive, you can change the color mode of a raw file at any time; the program simply remaps the colors into the new space.

Capture NX lets you *apply* a profile, which assigns a specific input profile to your image, or *convert* your image to a specific profile.

To apply a new color space to an image:

1. Choose Adjust > Color Profile. The Color Profile Settings palette opens.

2. Click Apply Profile.

3. From the pop-up menu, select the profile you want to assign.

The image on your screen might appear different from the original. But none of the color values in your image have been changed. In other words, if the profile you apply is smaller than the original profile, the colors in your image will not be clipped to the smaller profile.

However, when you convert an image to a different profile, the actual color values in the image are changed to fit the image into the new profile. There are a few occasions when you might choose to convert an image to a different profile:

- If you're going to post an image on a Web page, you might consider first converting it to sRGB.

- If you're sending an image to an online photo printing service, you might consider converting to sRGB since most online services expect sRGB images.

- If you're working with a printer or client that has very particular color space requirements, you might need to obtain a custom profile and convert your images to it.

To convert an image to a new color space:

1. Choose Adjust > Color Profile.

2. Click Convert to profile.

3. From the pop-up menu, select the profile you want to convert to.

4. Pick a rendering intent from the Intent menu. In almost all cases, you'll want to use Relative Colorimetric. You might also need to check Black Point Compensation. For more information on the rendering intents provided and on Black Point Compensation, consult the Capture NX Help file.

Note that like any other edit, a color space change is simply an edit in your Edit List, meaning you can undo it at any time. Because color space changes are nondestructive, you don't have to worry about clipping any of the color out of your file. If you convert to a smaller space and later decide you need your image in a larger space, you can simply change the Color Space edit accordingly.

Here's one way to think about the difference between applying a profile and converting to a profile: Applying a profile changes the look of the image but not the underlying numbers, whereas converting changes the underlying numbers but not the look.

CONTROL POINTS

So far, all of the edits that we've looked at have been global edits—that is, they have been applied to the entire image. While Levels & Curves, D-Lighting, and Highlight and Shadow protection let you adjust just one part of the *tonal range*, those edits aren't constrained to a specific geographic location in your image.

There will be times when you want to adjust the color or tone in a specific part of an image, just the way that darkroom photographers used to dodge and burn specific areas of a print to make them lighter or darker. Capture NX 2 provides an incredibly powerful set of localized editing tools, with capabilities that you won't find in any other image editor (unless you add expensive plug-ins such as Viveza or Silver Efex Pro). The most powerful of these features are the Control Point tools, which are just to the right of the Crop tool on the toolbar. While these tools don't let you make edits that you can't make in an editor like Photoshop, they do provide a level of ease and efficiency that is unmatched in any other program.

Tonal Control Points

The first three Control Points in the toolbar are used for making tonal adjustments. By themselves these tools don't allow localized correction, but they offer the same interface as NX 2's other Control Points, so we're going to look at them here. With the three tonal control points, you can perform many of the same type of tonal corrections that you can make with other edits, but the Tonal control points provide extra flexibility.

Neutral Control Point

In Chapter 3, we used the Levels edit to correct a color cast. While Levels is very effective, Capture NX's Neutral Control Point provides a much better, single-click solution for correcting casts.

To remove a color cast with the Neutral Control Point tool:

1. Open the image you want to correct (**Figure 5.17**).

2. Select the Neutral Control Point tool on the toolbar.

3. Click on a part of your image that should be a neutral, middle gray color.

4. Capture NX places a Neutral Control Point at the location you clicked and then automatically corrects your image (**Figure 5.18**).

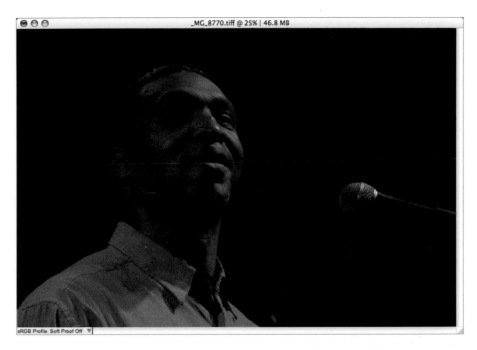

Figure 5.17 Shot in a dark club under pink stage lighting, this image plainly has some color-cast issues.

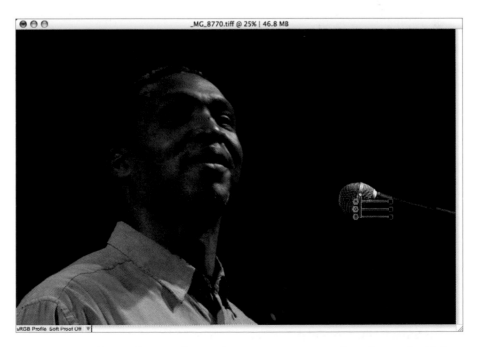

Figure 5.18 With a single Neutral Control Point, you can correct the color cast in this image.

Now try dragging the control point around. If you drag it to a different location, you'll get a very different correction (**Figure 5.19**).

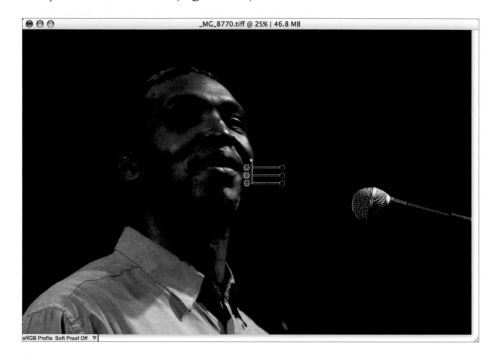

Figure 5.19 If you change the location of the Neutral Control Point, you get a very different adjustment.

The Neutral Control Point analyzes the color that you clicked on to determine how to equalize the red, green, and blue channels in your image, just as the Levels adjustment did in Chapter 3, "Basic Image Editing." So, if your initial click does not yield an image that's neutral enough, you can refine your adjustment by simply dragging the point around.

You can further refine the correction by dragging the red, green, and blue sliders that appear beneath the control point. If you drag any slider away from the control point, you'll add more of that color to your image.

For example, you can warm the image in Figure 5.18 by dragging the red slider to the right a little bit (**Figure 5.20**).

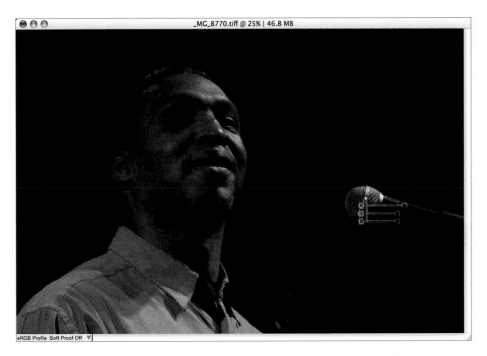

_MG_8770.tiff @ 25% | 46.8 MB

sRGB Profile Soft Proof Off

Figure 5.20 By adjusting the individual color sliders on the Neutral Control Point, you can change the color balance of your image. In this case, the image was warmed slightly by increasing the Red slider.

Advanced Controls. The Advanced Controls portion of the Neutral Control Point Settings palette provides a few additional options (**Figure 5.21**).

Show Selection shows the areas in your image that the control point will affect, just like the Show Selection command you saw earlier. White areas are completely selected, black areas are not selected at all, and gray areas are somewhere in between.

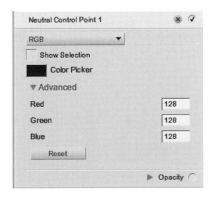

Figure 5.21 You'll find additional options for the Neutral Control Point in the Advanced Controls portion of the Settings palette.

Using the Color Picker. The Color Picker swatch affords you with yet another level of control for the correction that the Neutral Control Point creates. It allows you to correct the color in an area that doesn't actually contain any gray, such as sky or flesh tones.

To use the Color Picker swatch to correct a sky:

1. Click with the Neutral Control Point in the sky. The control point is added and the Neutral Control Point Setting is added to your Edit List (**Figure 5.22**).

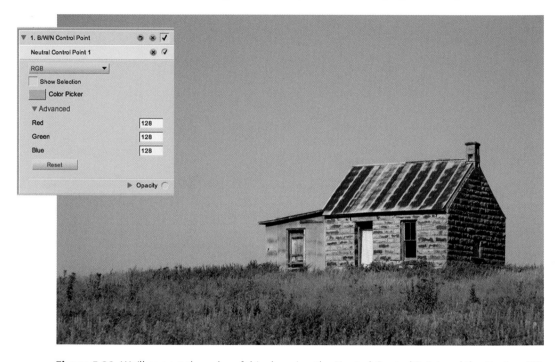

Figure 5.22 We'll correct the color of this sky using the Neutral Control Point and the Capture NX Color Picker.

2. Open the Advanced section of the palette. The Color Picker swatch shows the color that the control point is currently sampling.

3. Click the Color Picker swatch to open the Color Picker palette (**Figure 5.23**). When you select a color in the Color Picker palette, Capture NX calculates the difference between that color and the color that you clicked on in your image, and then subtracts that difference from your image. What makes the Color Picker palette especially useful are the predefined swatches, which give you sample sky, skin, foliage, and neutral tones.

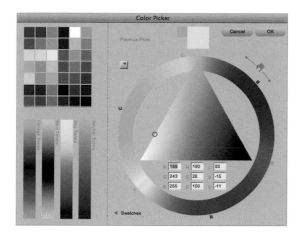

Figure 5.23 The Color Picker lets you pick a color that you would like for the sky. Capture NX calculates the difference between your original color and that destination color.

4. Click on a color in the sky swatch gradient in the Color Picker palette. Your image is immediately adjusted (**Figure 5.24**). By clicking on different colors you can easily try different corrections until you arrive at an overall tone that you like.

Additionally, you can use multiple Neutral Control Points to correct multiple casts in an image. When you assign multiple Neutral Control Points, Capture NX analyzes data from all of the points to determine a final correction.

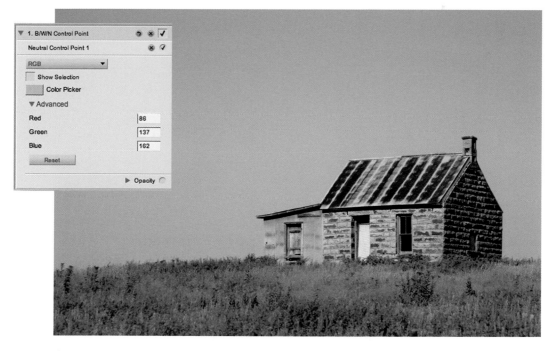

Figure 5.24 After selecting a color, Capture NX corrects the image.

White Control Point

Just as the Neutral Control Point lets you specify a neutral tone in your image, the White Control Point lets you define a tone that is supposed to be white. The white point in your image is adjusted accordingly.

To set the white point with a White Control Point:

1. Open the image you want to correct (**Figure 5.25**).

2. Select the White Control Point tool on the toolbar.

3. Click on a part of your image that should be white.

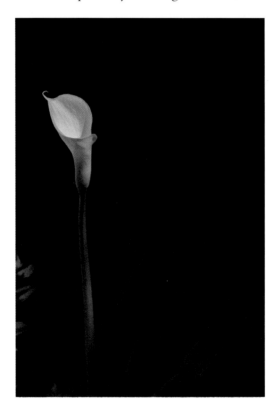

Figure 5.25 The "white" areas in this image are actually more off-white, meaning there's no real white in the image. This image needs a white point adjustment.

4. Capture NX places a White Control Point at the location you clicked and automatically sets the white point in your image (**Figure 5.26**).

Beneath the White Control Point is a single Luminance slider. By default it is set to 100 percent. Drag it closer to the point to darken your image (**Figure 5.27**).

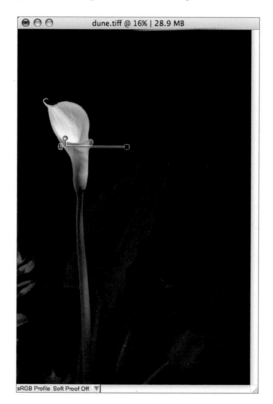

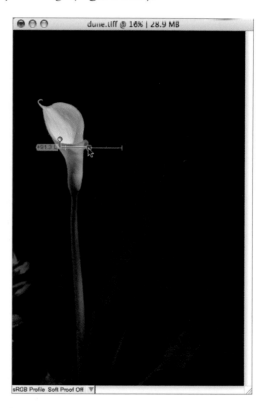

Figure 5.26 With a single click of the White Control Point tool, this image looks much better. As with the Neutral Control Point, you can drag the control point around to change your white point selection. As you move, Capture NX analyzes the underlying color to determine the correct white point adjustment.

Figure 5.27 The Luminance slider underneath the White Control Point lets you change the brightness of the new white point in your image.

Black Control Point

As you might have guessed by now, the Black Control Point lets you select the black point of your image. Click with the Black Control Point tool on something in your image that should be black. Capture NX adds a control point and automatically sets the black point in your image (**Figure 5.28**). As with the White Control Point, you can alter the Luminance value of the Black Control Point to change the amount of darkening in your image.

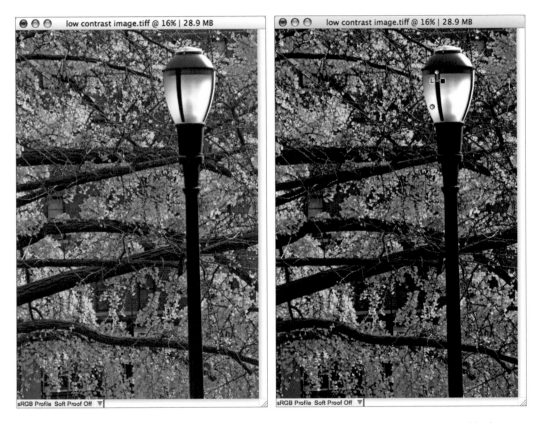

Figure 5.28 The contrast in this image was corrected by setting a Black Control Point on a black part of the street lamp and a White Control Point on the white part of the lamp.

Color Control Point

While the Black, White, and Neutral Control Points let you adjust the tonality of your image, the Color Control Point allows you to alter the hue, saturation, and lightness of specific areas in your image. The Color Control Point uses Nik Software's proprietary U Point technology, which is unlike anything that you'll find in any other image editor.

With it, you should find that you can make extremely complex adjustments with just a few clicks.

Using a Color Control Point is very simple:

1. Select the Color Control Point tool from the toolbar.

2. Click with the Color Control Point tool on the area that you want to adjust.

3. Drag the Size slider to adjust the size of the affected area (**Figure 5.29**).

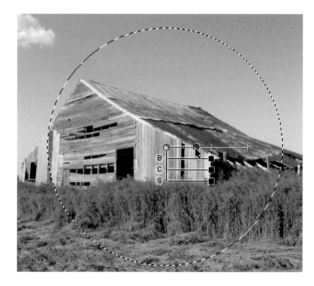

Figure 5.29 Color Control Points have a circular size parameter that controls their area of effect.

4. Alter the color sliders to edit the affected area. In this case, the Contrast slider was used to increase the contrast of the barn (**Figure 5.30**).

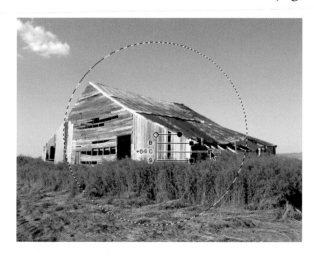

Figure 5.30 The B, C, and S sliders on a Color Control Point let you change the brightness, contrast, and saturation, respectively.

That's all there is to it. Based on where you click and the size of the area you choose to affect, Capture NX automatically calculates a mask for your chosen edit and applies the edit throughout that mask. For example, **Figure 5.31** shows the mask that Capture NX created for the adjustment that was defined in Figure 5.30.

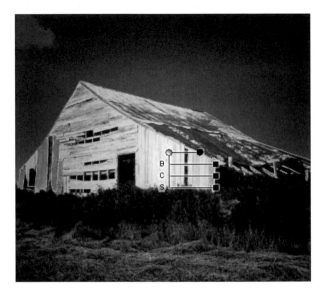

Figure 5.31 The Color Control Point that was defined automatically generates this selection mask.

At first, it may seem strange that Capture NX only lets you define a circular selection area. However, as you can see from the way that it builds a mask, this boundary is all that is needed for the Control Point to accurately calculate which pixels should be affected and which shouldn't, as well as how much effect each pixel should get. The Color Control Point does this by analyzing the color of the pixels at the location where you place the point.

Using multiple Color Control Points

Let's perform a more complex edit. **Figure 5.32** shows an image that needs a saturation adjustment in the sky and a contrast adjustment on the ground. What's more, we don't want either of these effects to alter the dorky-looking guy standing in the foreground, because we'd like to apply separate adjustments to him.

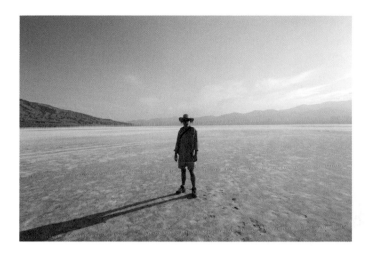

Figure 5.32 With only a few simple Color Control Points, we'll make a lot of corrections to this image—improving the brightness and saturation of the sky, increasing the contrast on the ground, and brightening the figure.

Adjusting the sky. Normally, this would require many different selection and masking operations to constrain the edits appropriately. With Color Control Points, you can achieve all of this editing with some simple clicking. Let's start by working on the sky.

Click with the Color Control Point tool to add a Color Control Point to the left side of the sky. Then drag the Size slider to cover as much of the sky as you can (**Figure 5.33**).

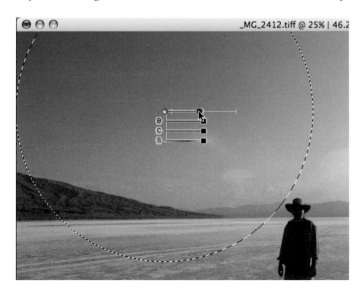

Figure 5.33 Begin by putting a Color Control Point on the sky and setting its size.

Don't worry that the Size circle extends into the foreground. Capture NX is smart enough to know that this area should be excluded from the mask. Obviously the entire sky hasn't been covered, but that problem will be taken care of in a moment. You first want to configure the control point's correction.

Make the sky a little brighter and more saturated by using positive adjustments on all three sliders. Capture NX updates the image in real time, so it's easy to fiddle with the sliders to get exactly the effect that you want (**Figure 5.34**).

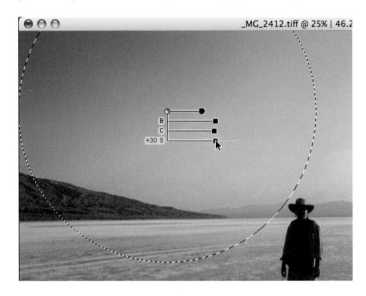

Figure 5.34 By adjusting the Brightness, Contrast, and Saturation sliders, you can add more punch to the sky.

As with any other type of color correction, Color Control Points work their effect by redistributing the tonal information in the red, green, and blue channels. As they do this, some data gets discarded. So, Color Control Points can lead to the same tone break and posterization artifacts that you saw in Figure 5.15. As you adjust the sliders, keep an eye out for those problems.

When you add a Color Control Point to an image, a control point entry is made to your Edit List. If you're the type of person who likes to work by numbers, then open the Advanced section of the Color Control Point edit and you'll find editable numeric readings for all four of the control point's sliders (**Figure 5.35**).

The sky is looking better, but only in the left half. You could add another Color Control Point to the right half, but it's easier to duplicate the first control point to be sure that you have the same adjustment across the sky.

You can duplicate a Control Point by Alt/Option clicking on it and dragging a copy to a new location. Alternately, you can right click on it to bring up a pop-up menu that provides a Duplicate option as well as some other commands (**Figure 5.36**).

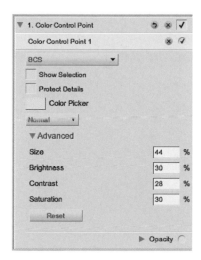

Figure 5.35 The Color Control Point Settings palette provides numeric readouts for the values of the Color Control Point sliders.

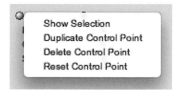

Figure 5.36 Additional options appear if you right-click on a Color Control Point.

After you make a copy and drag it to the left half of the image, the sky will get brighter because the new control point is working on the image, adding an additional round of edits (**Figure 5.37**).

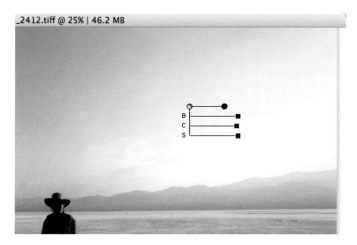

Figure 5.37 After duplicating the original control point, you can drag it to the right side of the screen to alter the other half of the sky.

The right half of the sky is now overexposed. As it turns out, the settings you defined for the control point in the darker, left side of the sky are a little too aggressive for the brighter right side. With a few simple parameter adjustments, you can bring things back in line (**Figure 5.38**).

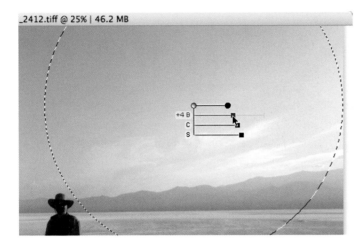

Figure 5.38 A few adjustments to the second control point and the sky is more reasonably exposed.

In the Edit List, you will see an entry for Color Control Point that contains a separate listing for each point you've defined (**Figure 5.39**). You can check and uncheck the check box next to Color Control Point to activate or deactivate it. Toggling the check box next to the top-most Color Control Point entry activates and deactivates all color control points. The lower portion of the Color Control Point edit shows parameters for the currently highlighted Control Point.

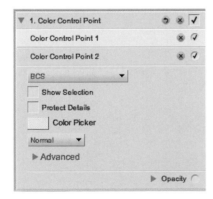

Figure 5.39 Using the controls in the Edit List, you can activate and deactivate some or all of your Color Control Points.

Even though your control point size circles overlap the ground, the ground receives almost no adjustment thanks to the selection mask that Capture NX has automatically calculated. You can see the actual selection by choosing View > Show Selection (**Figure 5.40**).

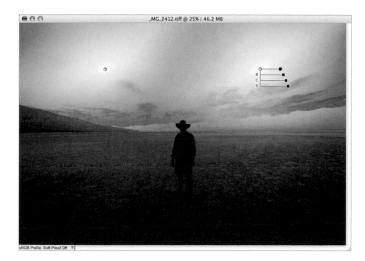

Figure 5.40 Using your two Color Control Points, Capture NX automatically creates a very complex mask that constrains the effects of the control points to only the sky.

The Color Control Points are interactive when in Show Selection mode. You can adjust their parameters and see the mask change in real time.

Adjusting the foreground. Now you're ready to work on the ground. It doesn't need a lot of adjustment, but a bit more contrast will make it a little more eye-catching. As before, begin with a Color Control Point on the left side of the image and adjust its size and parameters accordingly (**Figure 5.41**).

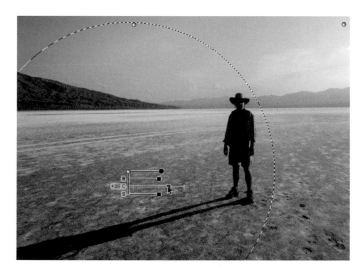

Figure 5.41 With your first foreground control point, you increase the contrast on the ground. Here you can see the difference between the left, affected area and the right side, which doesn't yet have any adjustment.

Again, duplicate your control point by Alt/Option-clicking on it and then dragging. Drag the copy to the other side of the image, but this time you don't need to make any adjustments to its settings. Because the ground is uniformly exposed, the same settings work for both control points.

As you drag the control point around, you should be able to see very small changes in its effect. Like the Neutral Control Points that you saw earlier, Color Control Points work by sampling the color that you place them over. They use this sample color as the basis for their selection calculations. So, when you move the control point around, the original sample color changes, altering the mask and affecting your image in different ways.

One of the most impressive aspects of the U Point technology that drives Capture NX's control points is its ability to properly calculate multiple overlapping masks. If you view your selection now with all four control points applied, you'll see a complex arrangement of different masking data with smooth transitions between each effect (**Figure 5.42**). Note that you have to be sure you select the top level of the grouping of edits in order to view all selections. If one of the individual edits is selected, only that area will show in viewing the selection.

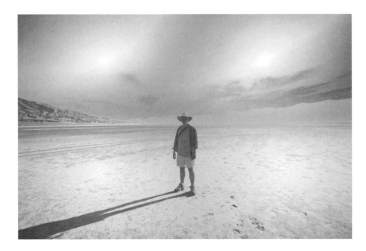

Figure 5.42 With four control points defined, your selection mask is a complex composite of overlapping masking information.

TIP: You can toggle the visibility of the control-point handles by selecting View > Show/Hide Control Points.

Adjusting the figure. So far a lot of brightness, contrast, and saturation adjustment has happened, but because of the sophistication of the mask that Capture NX has generated, the figure in the middle of the image has for the most part remained unaffected. You can use an additional control point to perform a final correction.

A single control point configured with a brightness, contrast, and saturation adjustment brightens up the figure (**Figure 5.43**).

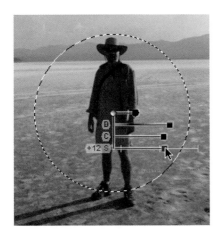

Figure 5.43 With one last control point, you can easily brighten the figure without altering any of your other adjustments.

You've now performed a lot of sophisticated localized editing operations, operations that in another application would have required you to hand paint masks or perform complex selections. With Capture NX's Color Control Points, all of that tedious work is performed for you on the fly.

Figure 5.44 shows the final result.

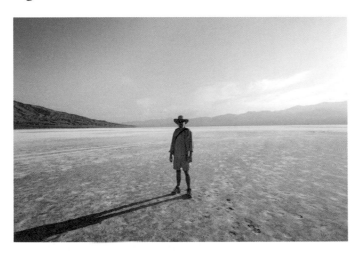

Figure 5.44 With just five control points, you created a complex series of adjustments that would have required lots of meticulous masking in most other image editors.

TIP: Note that if you crop an image, add some control points, and then change or remove the crop, your control points could end up in different relative locations. After changing the crop, simply move the control points back to where they should be.

Other Color Control Point settings

The Color Control Point edit provides a number of important settings (**Figure 5.45**).

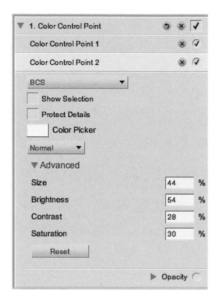

Figure 5.45 The Color Control Point edit provides a number of settings.

Show Selection lets you view the selection mask created by the selected Color Control Point. The control point's parameter sliders are still active in this mode, allowing you to edit the selection while viewing it.

Protect Details allows you to protect one part of an image from the effects of *another* control point. When you click Protect Details, the control point provides only a Size slider. You can drag the control point on top of an area affected by another control point and then adjust the size of the second point to protect your image from the effects of the first control point.

The **Color Picker** swatch lets you choose a color using the Color Picker palette. The area affected by the control point will be filled with that color, with the selection defining the opacity and tint of the color. This provides a simple way to add a little bit of tint to an area.

In addition, the pop-up menu lets you select the parameters that you want the control point to have (**Figure 5.46**). As you've seen, control points have Brightness, Contrast, and Saturation sliders by default. From the menu shown in Figure 5.45, you can opt to switch to RGB, which gives you Red, Green, and Blue sliders, or HSB, which provides Hue, Saturation, and Brightness sliders. Or you can select All, which displays every slider. All options provide a Size slider.

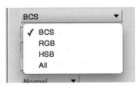

Figure 5.46 You can specify exactly what type of adjustment sliders you want a control point to have.

There's no right or wrong set of sliders to use; some will be more appropriate for some edits than for others. For example, if you're dealing with a color cast or warmth issue, RGB sliders might be easier to work with. Or perhaps you have more experience with one color model than with another and are already used to thinking in a particular way.

> **NOTE:** You may find yourself asking, "Where'd my control points go?!" Control points, watch points, and selection controls are automatically hidden when you move the mouse off the image. This provides you with a clear view of your image. When you mouse back over the image, the controls will return. If you'd rather your Control Points were always visible, change the Auto Hide option in the Display section of the Preferences dialog box.

SELECTION CONTROLS

If you've ever worked with other image-editing programs, you know that Capture NX 2's Control Points are not like the tools in other editors. With most editors, when you want to constrain an edit you must make a selection using a brush tool or any number of other lasso or marquee type tools. In addition to control points, Capture NX 2 does provide a suite of selection tools. You can use these to alter the effects of Color Control Points or to selectively apply any edit in the Adjust section of the Edit List.

Selectively Applying an Effect

When you apply any edit, its effect is automatically applied to the entire image. However, using Capture NX's selection tools, you can interactively create a mask that constrains your edit to specific parts of your image.

> **NOTE:** To use this technique, the edit must be selected in the Edit List before you begin brushing with the Selection tools. If no edit is selected, the tools will function differently, as we'll see later.

The Selection tools are in the rightmost palette, just below the menu bar (**Figure 5.47**).

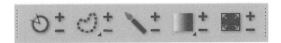

Figure 5.47 You'll find the Selection tools in the rightmost section of the toolbar.

Let's use a Selection brush to increase the contrast in the ground in **Figure 5.48**.

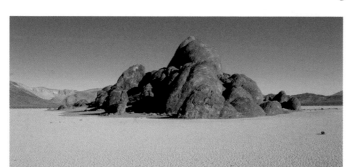

Figure 5.48 I'd like to increase the contrast in the ground texture.

1. Add the effect that you want to apply. In this case, add a Levels & Curves edit. Make sure the edit is selected (highlighted in the Edit List).

2. Configure the edit just as you normally would. The edit will affect the entire image, but while adjusting settings, I'm paying attention only to the area that I want to change. I want to increase the contrast in the ground to make the texture more pronounced, so I'm not concerned about how the rest of the image is getting screwed up (**Figure 5.49**).

    A selection is just like a stencil that controls which parts of the image are affected by the edit you've applied. Right now, the entire image is being affected by the Levels & Curves adjustment.

    Next to each Selection tool are + (plus) and – (minus) buttons. These allow you to change the mode of each tool. The + button sets the tool to add the effect to the image; the – button sets the tool to remove the effect from the image.

3. Click the + button next to the Selection Brush tool and then click on the ground in the image. The Levels & Curves adjustment will disappear, but note that it has not been removed from your Edit List. Also note that in the Edit List the Levels & Curves edit now has an additional Selection element in it (**Figure 5.50**). Capture NX has deselected the entire image, meaning that the effect is not being applied to any of it. Because you selected the + Selection Brush, you can add the Levels & Curves effect to the image simply by painting.

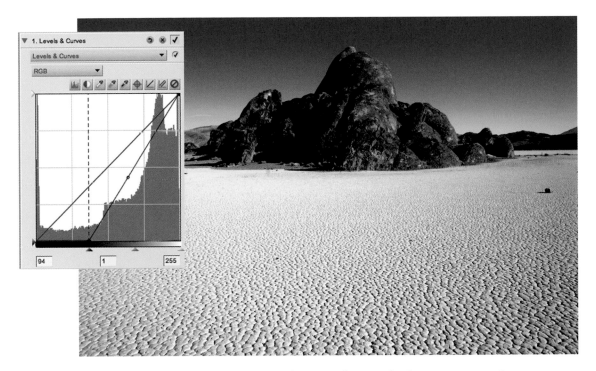

Figure 5.49 Here's the Levels & Curves adjustment that I used to increase contrast. As you can see, I moved the black point to the right. The result is an image that is, overall, too contrasty. But notice that the ground looks much better than it did before.

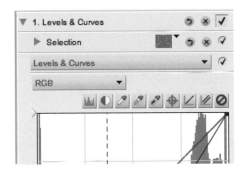

Figure 5.50 The Levels & Curves edit now shows an additional Selection control.

4. Paint anywhere in the image that you want the Levels & Curves effect applied. In this case, begin painting over the ground (**Figure 5.51**).

The texture on the ground gets more contrasty wherever I paint, because my Levels & Curves adjustment is being applied to those areas. Unfortunately, I slipped and accidentally painted over some of the rocks and part of the sky, rendering them too contrasty. Fortunately, it's easy enough to fix this problem.

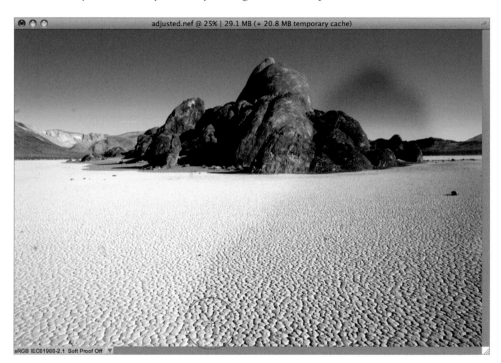

Figure 5.51 The Levels & Curves effect is applied to any part of the image that you paint into with the + (plus) brush. Here I'm about halfway through painting the ground.

TIP: You can change the size of the brush by using the bracket keys. The right bracket ( ]) enlarges your brush, and the left bracket ([ ) makes it smaller.

5. Click the – button next to the Selection Brush and brush onto any areas where you want to remove the Levels & Curves effect. The – brush removes the effect from the image so the Levels & Curves effect no longer affects that area (**Figure 5.52**).

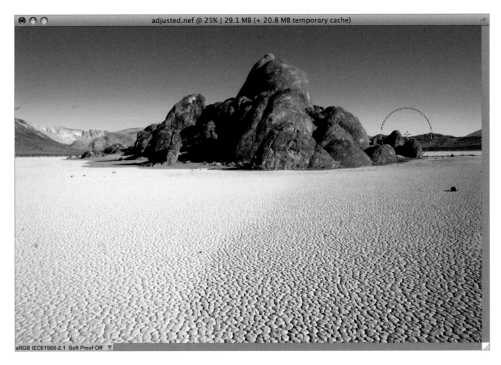

Figure 5.52 If you switch to the – Selection Brush, you can remove the Levels & Curves effect from the places in the image where it doesn't belong.

When using a brush, Capture NX changes the cursor to a circle that indicates brush size. It's hard to see in these screenshots, but there's a little + or – in the middle of the circle that indicates whether you're using the additive or subtractive brush. Also, note that the brush has a very soft edge, which means you won't see a sudden change in effect along the edges of your strokes.

Now that you've defined the selection, it's a little easier to see if you have the right amount of Levels & Curves adjustment. If you want, you can go back and change the Levels & Curves settings, just as you normally would. Your selection remains the same, so you will see the contrast change appear only on the ground.

View the Selection. When you use any of the selection tools, Capture NX adds a Selection property to the currently selected edit. You can uncheck, reset, or delete the selection by using the check box, reset, or delete icons, which are just like the ones you'll find on any other edit.

You can also use the pop-up menu to change the way the selection is displayed (**Figure 5.53**). By default, Capture NX doesn't show the selection—merely the effect. That's what you've seen in these examples.

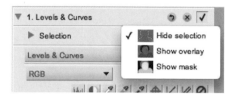

Figure 5.53 Using the pop-up menu in the Selection entry in the Edit List, you can change how the selection is displayed.

If you choose Show Overlay, a semi-opaque colored overlay will activate, to show you the area that the edit is covering. You can use this overlay while you're painting, which can make it easier to see where you have and haven't painted. Green indicates an area where you've used one of the + selection tools.

If you want a better understanding of what the mask does, choose Show Mask. Black areas indicate where the associated effect is being completely masked, white areas indicates where the effect is being completely applied, and gray areas indicate where the effect is being partially applied (**Figure 5.54**).

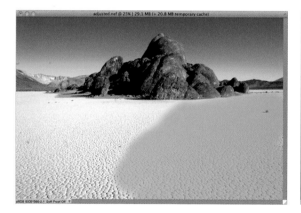 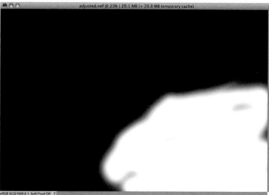

Figure 5.54 Show Overlay mode displays your edited area as semi-transparent green pixels. Show Mask displays your mask as a grayscale image, with black pixels indicating areas that are completely masked, white unmasked, and gray somewhere in between.

TIP: You can also access these selection options by right-clicking on your image with the Direct Select Tool.

Brush options

Capture NX provides brush options that let you control the opacity, size, and hardness of the brush edge (**Figure 5.55**). When you select the paint brush, the Options bar fills with a number of brush parameters.

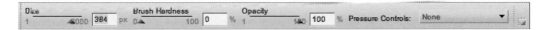

Figure 5.55 The Brush Options parameters let you change the size, hardness, and opacity of your paint brush.

Size simply changes the size of the brush. You can also change the brush size from the keyboard by using the left and right bracket keys.

Brush hardness controls how hard the edge of the brush is. Just as you can change brush size using the] and [keys, so can you change hardness using Shift-] and Shift-[.

Opacity controls how strongly the associated edit is selected. At 100 percent the full effect of the edit you've defined is applied. At 50 percent, the effect will be half as strong.

Pressure controls regulate pen pressure choices. If you have a Wacom-compatible pressure-sensitive tablet, you can use the options from the Pressure controls pop-up menu to specify whether pen pressure will change brush size, opacity, or both.

> **TIP:** *The Opacity setting is persistent—it's not specific to just the edit you're working on. For example, if you paint a selection on a Levels & Curves edit, set the opacity to 30 percent and then later make another edit, the brush defaults to 30 percent opacity unless you reset it to another opacity.*

> **TIP:** *You can use brushes to refine a color control point. While Color Control Points are incredibly powerful, there will be times when they will affect an area of your image that you want to leave untouched. To correct this, simply grab the – brush tool and paint those areas to remove the effects of the Color Control Point.*

Selection options

If you open the Selection controls that get added to your filter you'll find two sliders: Base Mask, and Paint & Fill Mask (**Figure 5.56**)

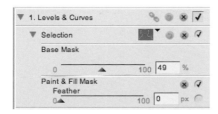

Figure 5.56 Base Mask and Paint & Fill Mask give you some additional controls for refining your selections.

When you paint with the + brush, you're painting masking data into the document's base mask, which is one of three different masks that are used for defining selections. Normally, the mask is completely empty. If you slide the Base Mask slider to the right, then the entire mask will begin to fill. You can see the exact effect by turning on Show Overlay (**Figure 5.57**).

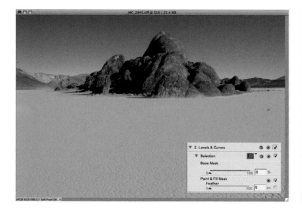 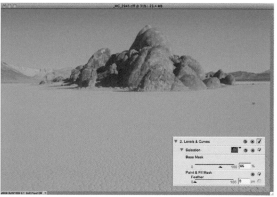

Figure 5.57 As you move the Base Mask slider toward the right, more of the Base Mask gets filled in.

Another Way to Create a Selection

In the preceding examples, I chose the type of edit I wanted first and then used selection tools to paint that edit into a particular area of the image. You can also work the other way around, and paint a selection *first*.

To define a selection before choosing an edit, *don't* click on an edit in the Edit List before you begin painting. Instead, grab one of the selection tools and start using it. Capture NX will show selected areas as green paint, and will add a *Select Adjustment* edit to the Edit List (**Figure 5.58**).

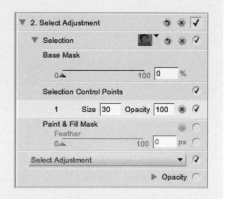

Figure 5.58 You can also define a selection before you choose the type of edit you want to apply.

These are the selection controls you've already seen, but without an associated edit of any kind. Once you've finished building your mask, open the Select Adjustment pop-up menu at the bottom of the edit and choose the type of edit you want.

There's no right or wrong to either of these methods. Personally, I prefer working interactively with the effect I'm applying. But if it's a subtle effect you're working with, it might be easier to first paint the mask.

If you slide the Feather slider to the right, then the edges of the areas you've painted will feather, making for a smoother transition between the areas that are affected and unaffected by the filter that you're masking.

> **TIP:** *Capture NX's selection tools don't work with Quick Edit adjustments, only with edits that appear in the Adjust section of the Edit List.*

Gradient selections

Sometimes you want to apply an effect that varies from one part of your image to another. While you can try to paint in this type of variation using a brush, it's much easier to use Capture NX's Gradient tool.

For example, let's increase the saturation of the sky in **Figure 5.59.**

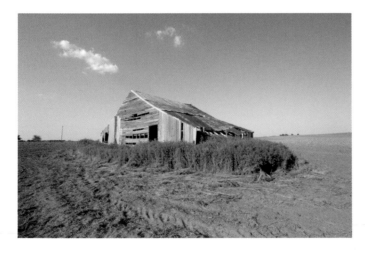

Figure 5.59 We'll use the Gradient tool to create a gradual change in the saturation of the sky in this image.

Since skies tend to get lighter closer to the horizon, you don't want to add a uniform saturation increase. Instead, you can use the Selection Gradient tool to add a gradient selection that extends from the top of the screen to the horizon.

To use the Selection Gradient tool:

1. Add the effect that you want to your Edit List. In this case, I'll add Saturation/ Warmth.

2. Select either + or – mode for the Selection Gradient.

3. Click to define where you want the gradient to start, then drag to define where you want the gradient to end. Your gradient selection is immediately selected, and you should see the effect in your image (**Figure 5.60**).

When using the + gradient, make your first click where you want the maximum effect, then drag to where the effect should stop. With the – gradient, do the opposite.

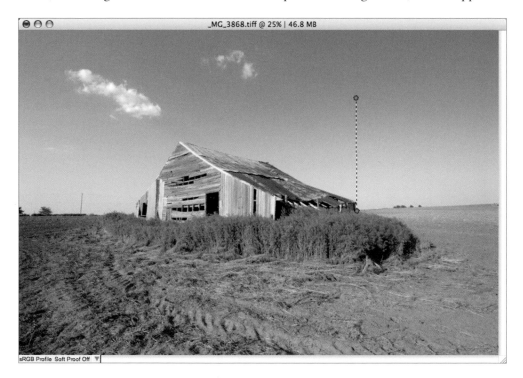

Figure 5.60 This gradient applies a gradual saturation adjustment to the sky in the image.

Note that while the Gradient Selection tool is still active you can drag either end of the gradient line to reposition it.

To illustrate what the Gradient Selection tool is doing, **Figure 5.61** shows what the selection for the image in Figure 5.61 looks like.

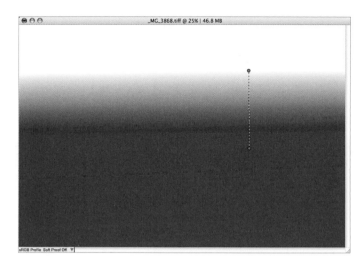

Figure 5.61 The Gradient tool created a gradual change from completely selected (white) to completely unselected (red).x

As you can see, most of the image is red, which indicates unselected (or masked if you prefer to think of it that way) areas. The white area at the top is selected (or unmasked) and transitions smoothly to unselected at the horizon. This has the effect of gradually applying the Saturation/Warmth adjustment.

Custom gradients. The Gradient Options on the options bar allows you to define a custom gradient (**Figure 5.62**).

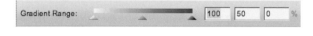

Figure 5.62 Using the Gradient options, you can change the gradient to select more or less at either end and to have a different midpoint.

For times when you don't want a gradient selection to be completely selected or unselected, you can change the white and black points. Remember, white means completely selected, black means completely unselected, and gray means somewhere in between.

The midpoint lets you shift where the middle of the gradient is. This lets you change the gradient from a straight linear gradient into a gradient that has more selection at one end than the other.

Radial Gradients. In addition to the linear gradient that you just saw, Capture NX can also create radial gradients, which allow you to create circular effects that blend in the same way that as the linear gradients.

For example, consider the image in **Figure 5.63**.

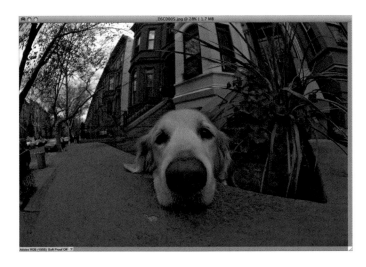

Figure 5.63 We're going to apply a radial gradient to this image to bring more focus to the dog in the center of the image.

While the image is okay on its own, it would be nice to bring a little more focus to the center. We're going to use a linear gradient attached to a Levels & Curves edit to create a darker image with a bright center. The result will be a very strong vignette effect.

To create the vignette:

1. Add a Levels & Curves edit, and configure it to darken the image. As with previous selection edits, don't worry about getting the adjustment exactly right. We'll be able to fine-tune it after we build the mask (**Figure 5.64**).

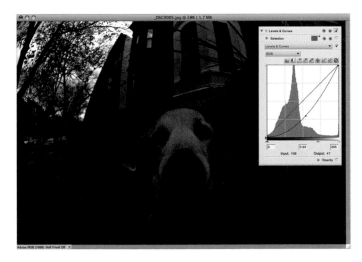

Figure 5.64 Apply a Levels & Curves adjustment to darken the image.

2. Click on the small arrow in the corner of the Gradient tool to switch the gradient tool to the Radial gradient.

3. Click on the – next to the Radial gradient to select the tool.

4. Click in the middle of the dog's snout at the point that you want to be the center of the circular gradient that we're going to create, then drag out a radius. This radius indicates the size of the circular gradient that will be created (**Figure 5.65**). When you release the mouse button, the gradient selection will be created and applied to your Levels & Curves adjustment. The center of your image should immediately brighten.

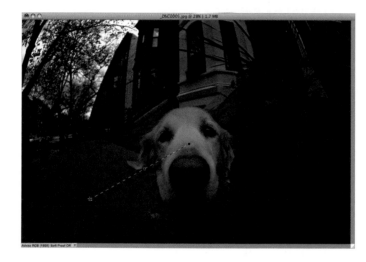

Figure 5.65 By creating a circular gradient with the – gradient tool, we've deselected the center of the image so that it is unaffected by the darkening Levels & Curves adjustment.

If you look at the selection created by the gradient tool, you'll see a circle that radiates from black in the middle to white at the edges. Remember, where there's black, the associated effect—in this case a darkening edit—does not get applied (**Figure 5.66**).

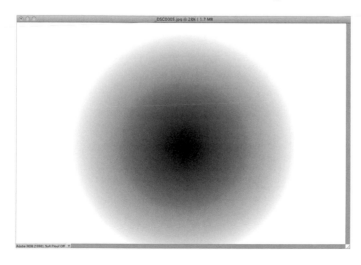

Figure 5.66 This is the selection mask created by our radial gradient.

While this looks pretty good, it would be nice if more of the center was bright. The problem is that our radial gradient progresses evenly from black to white. We'd like to skew the gradient so that it makes a slower transition, leaving more black in the middle of the mask so that more of the gradient ends up blocking the darkening effect.

5. On the Gradient options bar is a gray ramp with three arrows underneath it. You can use these to define the darkest and lightest ends of the gradient, as well as control the midpoint. Shift the midpoint of the gradient to the left and notice how the gradient effect changes (**Figure 5.67**).

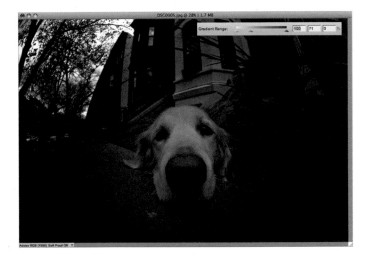

Figure 5.67 After adjusting the midpoint of our gradient, the center of the circle is a little brighter.

6. Let's refine the gradient further by making it a little bigger. If you mouse over the image with the gradient selected, its control handles will become visible. Drag the outside handle to a new location to make the gradient larger (**Figure 5.68**).

Radial gradients can be a handy way of making edits to people's faces and other round shapes that need brightening, darkening, saturation changes, or other edits. Because the gradient creates a very controllable feathering effect, it's easy to create edits that blend in with other tones in the image.

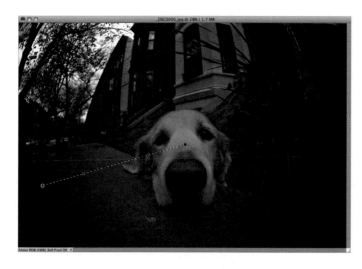

Figure 5.68 You can readjust the boundaries of the gradient by clicking and dragging the end handles of the gradient line.

Understanding How Masks Combine

While Capture NX 2 provides a number of selection tools, they don't all work together to create a single mask. Capture NX 2 actually has three different mask layers, each of which is altered by different tools. Together they combine to create your final masking effect. For the most part, you never need to think or worry about this, but there might be times when you do something with a masking tool and the results just don't make sense. When this happens, you might need to rethink your masking strategy.

Normally, the Base Mask is completely opaque. When you use any of the + (plus) tools, you're punching a hole in that mask to allow the associated edit to affect your image (**Figure 5.69**).

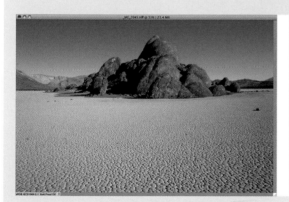

Figure 5.69 When I paint with a + tool, the Base Mask, which is normally completely black, gets white holes punched in it.

continues on next page

Understanding How Masks Combine *continued*

When you use the – (minus) tools, you are *not* refilling those holes in the base mask. Instead, you are painting into the Paint and Fill mask, which sits on top of the Base Mask. This means that any time you use the Base Mask slider to change the overall opacity of the base mask, any of the areas you've painted with a – tool will be unaffected by the change (**Figure 5.70**)

Figure 5.70 After I increase the Base Mask slider, the previously black area has become gray. But, the area that I had painted with the – brush remains unaffected. It is not part of the Base Mask.

In simplest terms, masking works as follows: There is the Base Mask. It is overridden by any strokes you make with the – tools. Finally, there is a separate mask for Control Points, which override both of the other masks.

Again, most of the time the way these separate layers work will not prove to be a concern.

Brush control and combining selections

You can combine any of Capture NX's Selection tools within a single edit. So, you can use whichever tool is appropriate for the area you're trying to select.

For example, the image in Figure 5.71 needs some localized saturation adjustment in the dirt. In Figure 5.60, you saw how to saturate the sky using the Selection Gradient tool. However, the gradient intersects with the top of the barn. I can remove the effect from the barn by using the Selection Brush in – mode (**Figure 5.71**).

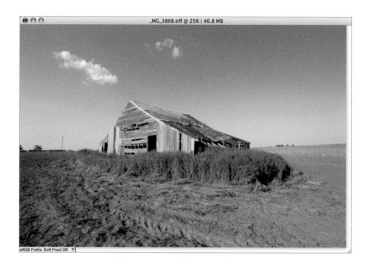

Figure 5.71 Using the Selection Brush in – mode, you can remove the saturation adjustment that was applied to the top of the barn.

To add saturation to the dirt in the foreground, use the + Selection Brush. However, the aggressive saturation adjustment that you defined, which is appropriate for the sky, is a little too much for the foreground. If you paint that saturation into the dirt, the dirt will be a little too "hot" (**Figure 5.72**).

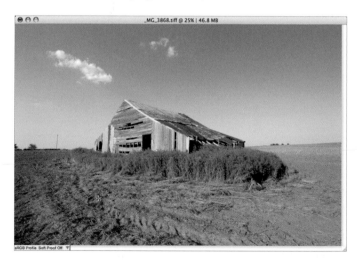

Figure 5.72 If you paint the dirt with the full saturation adjustment, the dirt ends up too "hot." You need a partial saturation adjustment on the dirt.

Fortunately, we can easily solve this problem by turning down the brush opacity. At 50 percent the effect will be half as strong, allowing us to paint a more appropriate level of saturation onto the dirt (**Figure 5.73**).

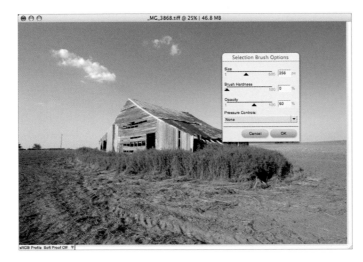

Figure 5.73 After painting the dirt are with our brush set to 50 percent, we get a less extreme saturation adjustment.

Note that opacity effects are additive. If you paint with 50-percent strokes, and then paint over those with 30-percent strokes, the 30-percent strokes do not replace your 50-percent strokes. Instead, the semi-opaque strokes build up as you layer on more strokes. So, if you paint with 100 percent and then paint over those areas with a *lower* opacity, you'll still see 100 percent of your effect.

Fill selections

The Fill tool lets you select or deselect the entire image. You'll probably only need this tool if you're painting a complex mask and screw up and want to start over. Click the + button next to the Fill tool and then click anywhere within your image. The associated edit will be added to the entire image. Click the – button next to the Fill tool and click anywhere in your image, and the associated edit will be removed from the entire image.

TIP: Change the Opacity slider on the Fill Options bar to change the opacity of the fill.

Selection Control Points

Earlier in this chapter you learned about Color Control Points, which let you apply color and tone adjustments using Capture NX's U point control technology. As you saw, with Color Control Points you never have to hassle with complex masking operations because Capture NX can automatically create a very sophisticated mask for you. However, Color Control Points only let you alter tone and color.

With Capture NX 2, you now have Selection Control Points, which let you use a U Point control to define a selection that can be used with *any* type of edit.

For example, a very popular postproduction effect these days is to convert an image to grayscale but leave one or two color elements in the scene. In the film days, this was accomplished by shooting black-and-white film and then hand painting colored areas with special tints. In the digital era, things are much easier because you can start with a color image and selectively change some parts to black-and-white.

The Selection Control Point makes this very simple. Consider the image in **Figure 5.74.**

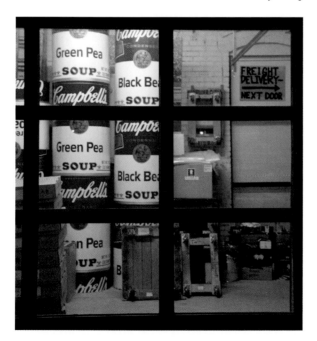

Figure 5.74 We're going to use Selection Control Points to apply localized black-and-white conversion. This will allow us to make this into a black-and-white image, but leave the soup cans colored.

Let's turn this into a grayscale image, but leave the red color in the soup cans.

To convert an image to grayscale, we apply a Photo Effects edit and set the Method to Black and White. This converts our entire image to grayscale.

Now we'd like to create a selection that masks the red parts of the soup can from the effects of the Photo Effects edit. So, I select the – Selection Control Point, and click on the red part of one of the soup cans (**Figure 5.75**).

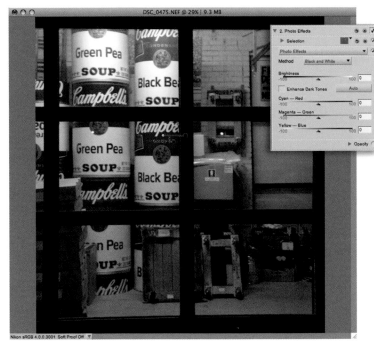

Figure 5.75 I click on the red of a can with the – Selection Control Point, and some of the color in the image is restored.

The Selection Control Point works just like the Color Control Points you saw earlier. It samples the color of the pixels beneath the control point and uses this information to automatically construct a selection. In this case, that selection is associated with our Photo Effects edit. Because I'm using the – brush, the black-and-white conversion is being removed to reveal the original color.

If we view the mask, you can see that most of the image—the white areas—is still being affected by the black-and-white edit. The black and gray areas are not, and so are retaining their color (**Figure 5.76**).

Now I simply duplicate my Selection Control Points onto the other cans until my image looks the way that I want (**Figure 5.77**). It took five Control Points to get all of the color back where I wanted it. Each one gets listed in the Edit List, just as the Color Control Points do.

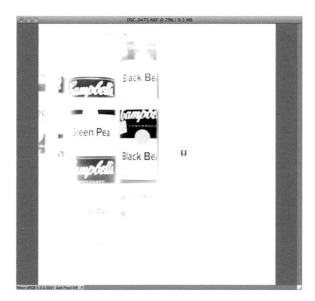

Figure 5.76 The mask created by our first Selection Control Point.

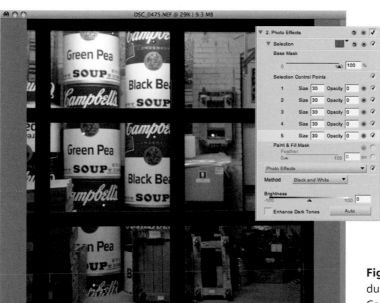

Figure 5.77 After duplicating my Selection Control Point four more times, I can restore the color to all of the cans.

Note that there's one extra bit of red on the cardboard box in the middle of the image. I can easily use the + paint brush to paint that area, thus adding the Photo Effects back to that small area.

TIP: *Don't overuse popular effects. As I've mentioned, the color/black-and-white combo image is very popular right now. The problem with using effects like these is that they will, one day, go out of fashion. So be careful about using such tricks too often. If you need to bring focus to one area of an image, consider all of your options.*

Selection Control Points are a great way to selectively apply sharpening, noise reduction, grain, and many other effects which we'll learn about in later chapters.

Using the Same Selection with Multiple Edits

Very often, you'll want to use the selections that you create for more than one effect— sometimes the same isolated area needs to be adjusted using several different edits. Fortunately, you can link edits together so that the same selection applies to all of them.

Let's return for a moment to the desert image we looked at earlier. In this image, I applied a Levels & Curves edit to increase the contrast of the image and then used the Brush tool to paint that effect onto only the ground (**Figure 5.78**).

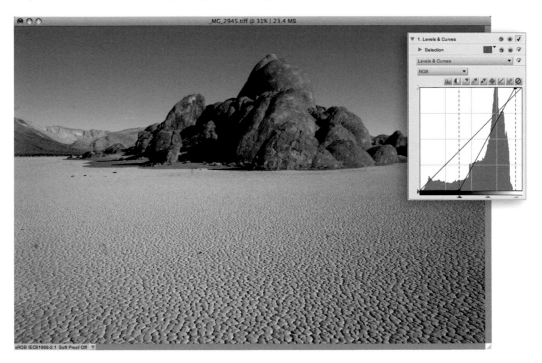

Figure 5.78 Earlier I used a Levels & Curves adjustment to increase the contrast in the ground texture. Unfortunately, that process also increased the saturation there.

While I like the improved contrast, the edit has also increased the saturation on the ground. I'd like to add a desaturation effect but I don't want it to impact the sky—I want to isolate the effect and restrict it to the ground. Fortunately, my Levels & Curves edit already has a selection that isolates the ground. By linking the desaturation edit to the existing Levels & Curves edit, both adjustments will use the same selection.

To link two edits together so that the first edit's selection affects the other linked edits:

1. In the Edit List, select the edit that you want to link to. This is the edit that has the selection that you've already made.

2. Hold down the Shift key while you choose the next edit that you want to add to the list. In this case, that will be Adjust > Color > Saturation/Warmth. The edit will be added to the Edit List but will not be listed as a new edit (**Figure 5.79**). The new edit will automatically be constrained by the selection that you defined in the first edit.

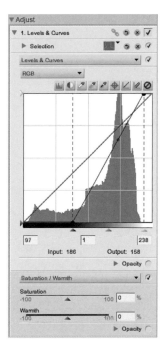

Figure 5.79 By holding down the Shift key when I select Saturation/Warmth, I can link it to the Levels & Curves edit, so that the new edit is affected by the Levels & Curves selection.

3. Adjust the new edit to taste.

With this image, I drag the Saturation slider in the Saturation/Warmth edit to the left to reduce saturation, and the ground returns to its more pastel tint, while my sky, and the rest of my image is unaffected (**Figure 5.80**).

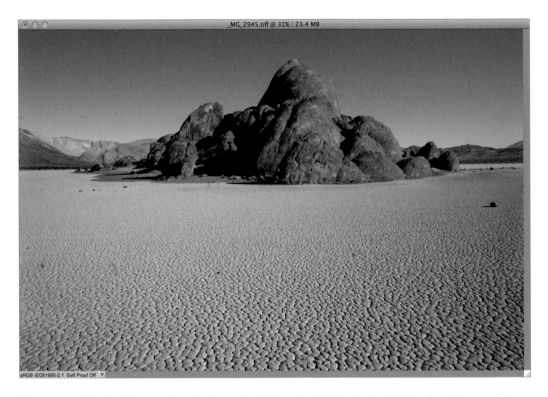

Figure 5.80 The final image after the Saturation/Warmth edit is linked to the Levels & Curves edit.

The Lasso and Marquee Tools

Strictly speaking, from a logical-organization standpoint I should have discussed these tools earlier. I've relegated them to the end of this section, though, because they're really just not that useful. The Lasso tool lets you define a selection by dragging around it. If you click on the Lasso tool in the toolbar, you'll get a menu offering some additional selection tools (**Figure 5.81**).

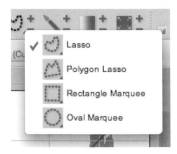

Figure 5.81 In addition to the Lasso, Capture NX 2 also provides a suite of Marquee tools.

DODGING AND BURNING

The Selection tools that we've been looking at allow you to perform many of the same types of adjustments that have traditionally been created using dodging and burning techniques in a wet darkroom. However, Capture NX's tools are far more powerful and flexible, thanks to their precision and to the fact that they let you adjust much more than just tone.

As you've seen, the tools are very easy to use—but what should you use them for? Sometimes the areas in your image that need brightening or color/saturation adjustments will be obvious. At other times it can be difficult to recognize where selective editing might improve your image.

Remember that light does more than just determine the brightness of your scene. Contour and depth are all indicated by the light and shadow in your image. An image like the one in **Figure 5.82** looks flat because the light is mostly uniform; the shadows are not significantly different from the bright areas.

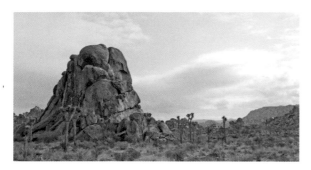

Figure 5.82 The overcast day made for diffuse lighting in this scene, which resulted in the rocks' appearing flat and evenly lit. You can add more depth to the scene using some selective lightening and darkening.

You can increase the overall contrast of the scene to make the image look much better (**Figure 5.83**), but there's still more depth that you can add to the scene with a little localized brightening and darkening.

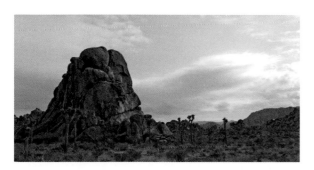

Figure 5.83 I darkened the shadow side of the rock by creating a Levels & Curves adjustment that darkens, and then painting the effect into only the dark side of the rock.

When this image was shot, the sun was not bright enough to cast strong shadows. There is little relief visible in the image, though one side of the rock pile is being lit slightly more than the other. Accentuating this difference will create more of a sense of the shape and depth of the rock.

By using a Levels & Curves adjustment, you can darken the image. Then use the Selection Brush to paint that effect into the dark side of the rock (**Figure 5.84**).

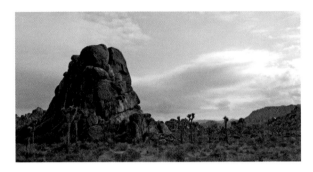

Figure 5.84 Next, I added an additional Levels & Curves effect, but this time configured it to brighten. With the Selection brush you can paint this lightening into the bright parts of the image. The result is that the rock has more depth.

Next, you can add another Levels & Curves adjustment, but set this one to lighten the image. Then paint that lightening into the bright parts of the image to lighten those areas (**Figure 5.85**).

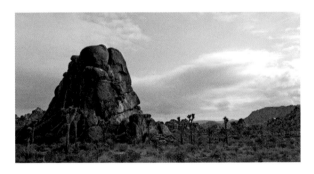

Figure 5.85 The final image has a more profound sense of depth on the rock, thanks to the extra shading that was introduced.

By the time you're done with the image, it will have three Levels & Curves edits: one for the overall (global) brightening, a second one for darkening the dark parts of the rock, and a third one that lightens the light parts.

> **TIP:** You can use the usual copy and paste controls to duplicate edits in the Edit List. Select an edit in the Edit List and choose Copy, then choose Paste to paste in a duplicate. This can be an easy way to create variations of the same edit.

Facial Retouching

The selective lightening tactic discussed in the previous section can also be used to reduce lines and wrinkles in peoples face. If you look closely at a wrinkle in a photo, you'll see that it consists of a dark line bordered by a light line, although sometimes it's only a light line (**Figure 5.86**).

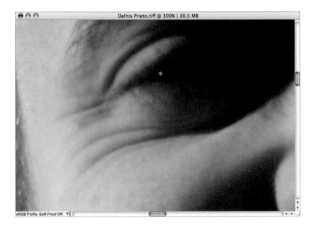

Figure 5.86 A wrinkle usually consists of a dark line with a light border.

You can use a Levels & Curves edit to create a lightening effect and then use the Selection Brush to paint that effect over the wrinkle (**Figure 5.87**).

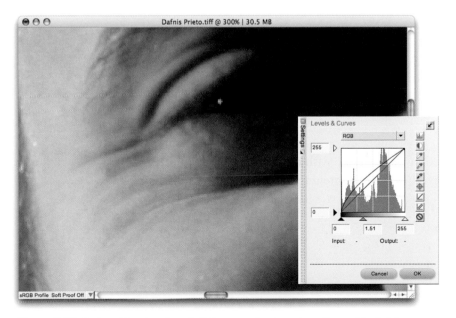

Figure 5.87 By brushing in a Levels & Curves adjustment configured to lighten your image, you can reduce the appearance of the wrinkle.

In most cases you'll want to use a midpoint, or gamma, shift in the Levels & Curves edit to perform the lightening. A white point adjustment will create too strong an effect, and one that might result in ugly tonal changes.

If your wrinkle also has a light edge to it, create an additional Levels & Curves edit that darkens the image and then paint that effect into the light part of the wrinkle.

ADDITIONAL ADJUSTMENTS

There are a few additional items under the Focus menu (Adjust > Focus) that we didn't cover in Chapter 3, "Basic Image Editing."

Gaussian Blur

The Gaussian Blur adjustment lets you apply a blur to your image (**Figure 5.88**). The Radius slider controls the amount of blurriness, and the Opacity slider controls the intensity.

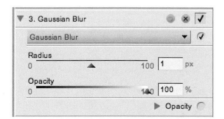

Figure 5.88 You can add a blur to your images using the Gaussian Blur adjustment.

High Pass

The High Pass filter is basically an edge detection filter. It converts the solid areas of your image to gray while leaving the areas of sudden contrast change alone. The practical upshot is that you end up with a map of the edges in your image (**Figure 5.89**).

The most common practical application for the High Pass filter is to combine it with some opacity adjustments to improve the apparent sharpness of your image.

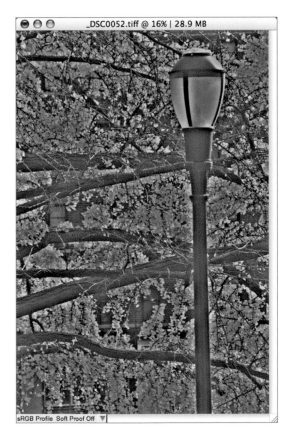

Figure 5.89 The High Pass filter identifies edges in your images.

To sharpen using the High Pass filter:

1. Add a High Pass filter to your image and set the radius fairly high—20 to 30 pixels, for example.

2. In the Edit List, open the High Pass edit's Opacity controls.

3. Change the All pop-up menu to Luminance and Chrominance mode. This allows you to blend the filtered effect into the Luminance and Chrominance information in different ways.

4. Set the Chrominance opacity to 0 percent.

5. Set the Blending Mode to Overlay.

6. Adjust the High Pass Radius setting to taste.

Using the High Pass filter in this way (**Figure 5.90**) can result in images with better detail without risking the sharpening artifacts that can occur with the Unsharp Mask effect.

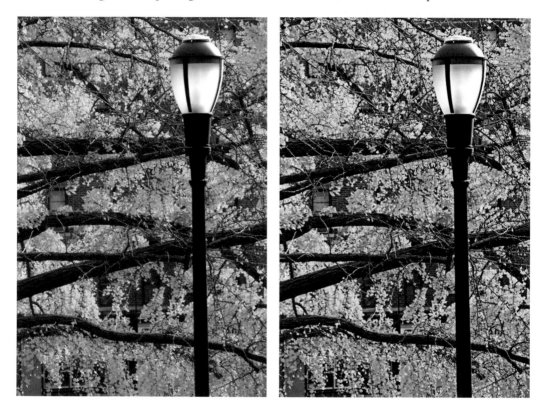

Figure 5.90 Using the High Pass filter and an opacity mix, you can dramatically increase the sharpness and detail in your image.

Noise Reduction

Located under the Adjust menu is a Noise Reduction edit that provides you with tools for reducing noise troubles in an image. There are two types of noise in a digital photo: luminance noise, which manifests as brightly colored specs, and chrominance, or color noise, which appears as colored pixels and splotches.

The Noise Reduction adjustment provides simple controls for applying noise reduction (**Figure 5.91**).

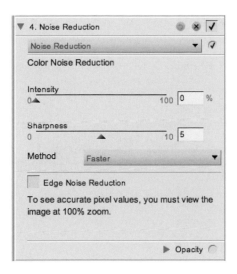

Figure 5.91 The Noise Reduction edit lets you lessen the amount of luminance and chrominance noise that appears in your images.

Intensity specifies how much noise reduction is applied. Increase the slider value to reduce the noise in your image.

Sharpness is a light sharpening effect that tries to counter the overall softening of your image that takes place when you apply noise reduction.

Method controls how noise reduction operates. Noise Reduction can be applied in a Faster mode or a Better Quality (but slower processing) mode.

Edge Noise Reduction reduces noise along edges in your image, resulting in stronger edges and therefore better sharpness.

As with sharpening, it's best to apply Noise Reduction while viewing your image at 100 percent.

CHAPTER SIX
Version Control and Batch Processing

In the previous three chapters you have seen how Capture NX's nondestructive editing architecture lets you easily add and change edits at any time. Unlike with destructive editing systems, you aren't limited to just a few "undos" (NX 2 provides unlimited undos), and you can change or remove edits in any order. You may find that once you're used to working nondestructively, going back to a normal destructive editor is very difficult.

But nondestructive editing has some additional benefits that we haven't explored yet. As you learned earlier, when you make an edit in Capture NX the specifics of that edit are stored in the Edit List. When Capture NX needs to display an image onscreen or output it to a printer or file, the edits in the Edit List are applied to your original image data file. Since it does all of this on the fly, you can alter the list at any time—the revised edits will be applied to your original image, and the updated, edited version will be displayed.

Because edits are kept separate from image data, Capture NX allows you to perform some handy version control and batch-processing features. We'll explore all of these in this chapter.

VERSION CONTROL

No matter what kind of image-editing software you've used in the past, you're probably accustomed to occasionally (or maybe frequently) making multiple versions of the same file. Sometimes you'll create additional versions because you want to try out several different approaches to an image but you want to keep each one. You might create multiple versions if you're trying to decide whether an image works better as color or grayscale. Or, you might create multiple versions when printing—for example, creating a version for each type of paper you want to print on, since different paper types often require slightly different tone and color adjustments.

In a destructive editor, you usually create a new version of an image by duplicating your original file or by using a Save As command to save a copy of your current image with a different name. You then perform a different set of edits on each new document that you create.

This scheme has a few drawbacks. First, it quickly uses up lots of disk space. Unless you're creating smaller versions, each new version that you save is the size of your original image. If you're working on a large file (25 MB or bigger), saving five or six versions can quickly consume a respectable amount of disk space. Second, these save operations can take time. Even a speedy computer can take a while to write out a very large file.

Additionally, saving multiple versions like this can create housekeeping problems. You have to come up with a naming scheme that makes sense to you, and you have to keep all of the files that you've created organized.

Nondestructive Versions

In a nondestructive image editor like Capture NX 2, creating multiple versions is much simpler. Since an edit in NX 2 is simply stored in a text file and then applied to a master image file later, there's no need to ever duplicate that master image file. Instead, you can simply create multiple text files full of edits with each one linked to a single image file. These different versions, each with its own Edit List, are all kept within the NEF file.

The Edit Lists that Capture NX creates are very small, usually just a few dozen kilobytes. So, you can easily create dozens of versions with very little impact on your storage space. What's more, writing out these tiny little files is a speedy process, so creating a new version doesn't take much time.

These last two features lead to something of a "meta" feature of Capture NX's versioning capabilities. Because creating a new version is so speedy and comes with so little storage penalty, you'll probably be more willing to create multiple versions, which you might find makes your work much easier.

Creating a New Version

To create a new version, choose New Version from the Version menu in the Edit List (**Figure 6.1**).

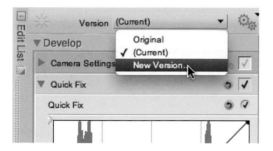

Figure 6.1 Choose New Version from the Version menu at the top of the Edit List to create a new version of any image.

Capture NX prompts you to enter a version name. Enter it and click OK to save the version. You won't see anything different on your document, but if you open the Version menu, you'll see both your new version and a new entry called (Current).

You can then make changes to your image and save another version. You can select either version from the Version menu to switch back and forth to either configuration.

When you make new changes, they are applied to the (Current) version, not to the version that you just saved. You can't make changes to a saved version. You can only load it, alter it, and save it again as a new version.

Note too that you can't save over a version with another version of the same name. You need to save altered versions under a new name, and then delete the old copy using the Edit Versions command on the Version menu. Edit Versions displays a dialog box that allows you to easily delete any existing versions.

At any time you can switch back to your original image by selecting Original from the Version menu.

If you want to save an image containing multiple versions, you must save it in NEF format. The NEF format keeps all alternate versions within the file, meaning you don't have to worry about keeping track of extra documents or sidecar files.

COPYING AND MOVING SETTINGS

Because an edit on a document is nothing more than an entry in a text file, it's possible to move edits around in your document or copy them from one document to another.

For example, there might be times when you want to rearrange the edits in your Edit List. Maybe you've accidentally inserted an edit in the wrong place, for example, or decided that your Levels adjustments should occur *after* your Saturation adjustment.

While Capture NX won't let you drag edits around to change their order, you can use the Copy and Paste adjustments commands to effectively move an edit.

To move an edit in the Edit List to a new location in the same document:

1. In the Edit List, click the edit that you want to move.

2. Choose Copy Adjustments from the Batch menu or from the Batch icon at the top right of the Edit List (**Figure 6.2**).

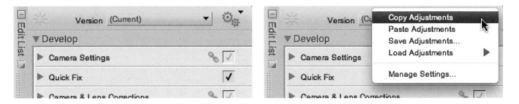

Figure 6.2 At the top of the Edit List is a pop-up Version menu containing simple commands for Copy and Paste Adjustments.

3. Deselect the Edit you just copied by clicking somewhere else in the Edit List.

4. Choose Paste Adjustments from the Batch menu on the menu bar or from the Batch menu at the top of the Edit List. The setting you copied is added to the end of the Edit List.

5. Delete the original copy of the edit.

Pasting a setting always adds it to the end of the list. It's not actually possible to use paste to insert an entry into the middle of a list. However, you can move multiple steps at one time using the preceding technique. Simply select each edit by Command/Control-clicking on it in the Edit List, and then use the Copy and Paste commands in the Batch menu. All of the edits are moved, in order, to the end of the list.

> **TIP:** You can also copy and paste edits between documents. So, if you have a bunch of similar images—such as a burst set—you can create an edit or series of edits that correct that image and then copy and paste those edits into the other images in your burst set.

BATCH PROCESSING

In the previous section, you learned how you can easily move edits around in a document or between documents simply by copying and pasting them. This is because an edit is nothing more than a note in a text file that is associated with your image. In addition to making it easy to move edits around, this architecture makes it possible to batch process your images. With batch processing, a series of edits can automatically be applied to a selected group of images.

Any type of edit can be applied in a batch process, including control points and selections. But before you can start a batch process, you need to save the edits that you want to apply to your target batch of images.

Saving Adjustments

The Batch menus on the Menu bar and at the top of the Edit List provide a Save Adjustments command that saves all of the settings that are currently defined in the Edit List. When you choose the command, the dialog box shown in **Figure 6.3** appears.

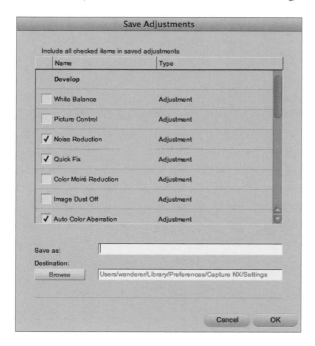

Figure 6.3 With the Save Settings dialog box, you can specify exactly which edits you want to save in a settings file.

TIP: *You can also access the Copy, Paste, Save, and Load commands by right-clicking anywhere in the Edit List palette.*

With this dialog box, you can specify exactly which settings you want to save in the set. In most cases, you'll probably leave all of the options set.

Note that each Edit Step also may have an associated Selection Step, which specifies whether the edit is applied to the entire image or just a selection. If you've defined an edit selection specific to the particular image you're working on, you may want to uncheck the selection before saving the set. This allows you to define a new selection for each image the edit set is applied to.

In the Save As field, enter a name for the settings.

Using the Browse button, you can specify a location for saving your settings. By default, settings are saved in the Capture NX Preferences folder, and unless you have a specific reason to save them somewhere else, it's best to save them to the default location simply because it is easier for NX to find them.

However, if you work with multiple machines or with other photographers, you might want to save your settings to a common location—on a network volume or external drive, for example.

After you've configured the dialog box, click OK to save the settings.

Loading Adjustments

After you've saved some adjustments, you can easily apply them to any other document by simply opening a document and choosing the Load Settings command from the Batch menu.

Any settings that you've saved automatically appear in the Load Adjustments pop-up menu. If the settings file you're looking for doesn't appear, choose the Browse option and then navigate to the desired file.

After you select the settings file you want, those settings are automatically applied to your image just as if you had applied each edit by hand. Your Edit List should show an entry for each adjustment in the settings file. You can alter any of these edits just as you normally would.

> **TIP:** You can also load and save settings and copy and paste settings or IPTC info using the Batch menu in the lower left corner of the Browser palette. This lets you move settings and metadata while browsing thumbnails.

Managing Settings

Over time, as you save more settings, the Load Settings menu will become longer and longer. You can hide or delete settings from the Load Settings menu by clicking the Batch menu and choosing Manage Settings, which takes you to the Manage Settings section of the Preferences dialog box (**Figure 6.4**).

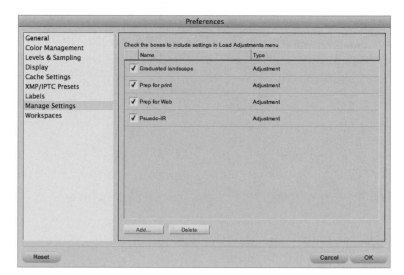

Figure 6.4 From the Settings Preferences dialog box you can manage saved settings files.

With Manage Settings, you can delete a settings file, add a settings file (such as one you might have received from someone else), or uncheck it so that it doesn't appear in the Load Settings menu.

Changing File Formats

The Capture NX File Browser provides a simple way to convert batches of images to a different file format without having to manually open and save each one. In the File Browser, select the images you want to convert and then choose File > Save As. Capture NX presents you with the Processing Queue dialog box (which you'll learn more about later). Using the controls in the lower half, you can select a destination and file-naming convention, as well as format and save parameters.

If you've been editing lots of images and saving them as NEF files, there will probably come a time when you want to convert all of those images to TIFF or JPEG files for use in another program. Using Save As from the File Browser makes it simple to output your final files.

Batch Processing

By using Save Settings and Load Settings, you can easily apply the same edits to multiple images. However, these commands require you to manually issue each Load and Save step, so they're not really practical if you have a huge number of images to process.

For times when you want to apply the same settings to entire folders full of images, you can use Capture NX's Batch Processing feature. Batch Processing does nothing that you haven't already done using the Load Settings and Save Settings commands; it just issues these commands automatically so that you don't have to continually open and save images (**Figure 6.5**).

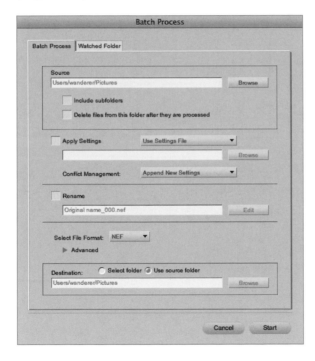

Figure 6.5 Choose Batch > Run Batch Process to configure and run batch operations.

To open the Batch Process dialog box, choose Batch > Run Batch Process. With the Batch Process dialog box open, you're ready to begin.

Choosing a source

Begin by selecting a source folder. In the Source section of the Batch Process dialog box, click the Browse button and navigate to the folder that contains the images you want to process (**Figure 6.6**).

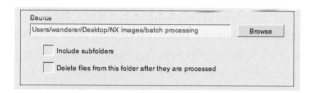

Figure 6.6 Select a folder of source images using the Source controls at the top of the Batch Process palette.

If the folder contains subfolders full of images that you also want to process, check the "Include subfolders" box.

If you want to automatically delete the source files after they have been processed, check the "Delete files from this folder after they are processed" box. Obviously, you'll want to be very careful with this option, lest you accidentally delete your original images.

Selecting settings to apply

Next, you need to choose the settings that you want to apply to the batch (**Figure 6.7**). Check the Apply settings check box. If you want to use a previously saved settings file, leave the Use Settings File pop-up menu as it is. If you want to use the settings from the currently opened image, change Use Settings File to Use Original Settings.

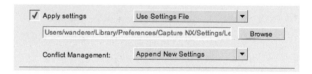

Figure 6.7 Use these controls to select and configure the settings that you want applied to each image in the batch.

If you will be using a saved settings file, click the Browse button to navigate to the settings file.

The Conflict Management pop-up menu lets you specify how to handle images that already have settings applied to them. Append New Settings adds the settings in the settings file to the image's existing settings, and Replace Current Settings completely overwrites any existing settings with the settings stored in the file.

If you select Show Differences, Capture NX displays a dialog box when the batch process is run. The dialog box lets you specify whether to use the image's settings or the settings from the settings file (**Figure 6.8**).

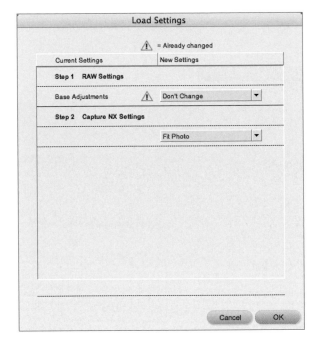

Figure 6.8 If you select Show Differences in your batch configuration, Capture NX lets you choose which edits to apply to an image if it encounters a conflict while the batch is running.

Renaming

If you leave the Rename check box unchecked, Capture NX saves the new file with the same name as the original file, possibly overwriting the original. In many cases, you'll want to rename the files as the batch process is performed.

To have the Batch Processor rename edited images, check the Rename box, and then click the Edit button to bring up Capture NX's File Naming dialog box (**Figure 6.9**).

In the File Naming dialog box, you can specify a file name that has the following components:

- A prefix that can be the file's original name, a new name that you specify, or no name
- A separator, which can be an underscore, hyphen, or space
- A sequential number (which you can format using the Starting number and Length of number controls), date, or date/time stamp
- Another separator

- A suffix, which can be the original name, a new name, or none

- A file extension, which is determined automatically by the file format that you specify in the Batch Process dialog box

The File Naming dialog box should provide you with all the controls you need to create any type of file name.

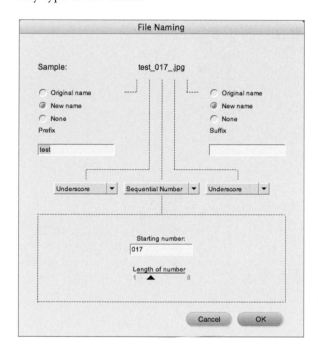

Figure 6.9 Using the File Naming dialog box, you can specify exactly how you want your images named during batch processing.

Format and destination

In addition, you'll want to select the file format and destination that you want to save your edited images to. From the Select File Format menu, you can choose NEF, TIFF, or JPG (the same formats that Capture NX's Save As command offers). Which one you select depends on what you want to do with the resulting images. If you think you'll need to adjust any of the edits that are applied by the batch process, select NEF. If you are batch processing images to create final deliverables for Web or print design, or for editing by users who don't have Capture NX, select TIFF or JPG.

In the Destination field, you can elect to save the resulting images back into the folder that contains the source images, or you can click the Select folder option to choose a new folder for saving.

Run the batch process

With the Batch Process dialog box configured, click the Start button to begin processing your files. Every Capture NX-compatible image in the folder that you selected as your source folder will be processed by the operation. If you checked Include subfolders, any compatible images in enclosed subfolders will also be processed.

Capture NX won't display any of the processed images. Instead, a simple progress bar indicates the number of images that have been edited. When the batch process is complete, your new, saved images appear in their destination folder.

You can expand the Processing Queue dialog box to show a more detailed view of your batch progress (**Figure 6.10**).

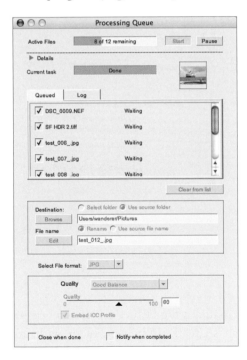

Figure 6.10 The Processing Queue dialog appears when your batch process is running. If you open the Details palette, you can manage the image queue, review the destination, and save settings that have been defined for the batch.

Watched Folder

A Watched Folder provides another way of starting a batch processing operation. If you specify a folder as a Watched Folder, any images that you place in that folder will automatically be processed; you won't have to issue a specific batch process command.

You configure a Watched Folder from the Watched Folder tab of the Batch Process dialog box. All of the same settings, renaming, and file format commands are provided. The only difference is that instead of selecting a source folder to process immediately, you select a folder to watch (**Figure 6.11**).

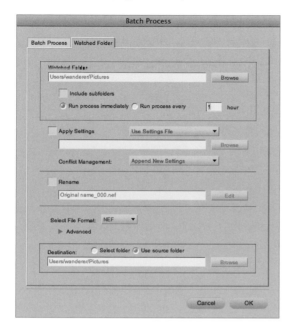

Figure 6.11 You can use the Watched Folder palette to configure a folder that automatically batch processes any image that you place into it.

Click the Browse button to specify the folder that you want to watch, and check Include subfolders if you want to watch any nested subfolders.

If you click the "Run process immediately" option, the batch operation will be applied to an image as soon as it's placed in the folder. If you click the "Run process every x hour" option, batch processing will only occur at the specified interval. If you don't need your images processed right away, processing at an interval might make more sense for your workflow.

The advantage of a Watched Folder is that it allows for further automation of your image production pipeline. For example, you can share the Watched Folder with other users on your production team. As they copy images into the Watched Folder, your settings can automatically be applied and saved to a final folder that is used by your print or Web designer.

Prepping for Output

In the next chapter, you're going to learn about Capture NX 2's output capabilities. We'll combine these facilities with some batch processing to create some cool automated-output routines.

CHAPTER SEVEN
Output

No matter what your organizational and editing workflows are, it's a safe bet that one of the last steps of your imaging process will be output. Whether you need electronic output, printed output, or some combination, Capture NX 2 provides fully color managed, easy-to-use output options.

RESIZING

Whether you're outputting your images to print or as digital documents, you'll probably need to resize them. Today's high pixel count cameras yield much more data than you need for most any electronic form of delivery, and unless you are printing very large prints, a 10+ megapixel camera produces files that are much larger than you need for printing out. Capture NX includes a few tools for resizing your images.

As you know, a digital image is composed of a grid of pixels, essentially one for each pixel on your camera's image sensor. For example, if you have an eight megapixel camera, the images produced by your digital SLR will have dimensions of roughly 3500 pixels by 2300 pixels. Your camera tags your image with an output resolution setting, which specifies how closely these pixels will by spaced (in pixels per inch) when they're output on a printer. The higher the output resolution, the closer the pixels will be to each other, so a higher output resolution means a smaller print size.

Capture NX provides you with two different ways of resizing an image: You can change the resolution setting, which doesn't change the number of pixels in your image but simply tags the image as having a different number of pixels per inch; or you can choose to change the size of the image by adding or removing pixels.

NOTE: *Capture NX uses the term "dots per inch" in its Size/Resolution dialog box. Technically, this is an inaccurate use of the term. Dots per inch is usually a measure of the number of printer dots that an inkjet printer lays down. "Pixels per inch" is the correct term for the pixels in an image.*

Changing the resolution of an image

To change the output resolution of an image:

1. Open the image.

2. Select Edit > Size/Resolution. A Size/Resolution edit is added to the Edit List (**Figure 7.1**).

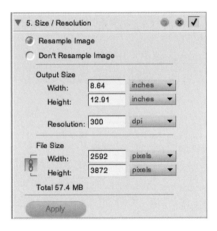

Figure 7.1 The Size/Resolution edit lets you change the resolution of your image as well as the number of pixels in your image.

3. Click the Don't Resample Image button. Resampling is the process of adding or removing data to increase or decrease the overall size of the file. We want to leave the total number of pixels as they are, and simply change the resolution setting. Resolution is simply a marker that indicates how tightly packed the pixels are.

    Note that when you select Don't Resample Image, the File Size fields become ineditable. This is because there's no way to change the number of pixels without resampling.

4. Enter a new size in the Resolution field. (You can change the dpi [dots per inch] measure to dpcm [dots per centimeter].) Note that the output size fields are updated to reflect the new print size that results from your resolution change. As you increase resolution, your print size will get smaller because the pixels in your image will be squished closer together.

    Note that the "Total" readout, which indicates the total size of your image, remains the same. You haven't changed the number of pixels—only their density.

You won't see any change in your image because you haven't altered any of the actual pixels. Instead, you've merely changed the output resolution setting in the document.

> **TIP:** *For printing photos on most desktop inkjet printers, use a resolution of 240 pixels per inch. In some instances, you can get away with less resolution. The only penalties for using a higher resolution are larger file sizes and possibly longer print times.*

Changing the number of pixels in an image

The Size/Resolution dialog box also lets you change the number of pixels in an image, a process called resampling. When you lower the pixel count in an image, Capture NX throws away as many pixels as necessary to achieve your desired target size. When you increase the number of pixels in an image, Capture NX concocts new pixels to boost the pixel count of your image to your desired size.

> **NOTE:** *Capture NX uses a bicubic interpolation for its resampling. This is a high-quality algorithm that is well suited to almost any photographic resizing task.*

To change the number of pixels (altering the native or original resolution) in an image (resizing by resampling):

1. Open the image.

2. Select Edit > Size/Resolution. A Size/Resolution edit is added to your Edit List.

3. Click Resample Image. Notice that the File Size fields are editable, indicating that the number of pixels in the image can change.

4. Enter new pixel dimensions in the File Size Width and Height fields. Alternatively, you can change the pixels' pop-up menus to % to enlarge or reduce your image to a percentage of its original size.

   By default, the Size/Resolution dialog box resizes your image proportionally: The lock icon between the Width and Height fields (**Figure 7.2**) indicates that the two values are proportionally related. You can click the lock to deselect it, which allows you to change each axis independently but results in image distortion.

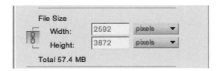

Figure 7.2 The lock icon between the Width and Height fields lets you choose whether or not you want to preserve the aspect ratio of the original image.

   Note that the Total readout changes. If you increase the image size, the total count goes up. If you decrease the size, the total count goes down.

If you prefer to think in terms of final image size, you can enter new values for the Output Size Width, Height, and Resolution. Your image will be resampled (either up or down) to yield an image with enough pixels to produce your intended print size and resolution.

Resizing an image for print

Your camera usually tags images with a resolution of 72 pixels per inch; this will vary from model to model. At 72, your image will have an unreasonably large print size—30 inches wide or more on an eight megapixel camera. (Obviously, if you crop an image, you'll have fewer pixels.)

Consider the image shown in **Figure 7.3**.

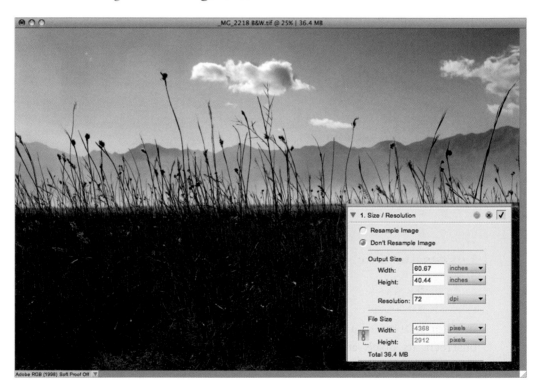

Figure 7.3 We'll use the Size/Resolution dialog box to resize this image for print on a desktop inkjet printer.

The Size/Resolution settings show that the image has pixel dimensions of 4368 x 2912 pixels at 72 pixels per inch, yielding a print size of roughly 60 x 40 inches.

Let's say that you know that the printer works fine with images that have a resolution of 240 dots per inch, so you can change the Resolution field to 240. The print size changes to 18.2 x 12.13 (the print size gets smaller because the pixels are closer together). You want to print an 8 x 10 image, so this is still larger than you want. So, you make sure the Resample Image button is checked, and then enter a width of **10**. Because the lock button is checked, Capture NX automatically calculates an appropriate height, to preserve the original aspect ratio of the image. It also *reduces* the total size of the image to yield a final image at the size and resolution that you want (**Figure 7.4**). Note that the total size and pixel dimensions have decreased.

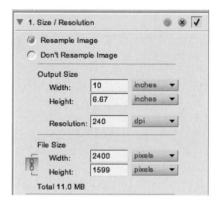

Figure 7.4 With the Size/Resolution dialog box you can resize your image to the precise size and resolution settings that you want.

NOTE: *If you're working with a raw file then your image might be larger, as Capture NX will open these as 16-bit images to give you more editing latitude. You can save these out at 8-bit later if you want smaller files.*

Resizing an image for the Web or email

Resizing for the Web or email is usually easier than resizing for print. First, output resolution is irrelevant for images that will only be viewed onscreen. The resolution of your monitor is fixed to a certain number of pixels per inch. When an image is displayed onscreen, its pixels are simply lined up, and the resulting number of pixels per inch depends on how close together the pixels on your screen are.

Second, images for screen display usually need to be made small. If you're shooting with a high-resolution camera, you'll need a fairly significant reduction.

In general, it's safe to assume that most users are capable of displaying an 800 x 600 pixel image on their screen with plenty of room for their OS interface. If you know your intended viewer has a larger screen, you might consider increasing the size to 1,024 x 768. If you want to play it very safe, stick with a small size such as 640 x 480. Simply plug the appropriate numbers into the "File Size" windows.

How much can you upsample?

Be careful with upsizing. Too much upsampling introduces noticeable artifacts into your image—jagged lines and an overall softening. That said, Capture NX does a very good job of upsampling, and you'll probably be surprised to find that you can enlarge your images quite a bit before they become noticeably degraded. This allows you to create very large prints.

Bear in mind, too, that larger prints are usually viewed from far away. You don't handle and examine a large print the way you do a 4 x 6" or 8 x 10" print. So you can usually get away with a little softness in a larger print.

If you need to upsample by more than 10 percent, you'll probably find that you get better results using multiple 10 percent resizings rather than one big resizing. You can easily stack multiple resize Edit Steps in your Edit List.

Nondestructive Resizing or "How I Learned to Stop Worrying and Love My Edit List"

In a normal, destructive image editor, if you resample an image—either up or down—you permanently alter the pixel count in the image. If you downsample, the pixels that are thrown away are permanently lost, whereas if you upsample, you end up permanently degrading your image with interpolated pixels. For this reason, you usually need to save multiple versions of your image at different sizes when working with a destructive editor.

In Capture NX you don't have to worry about resizing issues. Resizing is simply one more edit in your list of edits. Like the other edits, resizing is applied on the fly. So, if you want to return your image to its original pixel dimensions or resolution setting, you can simply delete the resize edits.

Because Edit Steps can be deactivated, you can even keep multiple resizings within one document. For example, you can have one resize step that resizes your image to 4 x 6", and another that resizes to 8 x 10", and yet another for email delivery. When you want to print a 4 x 6", you simply activate the 4 x 6" step and deactivate the 8 x 10" step. Then do the opposite for an 8 x 10" step or email output.

Fit Photo

A landscape-oriented image has a longer width than a portrait-oriented image, and a portrait-oriented image has a taller height than a landscape-oriented image. You can use the Fit Photo command to automatically resize an image to fit into a given size regardless of its orientation.

For example, you can use Fit Photo to prepare an image for email:

1. Open the image.

2. Select Edit > Fit Photo.

3. Make sure the pop-up menus are set to pixels, if necessary.

4. Enter a width of 800 and a height of 600, or whatever pixel dimensions you prefer (**Figure 7.5**).

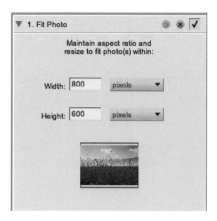

Figure 7.5 Fit Photo automatically resizes an image to fit into given pixel dimensions regardless of the image's orientation.

A Fit Photo edit is added to your Edit List, and your image is automatically resized so that it fits proportionally and is as large as possible inside the dimensions you specified.

Of course, you can do the same task manually by using the Size/Resolution dialog box. However, as you'll see later in this chapter, Fit Photo becomes very handy when you start batch processing large groups of images.

SHARPENING

Sharpening is an important step in your final output process. As you learned earlier in the book, sitting right in front of the image sensor in your camera is a filter that applies a slight blurring to your image. This is necessary to perform some of the color calculations that must be made. Fortunately, it's slight enough that it can easily be corrected with some sharpening in Capture NX 2. Sharpening can also help out if you have a lens that doesn't always yield perfectly sharp images. Sharpening *cannot* correct a wildly out of focus image or eliminate blur in a moving subject or in an image shot with a shaky camera.

It's not actually possible to increase the sharpness in an image—edge detail is either there or it isn't. However, it is possible to increase the *apparent* sharpness of an image by making the edges in the image appear more acute.

An edge is really nothing more than a sudden change of contrast in an image. Edges are almost always made up of dark or light lines. The Unsharp Mask filter in Capture NX changes the acutance of an edge by identifying the line of sudden contrast change, and then darkening the pixels along its dark side and lightening the pixels along the light side. This serves to make the edge more contrasty. However, too much of this additional contrast and your image can be plagued by *halos* around every high contrast line (**Figure 7.6**).

In this image the oversharpening is apparent in the bright whites of the highlights and the dark shadowy outlines that appear around all of the leaves. The overall effect is an image that's too contrasty and a little too "busy."

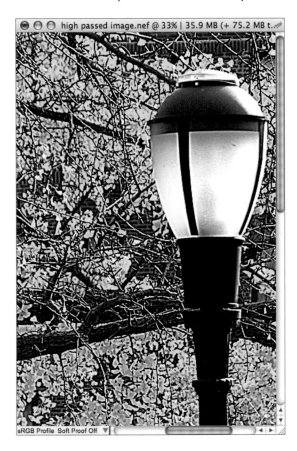

Figure 7.6 If you apply too much sharpening using the Unsharp Mask edit, your image will be plagued with ugly halos and an extreme level of contrast.

You'll find the Unsharp Mask edit under Adjust > Focus > Unsharp Mask. Unsharp Mask provides three simple controls (**Figure 7.7**):

Intensity specifies how much lightening and darkening should be applied.

Radius specifies how many pixels of halo should be created.

Threshold controls how much contrast change is required before the filter registers an edge as an edge.

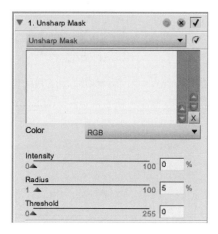

Figure 7.7 The Unsharp Mask Settings palette provides simple sliders for adjusting the Unsharp Mask parameters.

The Color pop-up menu lets you apply sharpening to individual channels. With one Unsharp Mask edit you can apply separate sharpening settings to each color channel as well as the RGB channel. Each sharpening that you make is added to the scrolling list at the top of the Unsharp Mask palette.

Here are some important guidelines to consider when sharpening:

*   Resize your image to its final output size before sharpening. If you apply sharpening and *then* resize, your sharpening effect may get lost in the resizing. In other words, make sure your resize edit comes before the Unsharp Mask edit in the Edit List.

    However, note that Capture NX *does* adjust sharpening amounts when you resize your image in an attempt to scale your desired sharpening amount to fit the new size of your image. Consequently, in Capture NX it's not quite as critical to sharpen at the very end of your workflow. But you'll still get more accurate sharpening if you adjust the settings yourself to conform to your final image size.

*   Sometimes, only parts of your image need to be sharpened. For example, flesh tones don't hold up very well to sharpening because pores, wrinkles, and veins get accentuated. For most faces, it's the eyes that matter. Use the Selection tools to apply the sharpening effect to only the areas that need it.

*   It's best to view your image at 100 percent when configuring your sharpness settings.

Sharpening operations often go hand in hand with Noise Reduction, since Noise Reduction achieves its results by applying blurs to your image. After Noise Reduction, you might want to try a little sharpening to see if you can bring back any lost detail.

OUTPUTTING ELECTRONIC FILES

If you need to deliver electronic files to a client, create images for use on a Web page, send pictures via email, or pass a file you've been editing in Capture NX to an additional editing program, you'll need to output files.

By default, when you save a file in Capture NX 2, it is saved as a NEF file, a proprietary Nikon format that includes both the original image data for your image and the list of edits that you've created in the program. Capture NX knows how to interpret and process the data to render a final image, but the edited files will not be readable by any other program. So, if you need a file that can be read by another application or by a user who doesn't have NX, you'll need to use the Save As command to save the image in a different format.

> **TIP:** You can change the default file format from NEF to JPEG or TIFF in the General section of the Preferences dialog box. The Default Save as preference also lets you opt to automatically save in the file's original format or in the last file format that you saved.

As shown earlier, if you choose File > Save As, you can elect to save in either JPEG or TIFF format (in addition to NEF) by choosing your desired format from the File Format pop-up menu.

Saving for the Web or Email

If you want to output an image for use on the Web or for sending via email, you'll most likely need to resize it before saving, as discussed earlier. In the last chapter, "Version Control and Batch Processing," I detailed some automation procedures that you can use for outputting to the Web or email. If you need to prepare a bunch of images for the Web or email, consider using a batch process.

For example, if you've just returned from a shoot, made your selects, and performed an initial round of edits, you might want to quickly dump those images onto a Web site or a photo-sharing site or to send them in an email. You can use Batch Processing to automatically resize and save them.

1. Open one of the images you want to prep for the Web or email.

2. Add a Fit Photo edit to the end of the Edit List.

3. Change the Fit Photo units to Pixels and enter the maximum width and height that you want your images to be. Choosing 640 x 480 or 800 x 600 ensures a good display on smaller monitors.

4. Save the settings file as Resize for Email. In the Save Settings dialog box, make sure that all edits except Fit Photo are unchecked. You want to create a settings file that contains only the Fit Photo command.

5. Close your image and choose Batch > Run Batch Process.

6. In the Batch Process dialog box, select your source folder, and then select your Resize for Email settings.

7. Set Conflict Management to Append New Settings. This adds the Fit Photo command to the end of any edits that you've already applied.

8. Configure your save and destination options accordingly, and run the batch.

When the batch is run, all of the edits that you made to the images are applied along with the Fit Photo edit, which resizes the image. The results are saved into the destination you chose and in the format you specified.

> **TIP:** I use Fit Photo rather than Size Resolution, because with Fit Photo I don't have to worry about whether the image has a portrait or landscape orientation.

Quick Web Preview

Sometimes when you come back from a shoot you want to quickly get your selects posted to the Web without having to engage in a lot of editing. If you're working for a client, being able to quickly produce a Web gallery of your selects can be essential: You'll want client approval before you begin a time-consuming editing process.

Create a settings file that applies an Auto Contrast edit and a Fit Photo edit, and then execute this settings file on your shoot using the Batch Processor. You'll quickly get a set of resized images that have had a reasonable initial contrast adjustment. This should be good enough for refining the selection for further editing.

Saving for a Print Workflow

Most printing workflows should use TIFF files rather than JPEG files for maximum image quality and to avoid potential compression artifacts. Most likely, you'll need to resize your images to particular specifications and save your TIFFs with specific settings. You might also need to attach a specific color profile. Consult your printer or art director to find out exactly what is expected for TIFF file delivery.

Batch Preparing for Print

Just as you can batch process images for Web and email delivery, you can build settings files that can prepare your images for printing. Printing workflows vary, but it's safe to assume that all print jobs will require resizing and possibly sharpening. As you did for the Web and email prep, create a settings file that resizes to your desired size.

For print you'll want to set both the image size and the resolution. You can do both with a Size/Resolution edit, but that edit will only work with images of a specific orientation. Instead, use both a Size/Resolution edit and a Fit Photo edit.

1. Open an image that you want to process.

2. Add a Size/Resolution edit.

3. Select "Resample Image" to Change the Output Size (DPI). Enter 240 into the resolution field (or whatever resolution you want to use for printing).

4. Add a Fit Photo edit and configure it to the width and height, in inches, that you want for your images. The resulting images will be sized to fit in the specified width and height and will have the resolution that you specified in the Size/Resolution Edit.

5. Add an Unsharp Mask edit and configure it appropriately.

6. Save the settings file.

Now save and process the images as you learned earlier. For best results, save the images as TIFFs rather than JPEGs to avoid JPEG artifacting.

Saving for Use in Another Image Editor

While Capture NX provides a full assortment of editing and retouching features, there will be times when you need to tweak or alter an image in another program. For these instances you'll want to output your images as TIFF files, which you will then open in your other editor. While you could use JPEG format to transfer files, every time you resave a JPEG file you introduce more quality loss.

TIFF files also give you the option of saving in 16-bit format to preserve more of the colors that your camera originally captured. JPEG files are automatically converted to 8-bit upon export. For maximum editing latitude, choose 16-bit in the TIFF Save Options dialog box. Even if your final files will be 8-bit JPEGs, making the transfer in 16-bit mode allows you to push your edits further before encountering posterization and tone breaks.

Printing

Capture NX provides powerful printing features that let you create single prints or contact sheets, with or without metadata captions. Capture NX's printing architecture is fully color managed and provides complete soft proofing capabilities to help you get a better screen-to-printer match.

Printing a Contact Sheet

Using the Browser, you can easily create contact sheets that display multiple separate images on one page.

To create a contact sheet:

1. In the Browser select the images you want to print.

2. Choose File > Print.

3. In the Print Layout dialog box, click Select Layout and then select the number of photos per page that you want on your contact sheet (**Figure 7.8**).

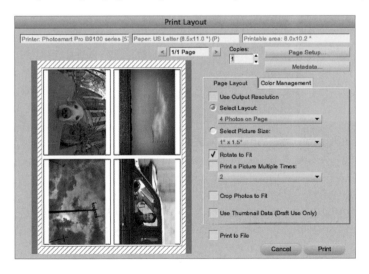

Figure 7.8 When you have opened multiple images, use the Select Layout menu to choose a contact sheet layout.

4. Check the Rotate to Fit button. This will automatically rotate your images to make the most efficient use of space. If you'd rather that all images were oriented with their tops toward the top of the page, then leave this box unchecked.

5. Configure any other options as needed. Note that the metadata controls allow you to choose a variety of information to be printed on or beneath each image on your contact sheet.

6. Click Print to move on to the standard Print Layout dialog box—the one you use when printing a single image.

Note that the Print to File option works with contact sheets as well as individual images. So, you can easily create JPEG images of your contact sheets for posting to the Web or emailing.

Printing an Individual Image

Printing an image is fairly simple. Select File > Print to invoke the Print Layout dialog box, and then configure as needed. Capture NX uses its own custom print dialog box, which looks a little different from the Print dialog box provided by your operating system (**Figure 7.9**).

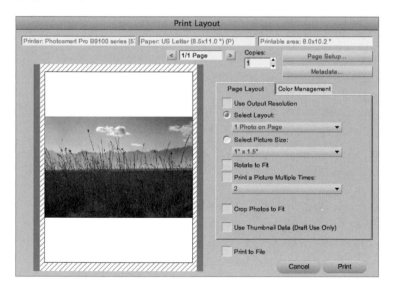

Figure 7.9 Capture NX has its own Print dialog box, which provides a full assortment of layout and color management features.

The printing controls are fairly straightforward. On the left side of the dialog box is a preview display that shows how your image will fit on the currently selected paper size. The three text fields across the top of the display indicate which printer is currently selected, what size paper you'll print on, and what the printable area of that paper size is.

Using the controls on the right side, you can configure and customize the printing process. The controls are grouped into two tabs, Page Layout and Color Management. I'll cover color-managed printing separately.

Page Setup. Click the Page Setup dialog box to invoke your operating system's standard Page Setup controls. These will vary depending on whether you're using the Mac or Windows OS.

Copies. Use this field to indicate how many copies of the page you want to print.

Metadata. Click this button to bring up the Metadata dialog box shown in **Figure 7.10**. From here you can turn on metadata sets that will be printed beneath your image. Using the Font controls, you can select the formatting of the printed metadata. You can also elect to print the date and time of shooting on top of the image.

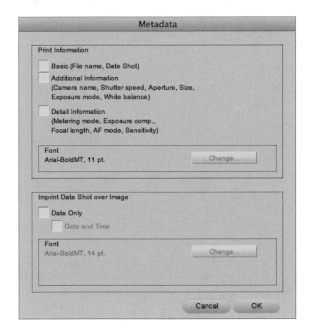

Figure 7.10 The Metadata dialog box lets you select metadata for display on or beneath your image in your final print.

Use output resolution. By default, Capture NX fits your image to the current page size. If you've meticulously resized your image by hand using a Resize or Fit Image command, you can check the Use output resolution option to force the program to use those settings instead.

Select Layout. When you're printing individual images, this pop-up menu has no effect.

Select Picture Size. The Select Picture Size menu contains some predefined images sizes (**Figure 7.11**). If you select one of these presets, Capture NX automatically resizes your image and outputs it at the optimal resolution for that size.

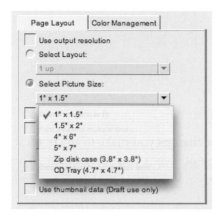

Figure 7.11 Use the Select Picture Size menu to select a predefined print size.

Rotate image(s) to fit. This option rotates your image to maximize the use of the page. Capture NX automatically determines which rotation will yield the largest image.

Print a picture multiple times. If your chosen print size is small enough to fit multiple copies of the image on the current paper size, this menu lets you select how many copies of the image to include on the page (**Figure 7.12**).

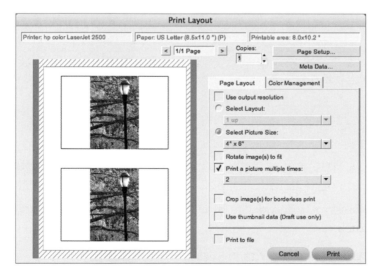

Figure 7.12 If your image size is small enough, you can choose to print multiple copies of an image on the same page.

Crop image(s) for borderless print. If you want to print an image without a border, and the image has a different aspect ratio than your current paper size, this option automatically crops the image to fit.

Use thumbnail data. This option prints using lower resolution data for those times when you're running your printer in draft mode. For the speediest printing, check this option.

Print to file. This option allows you to output the indicated page to a JPEG file. If you select this option, when you click Save Capture NX will ask you to select a location and then prompt you to pick a compression setting. Print to file allows you to easily export JPEGs formatted to a particular size along with metadata captions.

Note that the preview display updates to reflect changes you make to any of these settings, making it easy to understand exactly what type of layout you've specified. When you've configured the Print Layout dialog box to taste, click the Print button. The standard Print dialog box for your printer appears. You can then specify the printer, paper type, printing modes, and any other options necessary to get the type of print you want.

Printing a Batch of Images

You can use the Browser to batch print a group of images. This is different from printing a contact sheet in that each image will be printed on a separate page. Select the images that you want to print and then choose File > Print. Configure the Print Layout dialog box accordingly and then click Print. Capture NX will print each image according to the specifications that you define in the Print Layout dialog box. Obviously, when selecting images you'll need to select pictures that will print okay with the same print settings. For instance, you don't want to pick some images that need to be printed with the Use output resolution option and others that don't.

Capture NX's Rotate image(s) to fit option and other layout controls make it easy to define parameters that yield the optimal layout for each image in a batch.

When you have launched the Print Layout dialog box with multiple images selected, you can use the Forward and Back buttons next to the print display field (**Figure 7.13**) to view each image. These allow you to ensure that your chosen settings are appropriate for all of the images in your batch.

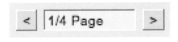

Figure 7.13 The page navigation tools let you thumb through multiple images if you've chosen to print multiple images from the Browser.

Color Managed Printing

Color management is simply the process of trying to ensure consistent color across different devices—usually monitors and printers—and from one program to another. For color management to work, your monitor and printers must be *profiled*. Running a color-accurate system is expensive. To get accurate onscreen proofs, you'll need a high-quality (read pricey) monitor as well as special profiling hardware.

Whether you choose to use onscreen proofing or not, over time you'll probably learn to better predict how the image on your screen will appear on paper. As you become more experienced with the traits of your particular printer, it will become easier for you to look at an image onscreen and say, "Oh, that will shift to red," or "Those shadows will turn out too dark."

In Chapter 2, "Workflow, the Browser, and Color," I talked in detail about profiling. If you skipped those sections, now would be a good time to go back and read them.

Installing printer profiles

For onscreen proofing to work, you must have ICC profiles installed for your printer. Most high-quality photo printers ship with ICC profiles that are installed along with the printer driver. Some vendors provide profiles as a separate installation and others provide improved profiles as a separate download. Check your printer vendor's Web site for more information.

Color management workflow

The process of color managed printing is fairly simple: You'll start by activating and configuring Capture NX's Soft Proof feature (see the next section). When you create a soft proof, Capture NX uses the information stored in your monitor and printer profiles to generate an onscreen simulation of what your image will look like when printed.

When you print, you have a number of options for specifying how Capture NX should process your color. You can simulate each of these options when soft proofing. So, one of your goals when soft proofing is to determine exactly which color settings you want to use when printing.

With the Soft Proof feature active, you may decide that you want to make some additional adjustments to your image to compensate for the effects of printing on certain types of paper. For instance, some glossy papers might introduce a green or blue cast into your image, so you may decide to perform a green or blue hue shift on your image to compensate.

Once you have your soft proof looking the way you want it to, you can execute your print operation.

Activating onscreen proofing

In the lower-left corner of the document window, you'll find the toggle button for activating and deactivating soft proofing (**Figure 7.14**). Click the button to activate soft proofing, and the Soft Proof Dialog appears (**Figure 7.15**).

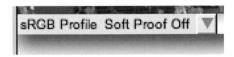

Figure 7.14 The soft proofing switch at the bottom of the document window lets you toggle soft proofing on and off.

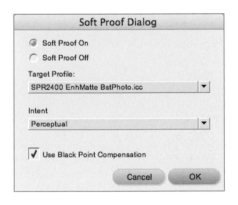

Figure 7.15 In the Soft Proof Dialog, you can select whichever paper profile you want to use and specify how you want Capture NX to process the colors in your document to fit within the gamut of your chosen paper.

Configuring the Soft Proof Dialog is fairly simple:

1. Select Soft Proof On to activate soft proofing. You'll most likely notice an immediate change in the appearance of your image. Don't worry, Capture NX has not done anything to the actual color values in your image. If you click Soft Proof Off, your image returns to normal.

2. From the Target Profile pop-up menu, select the printer profile you want to use when printing. You'll usually have separate profiles for each type of paper that you can print on, perhaps separate profiles for different settings that you'll use with each paper type and possibly even different viewing conditions.

3. Select an intent. These days, any printer you use will have a smaller color gamut than your document. Consequently, Capture NX has to map the broad range of colors in your document into the much smaller color space of your printer. The intent you choose will control how that remapping will occur.

Perceptual intent attempts to maintain the relationships between colors to produce an image that looks natural to the eye.

Saturation is only useful for very saturated images such as illustrations and business graphics—you'll never use it for photos unless you want a very stylized look.

Relative Colorimetric maps the white point of your image to the white point specified in your printer profile and then lines up all the other colors accordingly. Colors in your image that lie outside the gamut of your printer profile are mapped to the closest possible color. You'll probably use this intent most often because it preserves the greatest number of colors in your image.

Absolute Colorimetric doesn't map the white in your image to the white of your printer profile. Instead, it tries to reproduce the exact white that appears in your image. So, if the white in your image is actually a little bluish, Absolute Colorimetric reproduces it that way. All other colors are then mapped to their closest counterpart, as they are in Relative Colorimetric.

While the Soft Proof Dialog is open, try different rendering intents until you find the one that you like best.

4. Specify Black Point Compensation. The Black Point Compensation check box is available for all intents save Absolute Colorimetric. Black Point Compensation maps the black point in your image to the black point of your printer profile. You'll almost always want this option turned on unless your images lack a true black.

5. When you've determined the settings that yield the best soft proof, click OK.

   TIP: Once you've configured the Soft Proof Dialog, you can easily turn soft proofing on and off by pressing Control/Command-Y.

If need be, you can now perform additional edits. Your image is still being proofed in real time, so you can see the soft proof update as you work on your file. If you decide you want to change your proof settings, click the soft proof toggle again to invoke the Soft Proof Dialog. You can also deactivate soft proofing altogether by opening the Soft Proof Dialog and choosing Soft Proof Off.

Printing

With your proof adjusted, you're ready to print.

1. Choose File > Print and configure any page layout settings to taste.

2. Click the Color Management tab to view the Color Management controls (**Figure 7.16**).

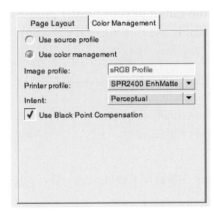

Figure 7.16 You'll use the controls on the Color Management tab to configure the Print dialog box to match the settings you determined during your soft proof.

3. If you used the Soft Proof controls, the Color Management tab will automatically be configured with the same settings—printer profile, rendering intent, and black point compensation.

4. Click Print to move on to the standard Print dialog box.

5. Using the controls in the Print dialog box, deactivate any color correction that is built into the printer. This is an essential step. Capture NX is already handling color correction, so you don't want the printer adding another layer of color correction. Consult your printer manual for details on how to deactivate built-in color management.

6. Configure the rest of your print options and then print.

Compare the results to your screen to see how well they match.

Improving soft proofing accuracy

As mentioned earlier, your prints will never exactly match your monitor. However, there are some measures you can take to try to improve the match.

- **Adjust your viewing environment.** When you're looking at your monitor, other colors in your field of view can influence your perception of the colors in your image. Try to remove any bright colors from behind your monitor. Also, make sure your computer desktop contains a neutral background.

- **Adjust the lighting in your room.** When you profiled your monitor, your profiling software probably asked you what the ambient lighting conditions were in your room. If these have changed, either put them back the way they were or make a new profile for the new conditions.

- **Get better printer profiles.** Often the profiles that ship with a printer are not very good, either because they were poorly made in the first place or because not every printer that rolls off of the assembly line is identical. Printer profiling hardware is not cheap (such devices start at $1000), but there are several online services that will make a profile for you. Most of these are reasonably priced ($25–$50), and the profiles they generate can make a great improvement in your printing accuracy.

Finally, remember that your monitor changes over time, so you should regularly re-profile it to keep it as accurate as possible. Most profiling devices include software that automatically reminds you to re-profile.

Printer-Controlled Color

Depending on the printer you have, you may find that you get as good or better results by letting the printer handle the color rather than Capture NX. To use printer-controlled color, click the Use source profile option on the Color Management tab of the Print Layout dialog box. Then leave color management on in your printer driver dialog box.

When you use driver-controlled color, Capture NX's soft proofing features are irrelevant. The preview shown by soft proofing won't necessarily be representative of what you get from the printer. The only way to determine if you prefer Capture NX or driver-controlled color is to try them both. A few years ago it was safe to say that driver-controlled color was inferior to application-managed color, but nowadays that has changed. HP, Epson, and Canon all have managed to greatly improve their printer drivers, and you can now get excellent results directly from the printer driver.

BACKUP AND ARCHIVING

No workflow is complete without an archiving step, and while you're working, you might want to consider regularly backing up your work files. The difference between backup and archiving is as follows:

- Backup is the process of creating duplicates of the files you're working on so that if you have a hardware malfunction or accidentally screw up an image, you can restore to your last backup.

- Archiving is the process of storing completed images when you're done working with them.

You typically create backups by copying your files to a second hard drive. Because you usually want to update your backup files as you continue to edit your images, hard drives make for quick, efficient backups and easy restoration.

When you're ready to archive your images for long-term storage, you can use hard drives or optical media such as recordable CDs and DVDs. Optical disks are cheaper per megabyte than hard drives, so you can easily create multiple copies, but hard drives allow for easy rewriting if you later decide to edit or alter an archived copy.

However you choose to back up and archive your images, remember that you should save *both* a NEF file and a rendered TIFF. The NEF files will allow you to return to a fully editable version of your image at a later date, and the TIFF files will give you an image that you can use in other applications. A TIFF file is especially handy in the event that you one day lack access to a copy of Capture NX.

WHERE TO GO FROM HERE

Many resources are available on the Web for Capture NX information and general image editing tips, including my own Web site at www.completedigitalphotography.com. But if you really want to improve your Capture NX chops, your best choice is to practice. Get out, shoot some images, and then put them through your Capture NX workflow. I hope by this point you have a good idea of how to find your way around the application.

If you have any questions or comments, I'd love to hear them. You can email me directly using the Feedback link on my Web site.

INDEX

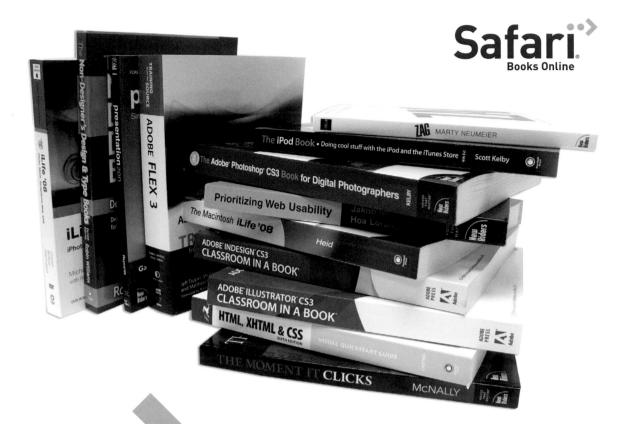